(Continued)

Fourth Edition

The CHILD as CRITIC

DEVELOPING LITERACY THROUGH LITERATURE, K–8

Glenna Sloan

Foreword by Bernice Cullinan

Teachers College, Columbia University
New York and London

To Charles and Mark

Published by Teachers College Press, 1234 Amsterdam Avenue, New York, NY 10027

Grateful acknowledgment is offered to the following for permission to reprint the poems indicated:

"Dark Girl" from *Personals* by Arna Bontemps. Copyright 1963 by Arna Bontemps. Reprinted by permission of Harold Ober Associates, Inc.

"In Time of Silver Rain" from *Selected Poems of Langston Hughes*. Copyright 1938, renewed 1966 by Langston Hughes. Reprinted by permission of Alfred A. Knopf, Inc.

"The Goblin" from *Picture Rhymes from Foreign Lands* by Rose Fyleman (J. B. Lippincott). Copyright 1935, renewed 1963 by Rose Fyleman. Reprinted by permission of HarperCollins Publishers, Inc.

"City Autumn" from *On City Streets* by Joseph Moncure March. Reprinted with permission from M. Evans and Company.

The original edition of this work appeared under the title *The Child as Critic: Teaching Literature in the Elementary School*. Copyright © 1975 by Teachers College, Columbia University.

Library of Congress Cataloging-in-Publication Data
Sloan, Glenna, 1930–
    The child as critic : developing literacy through literature, K–8 / Glenna Sloan.—4th ed.
        p. cm. — (Language and literacy series)
    Includes bibliographical references and index.
    ISBN 0-8077-4340-2 (pbk. : alk. paper)
    1. Literature—Study and teaching (Elementary) 2. Language arts (Elementary)
    3. Literature—Study and teaching (Middle school) 4. Language arts (Middle school) I. Title. II. Language and literacy series (New York, N.Y.)

LB1575.S53   2003
372.64—dc21   2003050761

ISBN 0-8077-4340-2 (pbk.)
Printed on acid-free paper
Manufactured in the United States of America

10   09   08   07   06   05   04   03   8   7   6   5   4   3   2   1

Contents

Foreword
to the Fourth Edition

Glenna Sloan declares that literature is the heart of the literacy curriculum. Everyday, my experiences affirm her convictions and strengthen my own beliefs in the power of literature. Children learn vocabulary, the rhythm of language, the joy of stories, and shape their own personality, character, and belief system through interaction with literature.

Recently, I was reading David Shannon's book *David Gets in Trouble* to my three-year-old grandson, Jamison (Shannon, 2002). In the story, David goes off to school with only his shirt and underpants on. As he leaves, his mother chases after him waving a pair of his pants in the air. David's excuse is, "I forgot." As Jamison and I were enjoying the book together, I said, "He forgot his trousers." Jamison echoed with delight, "He forgot his trousers." Later that day, Marguerite, Jamison's mother, spoke to me with pleasure saying, "I have never used the word *trousers* with Jamison, but suddenly he knows it. Isn't that amazing?" Jamison had just added a new word to his vocabulary from the books we read to him.

Research shows that students learn most of their vocabulary through reading. Thus, students who read more have larger vocabularies. Jamison's family often recites nursery rhymes and read poetry to him. He hears poems by A. A. Milne so often that he begins to join in and say them along with the reader. When he goes down a staircase, he stops in the middle, expecting to hear the poem "Halfway Down" to be recited to him. He laughs outloud at Mary Jane, who won't eat her dinner because it's lovely rice pudding again. He is learning the rhythms of language.

British writer Francis Spufford describes the way literature shaped his life in *The Child That Books Built: A Life in Reading*.

He writes, "I want to know why I read as a child with such a frantic appetite, why I sucked words off the page with such an edge of desperation" (Spufford, 2002). Spufford visits the books he remembered from his childhood and weaves together child development, personal reflection, and social observation to explain how fiction shaped his view of the world.

In this fourth edition of *The Child as Critic,* Glenna Sloan leads teachers into the process of turning children into avid readers. Her book is an excellent resource for teachers, and with each edition it becomes stronger. In this fourth edition, Sloan adds a section on the unifying principles of literature and stresses children's ability to respond to and to evaluate literature. She enriches our view of literature by explaining its connections and intertextuality, a primary goal of literary study. She shows teachers how to get started by adding an excellent short course in poetry. In a new section entitled "The Magic of Storytelling," Sloan provides an invaluable introduction to the art of how to "talk" a story so that children will hang on every word.

As its success over the years indicates, this a valuable book. Every teacher and librarian needs it. It will make life richer for many students.

BERNICE E. CULLINAN

REFERENCES

Shannon, David. (2002). *David gets in trouble.* New York: Blue Sky Press.
Spufford, Francis. (2002). *The child that books built: A life in reading.* New York: Metropolitan Books.

Foreword
to the First Edition

This book is an attempt to explain what the real place of literature is in primary education. Its place is to provide the verbal element in the training of the imagination. The imagination is not a self-indulgent, ornamental, or escapist faculty: It is the constructive power of the mind. Hence one should teach reading neither efficiently nor passively: Reading has to be a continuously active and leisurely growth, as is all genuine growth. Because it is active, the teaching of writing is inseparably a part of the teaching of reading, and the aim of teaching a child to write poetry is not to produce poets, but to produce articulate people, articulateness being the highest form of freedom that society can give to the individual. Mrs. Sloan quotes Kenneth Koch, who should know, as remarking that teaching children to write in this way is not really "teaching," in the limited sense, so much as a matter of allowing them to discover and exploit what they already have.

The author makes clear from the beginning her opposition to what she calls the "skills and drills" approach, which frustrates and stunts all genuine imaginative growth. Emphasis on skills tries to be efficient: It regards learning to read as a largely mechanical operation, to be taught with the least waste of time by repetition of familiar words, adding new words gradually as facility is gained. The argument for such teaching seems extremely plausible, and has only the flaw that the human mind, which always begins as a child's mind, is simply not built that way. Consequently such an approach is not merely immoral and anti-intellectual, it is also miserably inefficient, even in its own terms. Emphasis on drills is, again, an emphasis on a "teaching" process in which the teacher is the active agent, the one who knows, and the students are passive, learning through a mechanism of imitation. That doesn't work either.

I have had no firsthand experience with education below the university level, and while I believe that no theory of criticism is any good at all unless it can be adapted to kindergarten and grade one, I naturally make mistakes when I try to suggest how such an adaptation could proceed. I think most of my mistakes have really been much the same mistake: the mistake of underestimating what a child can respond to. Mrs. Sloan, with more experience, does not make this mistake. She knows that children can respond to tragedy and irony as well as to comedy and romance, and that children want difficulty: If they are practicing jumping over hurdles, they want the highest hurdle they can possibly get over, not a low one that they know they can manage. The author also makes it clear that the notion of there being some danger of distorting "reality" by introducing fantasy and myth to the small child is pure (except that it is very impure) superstition. Such dangers only arise in certain types of bad realism. As C. S. Lewis remarks, no child is going to confuse *Alice in Wonderland* with reality, but a pseudorealistic study about life in a British public school might lead him to expect that school life really was like this. Mrs. Sloan notes that there is now a fashion for realism in children's stories, probably because there is also a fashion for fantasy in adult stories, and adults tend to expect children to make up for their own deficiencies.

When I was about ten I once had to mind the little boy next door, who was about three. He wanted to know what the flowers in the front yard were. I told him they were hydrangeas, and this word, which came out something like "hyainzuz," he repeated all afternoon, chuckling to himself at intervals. Many years later I realized that I had confronted that afternoon one of the primary phenomena of literary education. It is the rare magic word, the mysterious polysyllabic word, that is most likely to become the educational focus, the beckoning light ahead: Similarly, it is the magic story, not the imaginatively squalid story, that is most likely to start the quest for awareness going. Ultimately, everyone exposed to literary education has to try to become a Prospero; otherwise he becomes a Caliban. From the stuttering Dick-and-Jane readers to the foul-mouthed blither of the Watergate transcripts, we realize how many Calibans there are who are quite right in saying:

> You taught me language; and my profit on't
> Is, I know how to curse.

But there are still some Prosperos who have learned how to control the magic of words and make it part of their own experience, and it is to increase their number in society that the present book is devoted.

NORTHROP FRYE
1912–1991

Preface

When the first edition of *The Child as Critic* was published in 1975, its basic premise, that literature belongs at the center of a viable program to develop literacy, was a revolutionary notion. In 1984, the year of the second edition, this was no longer a radical idea, although it was still a novel one. The third edition in 1991 reflected a widespread movement toward the use of literature—poetry, fine books of fact and fiction—in literacy development programs in elementary and middle schools. Today, influenced by results of standardized reading tests that have little to do with literacy and less to do with literature's place in its development, educational administrators in some places have reverted to an emphasis on *how* children read (e.g., phonics and exercises about reading) rather than on *what* they read and what they *want* to read: good stories, clever poetry, and interesting books of information. Still, among classroom teachers who know firsthand what motivates children to read, the use of literature is widely endorsed as a means of furthering literacy.

Endorsement is an important first step in the process of using authentic children's literature to help young students develop their abilities as readers and writers. Seventy-two teachers who responded to a survey on various aspects of literacy development through literature enthusiastically advocated its use but all expressed insecurity about which procedures to follow in implementing literature-based programs (Sloan, 1995). This fourth edition of *The Child as Critic* offers practical, research-based suggestions for their implementation. More importantly, it provides a theoretical substructure, a deductive framework intended *for the teacher*, to support an inquiry-based, inductive approach to learning. What this unique framework provides is a new way of looking at literature as a whole rather than work by work—an interrelated order of words stretching back to myth, legend, and folktale.

This is the Age of the Reader. We accept that meaning does not reside solely in a text; instead, it is created by each individual reader through a transaction with the text. The reader both brings meaning to and takes meaning from a work. In small discussion groups—the current jargon calls them "literature circles"—the empowerment of readers is properly celebrated. However, literary studies worthy of the term cannot be confined to conversations that are limited only to participants' personal responses to text.

Louise Rosenblatt's transactional theory (1938, 1978) has become a referent for responding to literary texts and the approach of choice for literature study in elementary and middle school. As an observer in classrooms and a reader of accounts of what takes place there, I am convinced that Rosenblatt's ideas often lack full implementation. Chapter 3, which now includes a brief history of literary studies as well as an overview of literary theories, presents a neglected aspect of her work: her argument for going beyond initial personal response to substantive study of literature. When they are informed in the history and theories of literature study, educators are better prepared to plan, set goals, and implement sound practice in their classrooms.

This edition supports the conviction that literature is the best means for developing genuine literacy, which includes both the ability and the desire to read and write. Literacy, not a point to be reached but a development over a lifetime, begins in wide reading, in discovering firsthand the delights and satisfactions to be found in the various forms of literature. Literacy through literature begins with each reader's personal response to a literary work, but it does not end there. It continues with study—critical, reflective consideration of what is read—undertaken through methods and materials appropriate to young students.

Works of literature, like musical compositions, cannot, of course, be directly taught. The study of musical compositions we call music appreciation; the study of literary works is criticism. Just how literary criticism may be appropriately and significantly undertaken in elementary and middle schools continues to be a primary concern of *The Child as Critic*.

One important function of criticism, as I see it, is to help students toward a conception of the interrelatedness of literary works. This aspect of criticism, which provides a sense of the unity of all literature, must be undertaken within the framework of a theory of literature that describes this unity. Like earlier versions of *The Child as Critic*, the fourth edition draws upon the theories of

Northrop Frye, the only literary theorist who has attempted a delineation of the unifying principles of literature. His theoretical model, intended, as he said, to be "a scaffolding to be knocked away when the building [literary criticism] is in better shape" (1993, p. 14), provides for teachers a deductive framework upon which their students may proceed inductively to build literary understandings.

The Child as Critic is based on research, both the author's and that of others. Data collected in classrooms where the language arts and other curriculum areas are taught and learned through literature are cited throughout as illustrations of good practice in teaching and learning. Many of the teachers in these classrooms were students in my graduate classes at Queens College of the City University of New York. I am indebted to all these colleagues and especially to Labiba Abdur-Rahman, Alice Brown, Susan Castellano, Christine Choka, Ann Carter, Kathleen Cunningham, Karen Curran, Regina Furnari, Jacqueline Gladden, Ellen Goldfarb, Aline Klinger, Bernice Levy, Kathryn Lewis, Yvonne Maddiona, Lisa Manfredonia, Ann Moynagh, Diane Peck, Joan Popper-Kane, Annette Sanchez, Sue Sgarro, Kalie Stern, and Jane Watson.

The book is intended for teachers, prospective teachers, librarians, language arts supervisors, designers of curricula, and others interested in the development of literacy in elementary and middle schools.

This new version of *The Child as Critic* offers educators a comprehensive program that combines theory and practice in developing literacy through literature. This program is purposefully free of jargon, reference to fleeting trends, and rigid adherence to a single approach in learning and teaching literacy. Teachers are encouraged to adapt the methods and the materials of the program to the unique needs of a specific group of children. Although unchanged in focus and philosophy from earlier editions, the fourth edition of *The Child as Critic* contains an entirely new chapter, Chapter 3, along with other additions and updates throughout. Relevant material from the earlier editions has been retained. The nine chapters of the book are arranged in three parts.

Part I, "Literature and Literacy," consists of two chapters. Chapter 1, "The Case for Literature," argues for the centrality of literature—reading material that speaks in the unique voice of an author with something to say—in programs to develop literacy. Chapter 2, "Toward Literacy Through Literature," discusses, from a research base, the efficacy of literature-based teaching and learning of literacy. Psycholinguistic principles derived from research demonstrate the importance of a holistic approach to all phases of literacy development. Genuine literature belongs at the center of holistic methods to teach reading and writing.

Part II, "The Unifying Principles of Literature," contains three chapters. Chapter 3, "On Teaching Literature," presents a brief history of how literary studies developed through various approaches to the present emphasis on the centrality of the reader's role in making meaning from texts. Discussion of literary theory in this chapter provides a basis for planning curriculum and for critiquing theory itself. In Chapters 4 and 5, "Likenesses Unify Literature" and "The Circle of Stories," the unifying principles of literature are delineated to provide teachers with a deductive framework on which to structure students' inductive learning.

The four chapters of Part III, "Theory into Practice," contain specific examples of practices and strategies in literary criticism. Chapter 6, "Poetry and Literacy," argues for the primacy of poetry in literacy education. Through "A Short Course in Poetry," the chapter provides direction and practical advice for bringing children and poetry together in the classroom. In Chapter 7, "Developing a Sense of Story," the discussion covers methods and materials, including a new section on the art and technique of storytelling, for broadening students' experience with prose literature. Included here are specific suggestions for implementing independent, individualized reading programs in the classroom. Chapter 8, "Growing as Critics," offers examples of techniques and activities that move students beyond personal experience and response toward a sense of the unity of literature and a conception of how the interrelatedness of literary and other verbal constructs affects both our imaginative and practical lives. In "The Process of Writing," Chapter 9, writing and other types of composing are presented as aspects of criticism. This chapter suggests, with examples, procedures useful in helping children compose their own stories and verse.

The book contains a list of resources in literature and language arts, which includes sources useful in book selection. In addition to general references, bibliographical information is provided for the children's literature cited in the text. In citing works of children's literature, I have used what are for me the best examples, realizing that older works may be out of print. However, these excellent old favorites are often available in libraries or as reissued paperback or other editions.

GLENNA SLOAN

PART I

Literature and Literacy

The Case for Literature

> The content of a children's book is basically unimportant. The sole purpose of that book is to convince the child that reading is great fun. The book must be so exciting and funny and wonderful that the child falls in love with it. Then the battle is won and the realization that books are easy and lovely and enthralling begins to dawn on the young reader.
>
> —Roald Dahl (1997, p. 74)

The National Assessment of Educational Progress (NAEP) in reading continues a 25-year mandate to assess and report the educational progress of students at grades 4, 8, and 12. The lowest achievement level defined for the NAEP reading assessment is the *basic* level. "Basic" means little or no mastery of the knowledge and skills necessary to perform work at each grade level. For the nation as a whole, more than a quarter of the students in each grade failed to reach this lowest level (Williams, et al., 1995, p. 19).

In this electronic age, children are likely to feel no urgent need to read and write. In the world outside of school, whole days may pass without the necessity for reading and writing. Televised situation comedies and police shows provide the entertainment once supplied by comics and series books like Nancy Drew and the Hardy Boys. Tape recorders answer phones and take messages with never a word written or read. It is quicker and more convenient to pick up the phone instead of a pen to communicate for business or pleasure. Reading and writing always required more exertion than talking and listening. Now that alternatives are available, why make the effort?

For many children, reading and writing have become activities almost exclusively associated with school. One major study of fifth graders revealed that reading books occupied less than 1% of the children's free time (Anderson, Hiebert, Scott, & Wilkinson, 1985). While some of these children may be *illiterate*, unable to read beyond the most rudimentary level, more of them are likely to be *aliterate*, able to read but choosing not to.

LITERATURE *IS* A "READING PROGRAM"

Literacy is a state of becoming, not a point to be reached. It has barely begun when children acquire the basics of reading and writing, which in themselves are only passive skills, having to do with being an obedient citizen: able to read traffic signs and fill in the blanks of official forms. Knowing *how* to read—and write—is essential, but not in the long run what is important about literacy. What is important is how the skills are developed and what nourishes their development. The truly literate are not those who know how to read, but those who read: independently, responsively, critically, and because they want to. The first real business of reading instruction is to make children want to read. To do that, we must be as concerned with *what* they read as with *how* they read.

Since literature—unique writings that demonstrate excellence of form and expression—addresses itself principally to the imagination, many educators have difficulty in accepting it as more than a diversion. Confronted with the low scores on standardized reading tests of children who read "below grade level," if at all, they insist that the business of the elementary school is to teach "basic skills." Too often this means a tedious program of skill drills. For children who have already learned to hate reading, there could hardly be a more futile approach.

"Is this all there is to reading?" young students must think, struggling with one more workbook exercise in phonics. If children's school experience convinces them that there is no more to reading—and writing—than ho-hum exercises, it is not surprising that they show little interest in becoming consumers or creators of written words.

Children develop their ability to read and write by reading and writing. But reading and writing require considerable effort, and children will not bother to expend it unless their experience convinces them that written words have significance in their lives.

The conviction that reading and writing are worthwhile may well be the single most important ingredient in any program to develop literacy. The promise of better jobs or higher salaries motivates adults to apply themselves in night-school classes. Children are seldom so practical. Prospects of earning a living or succeeding in college are too remote to influence their effort. The young are notorious hedonists, preferring to expend their energies on activities that offer satisfaction here and now.

Unless printed words make a strong appeal to their emotions and imaginations, children will remain indifferent to reading and writing them. For children, printed words must provide wonder, delight, interest, and pleasure, or they won't bother to read, even though they may have learned the rudiments of reading.

Among the masses of printed material available to readers, the works for which we reserve the term *literature* possess the greatest potential to influence the feelings and the imagination. Born of imagination, the unique literary work influences through a direct, intense appeal to that faculty. At its best, literature is art created in words, where, driven by imagination, language is chosen with artistry and skill to construct stories, poems, and informational material with potential to engross, enchant, and enlighten.

Children will become readers only if their emotions are stirred and their imaginations stretched by what they find on printed pages. One way—a sure way—to make this happen is through genuine literature, works that claim consideration because, having something to say, they use language to greatest effect in saying it.

Nothing is more important or practical in the long run than genuine literature. Nothing should come before it. All efforts to teach reading must begin with it. It is only the art of literature that can successfully counter the drawing power of television. Literature, because it is worth reading, nourishes the desire to read.

What does a teacher do when a survey of her students reveals that in their spare time they "would rather do chores than read?" The answer: make a concerted effort to convince the children that reading is well worth their time. In a study that I conducted in 1995, teachers of grades four through six in a graduate class in literature armed themselves to fight aliteracy with literature (Sloan, 1995). In addition to surveying the children on their attitude toward reading, the teachers questioned the children about their interests. The teachers' assignment was to use what they knew of the children's interests in order to choose ten to twelve of the best books available in this area and to begin to tempt their classes with lively book talks, which included reading aloud tantalizing tidbits from the chosen books.

In every case, children's negative attitudes toward reading were changed for the better. Copies of the books that teachers enthusiastically introduced were made available for the children to complete independently. All that was required of the students, if they recommended the book they selected to read, was to tell the class why and to share a short excerpt. Teachers were astonished at the success of this simple exercise in changing students' attitudes and behavior toward reading. Here is a selection of their comments: "Finding the books I needed took a lot of my time, but it was well worth it;" "I had good books to share, but I believe that my own enjoyment of them was what got my children excited;" "If I didn't know about the really good books available—and I didn't—how would children know without help?" "If you want to change children's bad attitudes about reading, you have to introduce them to the best stories, the ones that capture their attention and make them wonder."

Literature is far and away the most effective "reading program" ever devised. Unfortunately, it has not been the one widely used in the United States.

Pervasiveness and Limitations of Reading Systems

For several decades most children across this nation have been taught to read, from kindergarten through eighth grade, with basal reading programs or packaged systems for teaching reading. These programs are based on the premise that learning to read consists of mastery of a sequential series of skills, best presented through material in which syntax is simplified and vocabulary is controlled.

Complete packages of teaching materials provide the scope and sequence of an entire reading curriculum. Included in them are graded anthologies of selections in children's "readers," instructional strategies detailed in teacher's manuals, practice exercises in workbooks, as well as supplementary material: tests, management systems, visual aids such as word and sentence cards, audio tapes, film strips, games, and phonics and skill development charts. The trappings of a basal reading system, besides taking up considerable space on classroom shelves, are major items in school budgets.

Over the years, publishers have responded to the literature-based literacy development movement with revamped versions of the basal reader. In its new guise, the "reader" includes stories, poems, and factual material. In some cases it is unabridged. More often, it is "basalized," to use Kenneth Goodman's (Goodman, Shannon, Freeman, & Murphy, 1988) term, through simplification, censoring, and leveling, leaving literary works mutilated.

Along with these new readers come the inevitable teacher's manual and teaching guides (some with more pages than the literary work they accompany). Although these aids deal with literature, their way of treating it often echoes the earliest and worst basal reader manuals: questions that emphasize bits and pieces of content, fill-in-the blanks exercises, questions with suggested answers, and the like.

Now that illiteracy—and aliteracy—are recognized as serious problems, educators question the efficacy of systems which suggest that *how* children read is always more important than *what* they read. They question lock-step skill and drill exercises and exclusively teacher-directed questioning as the way to develop genuine literacy.

In light of research in language learning that showed widely-held conceptions about literacy development to be erroneous (Harste, Woodward, & Burke, 1984; Smith, 1983), we cannot accept the idea that reading merely involves sequential mastery of dozens of separate and distinct skills and abilities. Does it make sense to control vocabulary when, after all, word sense develops through encounters with unfamiliar words, not suppression of them? Children are thrilled by the sight and sound of polysyllabic wonders. Aware of this, Beatrix Potter (1912) used five-dollar words like *alacrity* in her nursery tales.

Yet, reading systems are so entrenched as the methods and materials used across America in reading instruction that objective evaluation of them is rare. They, together with the standardized reading tests that complement them, are so much a part of school culture that it seems difficult for everyone—supporters and detractors alike—to imagine school without them. The Commission on Reading (Anderson et al., 1985), advocating their use while acknowledging their limitations, did not seriously consider alternatives to the basal.

Literature as an Alternative to Readers and Reading Systems

An alternative does exist, however, in literature-based literacy programs. Learning to read trade-book literature, a growing body of research informs us, is another way—and a highly effective one in terms of motivation and improved performance—to learn to read (Eldredge & Butterfield, 1986). The exclusive use of basal systems has not and will not lead children toward genuine literacy, which includes both the ability and the desire to read. Learning the basic skill of decoding is essential, of course, but as soon as children can read, they must read real texts. So-called skill building can, and often does, become an end in itself. Readers, workbooks, and audiovisual kits of reading exercises are only skill builders. They are not actual reading material, any more than scales are musical compositions. Participation in a reading program that does not go beyond drills of skills is like learning to play the piano by practicing scales without ever playing a piece of music.

To those who would prescribe increased doses of drills as the cure for illiteracy and aliteracy, advocates for literature respond that even the slowest learner will profit more from the injections for the imagination that literature provides. The capacity of children to experience and enjoy stories, poems, and informational books is not dependent on their ability to decode or read fluently. Like the telegraph operator, they are able to "read" what they hear. Although being read to is not reading for oneself, if what one hears is worth listening to, the desire to read is sure to follow.

Interest in the exploits of storybook characters like Curious George, Madeline, Henry Huggins, Anansi, George and Martha, Encyclopedia Brown, and Frog and Toad keeps children listening or turning the pages of books. Learning about the eccentricities of long and short vowel sounds does not. Nor do reading snippets of trivia written in flat-footed prose and answering reams of questions on its content. Too much emphasis on skill and drill, far from turning children into readers, turns them against trying to read. From the beginning, they must experience printed words at their best, in continuous texts with the power to involve and engross them.

Detecting Basalized Literature

Responding to criticism that the selections in basal readers were bland, trivial, and lacking in literary quality, publishers moved to include "literature" in their basal readers. The result, however, is often a "basalization" of an author's text to fit the readability, vocabulary, and sequential skill requirements of the reading system of which they are a part. In most cases, works are shortened, simplified, or rewritten with changed vocabulary, shortened sentences, and modified story lines.

As an example, here are the original first two paragraphs of the tale, "Two of Everything" (Ritchie, 1949).

> Mr. and Mrs. Hak-Tak were rather old and rather poor. They had a small house in a village among the mountains and a tiny patch of green land on the mountain side. Here they grew the vegetables that were all they had to live on, and when it was a good season and they did not need to eat up everything as soon as it was grown, Mr. Hak-Tak took what they could spare in a basket to the next village, which was a little larger than theirs, and sold it for as much as he could get, and bought some oil for their lamp, and fresh seeds, and every now and then, but not often, a piece of cotton stuff to make new coats and trousers for himself and his wife. You can imagine that they did not often get the chance to eat meat.
>
> Now one day it happened when Mr. Hak-Tak was digging in his precious patch, he unearthed a big brass pot. He thought it strange that it should have been there for so long without his having come across it before, and he was disappointed to find that was empty; still, he thought they would find some use for it, so when he was ready to go back to the house in the evening, he decided to take it with him. It was very big and heavy, and in his struggles to get his arms around it and raise it to a good position for carrying, his purse, which he always took with him in his belt, fell to the ground, and to be quite sure he had it safe, he put it inside the pot and so staggered home with his load. (pp. 142–143)

The following is the beginning of a version of the same story that appears in *Jumping Up*, a reader in the Lippincott Basic Reading series (Walcutt & McCracken, 1981):

> One day Mr. Hak-Tak found a big brass pot. He was sure there must be some use for it. Mr. Hak-Tak decided to take the pot home with him.
>
> As he was going along, his wallet fell to the ground. To make sure he did not lose it, he placed his wallet inside the big brass pot. (p. 150)

In the ruthlessly abridged basal reader version, nothing whatever remains of the leisurely charm and folktale flavor of the original. All detail that establishes who the Hak-Taks are and where and how they live is omitted. The style of the original is lost, leaving readers with a mere summary of the story in language that utterly lacks the storyteller's rhythmic, conversational style.

If well-told tales and carefully crafted poems are not children's reading material in school from the beginning, why should we be surprised that children refuse to read? Where is the motivational power in the thuds and thumps of graceless textbook prose? When it comes to charm, inventiveness, freshness of approach, and imaginativeness, there is no contest between literary language of distinction and language fabricated to serve the questionable purposes of a reading scheme.

LITERACY BEGINS IN LOVE OF LANGUAGE

In the introduction to *The Acts of King Arthur and His Noble Knights,* John Steinbeck (1976) writes:

> Some people there are, who being grown, forget the horrible task of learning to read. It is perhaps the greatest single effort that the human undertakes, and he must do it as a child. . . . For a thousand thousand years humans have existed and they have only learned this trick—this magic—in the final ten thousand of the thousand thousand. . . . I remember that words—written or printed—were devils, and books, because they gave me pain, were my enemies. Then one day, an aunt gave me a book. . . . I stared at the black print with hatred, and then, gradually the pages opened and let me in. The magic happened. (p. xi)

The book his aunt gave Steinbeck was a cut version of the Caxton *Morte D'Arthur* of Thomas Mallory. Steinbeck continues:

> I loved the old spelling of the words and the words no longer used. Perhaps a passionate love of the English language opened to me from this one book. . . . The very strangeness of the language dyd me enchante, and vaulted me into an ancient scene. (p. xii)

A similar story is likely to be found in the biography of every writer. Poets, columnists, and novelists all acknowledge the role of reading in making them writers. Early acquaintance with favorite books instilled in them a passionate love for words. These are the truly literate, who know from experience the power of written words, because these have made a difference in their lives.

The emotional impact of hearing or reading a fine piece of writing can be profound. It may well be the goose-bump experience that leads a child to a lifetime love of carefully crafted language. At the age of seven, Henry James, hiding under a table to hear a chapter of *David Copperfield* read by a relative, was discovered and sent to bed when he burst into tears at the cruelty of the Murdstones. Novelist Walker Percy remembers his father reading *The Jungle Book* and *Treasure Island* aloud to him: "To this day I remember certain passages from Kipling and every concrete detail of the way he read them" (Tyler, 1977, p. 17).

Donald Barthelme has a vivid recollection of being read to as a child, one book in particular whose title he can't recall: "I've been searching for that book all my life. The feeling of it, the tone, I remember: the music, but not the words" (Tyler, 1977, p. 16). Those familiar with the cadences of Dylan Thomas' poetry will not be surprised to learn that his father, a teacher, read him Shakespeare and only Shakespeare from the time he was a toddler.

John Updike (1975), master writer in several literary forms and frequent contributor to the prestigious pages of *The New Yorker*, recalls: "When I was thirteen, a magazine came into the house, *The New Yorker*, by name, and I loved that magazine so much I concentrated all my wishing into an effort to make myself small and inky and intense enough to be received into its pages" (p. 37).

Poet Eve Merriam acknowledges that certain favorite poems, like the parodies of Mother Goose by Guy Wetmore Carryl and his brother Charles, directly influenced both the style and content of her own writing (Sloan, 1981). Robert Cormier (1997, p. 46), speaking of his discovery at the age of 13 of *The Web and the Rock*, writes: "I found in Wolfe . . . the tumultuous language that shook my senses, the theme that excited my soul. . . . I knew when I finished that novel the inevitable course my life would take. I would be a writer. No other life would be possible for me."

Andrew Wilkinson, in *The Foundations of Language* (1971), comments: "Many people do not feel a need to develop their language, and the reason is that they are unaware of the possibilities of language. They imperfectly appreciate the nature, the uses, the joy of language" (p. 139). Through encounters with genuine literature—art in words—children can begin to learn about "the nature, the uses, the joy of language."

Literacy begins in hearts, not heads. For some it may begin in the moment of silent awe that follows the reading of a poem like "The Ballad of the Harp-Weaver," by Edna St. Vincent Millay (1924). For others it might start with laughter at the mishaps of Pooh and Piglet or in tears at Charlotte's death. For little ones, chanting the refrain of *Millions of Cats* (Gág, 1928) might be all it takes. There is a story or poem to raise a goose bump on the toughest skin, and we are well advised to help each child find it. A child who has never thrilled to words will remain indifferent to reading and writing them.

LITERATURE EDUCATES THE IMAGINATION

If literature is essential to the development of readers and writers who are genuinely literate, it is also essential to the education of the child's imagination. There is no single definition of imagination. We have no standardized tests to measure it, but this does not mean that its education can be neglected. We know that this creative and constructive power is not exclusive to the artist or inventor. Nor is imagination secondary to intellect or emotions; it is the very core of them. It is through the imagination that we participate in every aspect of our daily lives: in conversation, in relating to others with sympathy and consideration, in making choices and decisions, in analyzing news reports and the speeches of politicians, in evaluating advertisements and entertainment.

Why can literature and the study of it educate the imagination? One reason is that literature itself is born of imagination. The imaginative writer constructs a world that is but never was; within each world there is room for endless imaginative possibilities. A story is not real life; anything can happen; anything goes. Literature illustrates what it is essential for humans to realize: there are no limits for the imagination. Literature makes carpets fly and rabbits talk; it overcomes the tyranny of time and conquers death itself. A Yellow Brick Road leading to an Emerald City will never be found on a road map, but it exists, along with other literary locations and their inhabitants, as an imaginative reality.

Literature, furthermore, has the capacity to develop our imaginative perspective on reality. What we call reality is a confusing tangle of experience: Radios blare at us, advertisers bombard us, we are harassed and hurried, torn in a dozen directions. We have all had the desire, when the confusion of life is at its height, to "get away from it all," "to sort things out," "to see where we are," "to get ourselves together." We feel a need for perspective on our fragmented experience. One way to get it is through literature, the art that describes what happens to human beings as they try to come to terms with living. Literature gives shape to shifting human experience.

Another property of literature worthy of the name is its ability to call forth, as we experience a work, our own imaginative experience, something we "have always known" but couldn't express until a poem, play, or story put it into words and images for us. Thus literature puts us in touch with our own imaginative powers. Nothing is more important for creating a truly human world than realizing the power of the imagination. William Blake said that nothing is real beyond the imaginative patterns we make of reality. Imagination, in Blake's sense, creates reality. In the real world there can be no change or reform of any kind unless we first use our imaginations to describe what sort of life we want to lead, what kind of world we want to live in. The experiencing of a variety of literary works and the appropriate study of them can lead gradually to the transferring of the imaginative habit of mind that literature embodies.

SOCIAL VALUE OF THE STUDY OF LITERATURE

A culture's beliefs and actions take shape around a social vision constructed by the imagination. It is in literary works, particularly myths, legends, and folktales, that these informing social myths are expressed most clearly. Much of the mythology of the United States reflects ideals of self-reliance, independence, industry, tolerance, and respect for democratic process. Mythical figures such as the explorer, the pioneer, and the cowboy embody these ideals. Through encounters with our earliest stories, understanding of subsequent developments in history, politics, religion, and social life is deepened and clarified. Attention to the traditional and classical stories of a culture provides a kind of key to its history. They are more than "just stories." But because they are stories—imaginative constructs—it is possible to examine them with a certain detachment and discover things about our beliefs and actions as a society that we could never learn in any other way.

Every use of words, from the advertisement to the politician's speech, is a verbal structure, just as a literary work is a verbal structure. The same myths—imaginative verbal structures—inform both uses of words. Those who wish to influence others, for good or evil, make use of the same myths we find in literature: pastoral myths, hero myths, quest myths, sacrificial myths. The politician promises to take us back "to the good old days." The advertiser lures us with a description of a holiday retreat "away from it all," or promises to make rugged achievers out of those who eat the right breakfast food. With guidance in developing critical literacy, students who have encountered the genuine form of the myth in literature will be less likely to fall prey to its perverted form in the advertisement. They will know as questioning, critical readers that an advertisement showing the plain, unpopular girl suddenly made beautiful and popular by the use of the right face cream is nothing more than a version of the Cinderella story. They will recognize that an advertisement showing idealized young men and women drinking a certain brand of cola while they frolic joyfully in a summer setting has stolen its conventions from the romance, a literary form given more to fantasy than to realism.

Such use of language and myth is part of a pervasive social mythology whose purpose is to persuade us to accept—usually for another's gain—the standards and values of the society in which we live. It provides a means of making us adjust to things as they are or as a profiteer would have us believe them to be. Some adjustment to society is necessary, of course. But it is important to guard against too much passive acquiescence. Children especially need a means to fight the effects of the propaganda and social conditioning of advertising and popular entertainment.

Literacy and critical literacy develop cumulatively over a lifetime. Becoming literate involves more than reading at a rudimentary level. It embodies some conception of how the imagination works in creating verbal constructs and how these constructs, literary and subliterary—advertisements, political speeches, formulaic fiction, pop songs, and the like—not only share the same elements but also come from the same roots. Raised on genuine literature, the truly literate will recognize, in the speeches of politicians, in popular books and television sitcoms, in pop songs and advertisements, perversions of quest myths, hero myths, and pastoral myths.

The structures of literature are self-contained; the reality they present is an imaginative reality. Contemplating these structures critically and reflectively can help us to develop the capacity to view with detachment other verbal structures that surround us. A well-developed imagination, educated on literature, is protection against social mythology in all its forms: entertainment, advertising, propaganda, the language of cliché and stereotype, the abstractions of jargon and gobbledegook. In an irrational world the trained reason is important, but an educated imagination is fundamental to the survival of a sane society.

2

Toward Literacy Through Literature

Actual stories are the kind of reading that I think most familiarizes children with written language. These can range from the contemporary material found in newspapers and magazines . . . to the traditional content of fairy tales and adventure stories, to history and myth. These traditional stories fascinate children—possibly fulfilling some of their deepest needs (Bettelheim, 1976)—without pandering to an alleged inability to handle complex language or ideas. . . . Indeed, it is through exposure to such meaningful complexity that children are able to develop and test their hypotheses about the nature of spoken or written language.
—Frank Smith (1983, p. 48)

For whatever misguided reasons, courses in children's literature—where knowledge about *what* is available for children to read is provided—are not considered essential for teacher certification in New York State. Only courses in so-called basic reading skills—the *how* of reading—are required. Despite this, teachers enroll each semester for our graduate courses in children's literature at Queens College.

They want to learn about children's literature primarily because they see it in terms of its usefulness: The right books can supply children with the sociological and psychological insights they need to interpret the world and survive in it; certain books are valuable as supplemental learning aids in social studies and science curricula; literature entertains and has potential for motivating children to read. However, at the beginning of the course, talk of actually teaching literature is likely to draw blank looks and the occasional objection. Like their supervisors and administrators, most teachers regard the teaching of "basic reading skills" as the proper major concern of the elementary school. For the most part familiar only with the behaviorist-psychology approach to reading instruction, and believers in its sacred books—the basal reader with its manual—too many educators are convinced that reading "real" books has nothing to do with teaching the basics of beginning reading.

"How will we find time to teach literature," teachers ask, "when we have to teach reading?" The answer: *Use literature effectively to develop literacy, and you are teaching reading.*

Studies show that the narrative structure of well-written stories "teaches" children to read, that learning to read literature is—or can be—learning to read. What children read does matter. Important lessons about reading, notably through narrative structure and convention, are taught by the material read, and it need not be simplified to the point of inanity, as researchers have discovered (Bennett, 1979; Fox, 1985; Meek, 1982; Wells, 1982).

Published articles and books about the teaching of reading to elementary and middle school children number in the hundreds of thousands. However, in this flood of words there is little agreement on the ways and means best suited to teaching reading. We revere research, but even when we sift through the multitudinous studies looking for those of significance, they do not provide us with definitive methodology. We soon discover that reading means different things to different people.

There exists in the field of literacy education a difference in world view not unlike C. P. Snow's "two cultures," the phrase he coined to refer to a polarity in mental attitude between the sciences and the humanities (1959). These different perspectives, for the most part, are representative of two distinct points of view, which psycholinguist Frank Smith (1983) has characterized as outside-in and inside-out.

LEARNING TO READ:
OUTSIDE-IN OR INSIDE-OUT

The stimulus-response perspective of the behaviorist psychologist, which has dominated reading instruction for decades, views reading as separate from other aspects of language development.

This "outside-in" viewpoint focuses on programmatic technology, exemplified by the basal reader and the standardized test. It insists that reading is learned by following a rigid sequential program of skill development. To serve this program, reading material must be simplified by "controlling" vocabulary and sentence structure. Control extends to teachers and pupils, who are led lock-step through texts and workbooks.

Central to the approach is teaching and testing on letter–sound relationships, isolated words, and fragmented texts. Fragmentation is a key word of the process. The complex task of reading is split up into discrete segments—ideal, it should be noted, for quantitative testing.

A different perspective is offered by psycholinguistics, a discipline that combines the disciplines of linguistics and psychology. This discipline was established mainly on the theory and research of Noam Chomsky (1957) and George A. Miller (1962), challengers of behaviorist views of language development, in particular those of B. F. Skinner (1957).

Psycholinguists see reading as but one aspect of general language development. The "inside-out" viewpoint is exemplified in the holistic approach to all language development, of which reading is an integral part. It deplores the behaviorist point of view with its initial emphasis on isolated skills, sounds, letters, and lists of words. The psycholinguistic emphasis from the beginning is on helping children to extract meaning from complete texts, to consider the whole before the part. Psycholinguistic theory insists that learning to read can proceed as simply and naturally as learning to speak, when the constraints of testing are lifted and learners are freed to make sense of authentic texts that they find relevant and interesting (Harste, Woodward, & Burke, 1984; Meek, 1982).

In opposition to the behaviorists, psycholinguists emphasize that language is not learned in bits and pieces along a continuum; rather, it develops holistically, all aspects interrelating in the development. Since the linguistic approach to reading denies that we process language piecemeal, it does not lend itself well to the relentless, quantitative testing on separate aspects of reading, which the behavioristic approach has made the norm in our schools.

Psycholinguistic research confirms that human language behavior is not learned on a stimulus-response model. Language develops functionally, through use that allows learners to grow using trial and experimentation, all their efforts reinforced and encouraged with positive feedback. Notions of word-perfect reading and spelling are rejected as inhibiting. Guessing is encouraged, just as the infant's early attempts to speak, however far from standard speech, are applauded and fostered. Far from favoring constant testing, with its emphasis on right and wrong answers, psycholinguists speak persuasively against the negative, trivializing effects of constant testing on teaching and learning. A far more liberating form of evaluation is determining through observing what language users are trying to do and what help they need in developing their linguistic skills. As for evaluation, the developmental nature of language ability is more appropriately studied through successive samplings of a child's speaking, reading, and writing as these language uses develop in meaningful contexts, than by tests that deal in right or wrong responses (Goodman, Shannon, Freeman, & Murphy, 1988; Goodman, Y., 1989; Shuy, 1981; Smith, 1986).

The inside-out perspective insists that children learn to read by reading, just as they learn to talk by talking. The child who picks up a familiar book and pretends or attempts to read it is more of a reader than the one who can call out correctly words in a list. Reading is understood as something a reader works at in a quest for meaning, often puzzling out a portion that isn't readily understood. The quest for meaning involves desire: to find out what happens next, to learn more about a fascinating character, to find answers to interesting questions. In this perspective the emphasis is on development of ability through encounters with meaningful language in a supportive environment.

The Behaviorist Perspective

Report Card on Basal Readers, the report of the National Council of Teachers of English Commission on Reading (Goodman et al., 1988) is both a historical and an evaluative examination of the basal reader phenomenon. A comprehensive study of basals indicates that even the best and most recent are based on the "outside-in" perspective of behavioral psychology, which views language as habitual behavior learned through response to stimuli. The flowcharts in the handbooks accompanying basals and reading schemes reflect notions of reading as the sequential development of a series of skills. The alphabetic nature of written language is emphasized in exercises, which implies that reading is decoding alphabetic symbols into sound by the application of spelling-to-sound correspondence rules. Learning, which is teacher-directed, proceeds lockstep in a prescribed sequence, according to a script of questions and expected answers.

Behaviorists, notably Edward L. Thorndyke, influenced William S. Gray, who in 1919 published "Principles of Method in Teaching Reading, as Derived from Scientific Investigation" (Seashore, 1919). Educators, enamored of the results of "scientific investigation," looked for ways to make foolproof the process of learning to read. The basal reader, with its sequenced, fragmented approach to reading and accompanied by the teacher's manual—the stimulus that could exact the correct response from teachers (and ultimately from students)—was settled on as the once-and-for-all answer to reading instruction. For more than 60 years the supremacy of the basal reader, on the surface changing with the times but at the bottom still based on old behaviorist theories, has largely gone unchallenged.

Generally, the entrenched methodology exemplified in basal reader systems emphasizes phonics, either implicit (the sound associated with a letter is never pronounced in isolation) or explicit (the sounds associated with letters are identified in isolation and blended to form words). While most experts advocate some use of phonics in teaching reading, they agree that teaching letter-sound relationships apart from actual reading of text is of little value. Filling workbook sheets with phonic abstractions is unprofitable. Instead, readers need to be taught to rely more on syntactic and semantic clues—the context—in their efforts to make sense of text.

Criticisms from Psycholinguistics

Stressing meaning-making as primary in reading, psycholinguists charge that emphasis on word study, which includes heavy doses of phonics, distracts the reader from using syntactical and other clues to meaning imbedded in the language itself. Most words derive meaning from their contexts. The fact that language, by its very nature, is predictable is evident in the conventional structures in which it is used. Sentences as well as stories follow predictable patterns; the subject-verb-object order of the sentence and the ubiquitous quest in stories are examples. Predictability is built into poetic forms through repetition and rhyme (Goodman, K., 1968; Smith, 1978).

In actual practice, language is learned not from part to whole but from whole to part, through use, in response to a learner's felt need (Halliday, 1975). Spoken language develops in actual social situations, through trial and error, experimentation, and with the help of feedback. *Learning to read and write can and should proceed the same way.*

Yet here we employ a double standard. Any early attempts of a child to speak are applauded, no matter how far these productions stray from standard or adult speech. However, when a child begins formal literacy instruction, it is common for teachers and parents alike to demand nothing less than word-perfect reading and standard spelling.

In learning to read—and write—there needs to be freedom to make mistakes and learn from them. Miscue analysis research (Goodman, Watson, & Burke, 1987) shows that even the so-called "errors" readers make as they read are indications of an active effort to discover meaning. As an example, when the child reads "with a weight of black hair," for "with a wealth of black hair," there is evidence that the text is being interpreted, not merely misread. Furthermore, given the opportunity, readers frequently correct their own miscues in the process of considering the text as a whole.

Basal reader systems, built around control, leave little room for trial and learning through taking risks. The goals for their readers are accurate calling of each word in the text and ability to give prescribed answers to questions on bits and pieces of text.

> The whole justification for an all-inclusive and carefully se-
> quenced basal reader series depends on controlling passive
> learners. . . . Nowhere in the basals are learners encouraged
> to decide what is for themselves a good story or text. There
> is little choice, little self-control, little sense of ownership of
> their own learning and their own reading. That's not just bad
> for reading development. It's also bad for their development
> as thinkers, as learners, as participants in a democratic so-
> ciety. (Goodman et al., 1988, pp. 125, 129)

THE HOLISTIC APPROACH TO LITERACY

Across the United States and in Canada, New Zealand, and Australia have grown up, from grass roots, groups of teachers applying the principles of psycholinguistic research to literacy learning. Alliances within this movement informally provide, through conferences and newsletters, support and resources for educators who believe that all language learning—speaking, reading, and writing—should be fully integrated, meaningful, and child-centered. *That is to say, teaching and learning of language need to grow naturally from the actual experience of each specific group of children.* Reading, listening, speaking, and writing develop together functionally, in actual situations. Prepackaged reading systems—where language functions are considered as separate entities and activities, ordered and prescribed—cannot be tailored to the needs of a particular group of individuals and therefore are not welcome in classrooms favoring a holistic approach to literacy development.

On the basis of research, this is the approach with most validity. However, in some places in the United States, holistic, or so-called "whole-language," programs are in disfavor, largely through misconceptions concerning their implementation. Programs featuring actual reading of genuine literature with attendant talking and writing in real-life situations are far from establishing themselves to displace the canned and processed fare of reading systems. In many of the so-called literature-based literacy programs I have observed, the basal reader approach persists; the reading material may be more literary, but the methodology reflects the ingrained thinking that results from years of basal brainwashing.

Frank Smith (1986) attempts to explain why holistic theories of language, though informed by research, are questioned and criticized:

> The view of language and learning that psycholinguists promised was superficially examined by the educational planners and set aside as too vague. Notions that children learned best by being immersed in everyday experience did not fit well with the philosophy that believed in quality control and the delivery of instruction to children as if they were on a production line. (p. 26)

There are other reasons, of course. Supplying readers and reading systems represent a big business enterprise, and their publishers are willing to make superficial changes in their products in a hard-sell attempt—too often successful—to convince the unwary that their methodology is based on the latest research. Furthermore, funds are typically allocated on the basis of need, invariably proven by test results. The basal reader instructional program, which presents reading as a series of discrete, simple steps, translates well into the format of the standardized test. Until alternative ways of assessing reading ability are accepted, the tyranny of the test will prevent holistic literacy education from coming into its own.

The tyranny of the reading test is an ongoing educational scandal. There being so many factors involved in the process of learning to read, and many of these not fully understood, it is absurd to blame teachers for their students' failure to score at grade level on standardized tests. In 1999, I was privileged to work with teachers in several SURR (Schools Under Registration Review) schools in Bronx, New York. SURR schools are about to be reorganized, possibly even shut down, because reading scores are below grade level. The teachers in the schools where Queens College faculty participated, already well-trained and dedicated, were willing to spend part of their summer and several Saturdays in study groups to find out "what we can do [to help the children] after we've done everything."

Working in the classrooms with the teachers, I and my colleagues found that the children—many of them Latino and newly come to this country—were clearly performing as well as they could at their level. To improve the developmental skills of reading and writing, learners can only work from the point where they find themselves, whether at grade level or below. There are no literacy pills to pop. Nor does skill in reading and writing develop on the demand of politicians; instead, it develops with constant practice in a supportive environment where children's successes, not their failures, are measured (Robb, 1993).

Holistic-language teaching and learning place emphasis on constructing meaning from authentic texts in the belief that literacy develops from whole to part in a setting that allows for trial and error as language is used purposefully. The reading program is literature-based. It features genuine reading material, whether literary or subliterary: children's trade books, both factual and fictional; poetry; periodicals; newspapers; television guides; catalogues; songs; advertisements; even signs and the labels on products.

Implementing a Literacy Program Based on Holistic Principles

Educators in Australia and New Zealand have for years built successful literacy programs based on psycholinguistic principles

(Clay, 1980; Guthrie, 1981). It should be noted that New Zealand, even with an influx of non-English speaking immigrants from the Pacific Islands and Vietnam, has one of the highest literacy rates in the world. Educators in Canada and the United States have adopted much of their good practice. If these sound practices could be summed up in two words, these would be: *use literature*.

In *The Foundations of Literacy*, Don Holdaway (1979) describes how children in Australia and New Zealand are taught to read not with the primers of a basal reader system but with prose and verse from children's literature. Nursery tales and rhymes, their language made predictable through repetitive patterns, rhyme, and rhythm, supply naturally the repetition of words and phrases considered necessary for success in beginning reading. Furthermore, these authentic stories and verses provide readers with the predictable structures psycholinguists insist are essential for learning to comprehend written language (Stein & Trabasso, 1982).

The developmental program to foster literacy, as described by Holdaway (1984), places literature at its center. Stories and poetry are the reading material; discussing, writing, dramatizing, drawing, listening, reading, and retelling are among the responses to it.

> Over the weeks the children's responses to these opportunities for reflection, discovery and clarification become more and more sophisticated. They always bring to the surface the compelling necessity for sense and meaning. They concede the usefulness of predictable structures of rhyme and rhythm. . . . Aspects of story pattern and new linguistic structures are introduced in memorable and generative ways. . . . Children are likely to attempt a story of their own following this sort of structure. (p. 52)

Planning and implementing a holistic literacy-development program for a specific group of youngsters, without teachers' guides and all the other paraphernalia of basal systems, understandably present a formidable challenge to many teachers. Meeting the challenge, as converts to holistic-language teaching testify, results in renewed enthusiasm for teaching (Henke, 1988). Freed by knowledge of how children actually become literate, these professionals discover in themselves remarkable resources of creativity and inventiveness as they design literacy programs tailored for *a specific group* of students. A major goal of this text is to support teachers as professional experts, able to operate independently of systems and schemes created by others.

But what of control, ask the teachers and administrators from outside-in? How are skills taught? How are records kept? How do you evaluate? How do you organize?

Characteristics of Classrooms Practicing Holistic Techniques

Perhaps the best way to find answers to these questions is to watch successful classrooms in action. Detractors object that a child-centered curriculum leads inevitably to chaos. This is nonsense. I have observed in these settings for years; what I have seen were organized, creative teachers helping children to be responsible for their own learning and their use of time—in short, to be active learners.

The following are some of the characteristics of the classes where I have observed as one particularly interested in literature-based literacy development.

● Teachers and children meet together daily to plan activities for morning and afternoon sessions. Children articulate their own goals based on needs and interests; classroom resources and facilities (e.g., learning centers) are shared on a rotating basis.

● Good books and other reading material are readily available. Although directed reading lessons may also take place, time is allotted daily for classroom reading of self-selected books for pleasure and information. Teachers conference regularly with children about their reading and writing, keeping anecdotal records on children's progress. Skills practice is based on the actual need of individual students, as perceived by the teacher through observation and as requested by the children themselves. Pairs of children often read together. Small groups of children discuss books each of them has read. Children talk knowledgeably about themselves as readers: "I read too fast." "I used to read one word at a time, but I got over that." "I'm a good reader for my age."

● Teachers read aloud to children of all ages. Both teachers and students give book talks to recommend books they enjoyed. "Teaching" of literature proceeds through an inductive process of discovery by children talking together in small groups. One group of fifth graders was able to describe the conventions of the fable (and subsequently wrote original fables) after reading and hearing a selection of fables from La Fontaine to Thurber.

● Research in informational and reference books is in relation to actual situations. In preparation for an apple-picking expedition, one second grade class researched apple-picking procedures and learned about the varieties of apples they would pick.

● Writing, often growing out of reading, is a process in which groups of children work on projects in a workshop setting, critiquing each other's work, revising, and rewriting. Each member of one eighth-grade class possessed a dog-eared copy of the first paragraphs of the short story on which the students worked for many weeks, laboring to get this all-important part of the short story "right." From their extensive study of the short story form, they were aware, as one boy told me, that "the first couple of paragraphs are the key to the whole thing."

● "Publications" of children's work are commonly part of classroom or school libraries. In the apple pickers' class, reports of the experience, which took whatever form the writer favored, were presented in apple-shaped booklets. Included were poems, factual accounts, stories, picture essays, and a play.

● For evaluation, children maintain folders of their written work from the beginning through the end of the school year. These are used in self-evaluations and teacher evaluations. Emphasis is not on "right and wrong" but on making progress. Teachers keep anecdotal records of children's progress; their records are the basis of lessons for individuals and groups, which are tailored to the needs of the children.

● There is evidence of cooperative group learning and peer teaching (buddy reading and writing); teachers are not seen as the only source of assistance and information.

● Second-language speakers benefit from peer tutoring and cooperative small-group learning. They are helped toward full, rich literary lives by reading genuine literature, listening to others read it aloud, and hearing it on tape as they follow a printed text.

● Classrooms are filled with evidence of children's productivity as readers and writers:

Books created by children on such subjects as computers,
    sports, Martin Luther King, and dollhouses
Bulletin boards filled with magazine and newspaper articles
    on topics like acid rain and terrorism
Displays of writing in every form, including biography, nar-
    rative poetry, fantasy, and realistic fiction
Copies of letters sent to members of Congress
Copies of fan letters to authors
Newspapers and magazines created by students, containing
    everything from reviews of television shows and movies to
    parodies of them
Lists of books recommended by children
Diaries and personal journals
Children's own scripts for Readers Theater, prepared from
    novels they have read (In Readers Theater, a brief play
    script of a key scene is created by using actual dialogue
    from the book; see Chapter 9 for an example.)

There is no single blueprint for the classroom that operates
on sound psycholinguistic principles in developing literacy. Each
will be different, for *the curriculum and methodology must be
designed with the needs and abilities of a particular group of children in mind*. Language activities are natural and real, arising
out of the actual experiences of the children. Talk centers on a
story they have heard. Research grows out of a need to know.
No textbooks in language or literature are required, but authentic reading materials are in abundance.

Teachers in these classrooms serve as guides and facilitators,
motivators and mentors (Robb, 1994). They are open, organized,
flexible, involved, interested, knowledgeable, and enthusiastic.
They know their students well because they listen and observe to
ascertain what the students need to help them grow. Those who
guide literacy development holistically know that education has
very little to do with explanation but everything to do with engagement and involvement.

LITERATURE DEVELOPS LITERACY:
REVIEW OF CLASSIC AND NOTABLE RESEARCH

Reading rewritten literature in textbooks is not the way children learn to read by reading. Reading authentic literature in its

original form is the way. To make this statement is not to present a new idea. For decades, there have been educators who recognized the limitations of basal reading systems in the development of literacy. Shirley Koeller (1981), reviewing 25 years of *The Reading Teacher*, discovered continuous advocacy, supported by the results of research studies, for the use of children's literature in programs to teach reading. Among those who have insisted that literature belongs at the center of any program to develop literacy are Jeanette Veatch (1959), Walter Barbe (1961), Charlotte Huck (1961), Leland Jacobs (1965), and myself (Sloan, 1975, 1984, 1991). The impressive results of extensive research support this advocacy.

Dorothy Cohen's (1968) classic study with 580 academically retarded inner-city second graders provided clear evidence that the daily reading aloud of appealing, well-written stories resulted in dramatically increased ability in word recognition and comprehension, as measured by standardized tests, particularly for children with the lowest initial scores.

The Cohen study, replicated by Bernice Cullinan, Angela Jaggar, and Dorothy Strickland (1974) with second graders from low socioeconomic backgrounds in New York City, again demonstrated that the groups who were read to, who became involved with actual books, and who had their own trade books to explore far outstripped in standardized reading test results control groups who used basal readers during the same period.

Nancy Larrick (1987) reports similar successes with 225 kindergarteners in a New York City school where 92% of the children were from non-English speaking homes, 96% were below the poverty level, and 80% spoke no English on entering school in September. The experimental treatment for these children was Open Sesame, a program offering immersion in the best books written for children through daily reading aloud; unpressured, pleasurable opportunities to practice reading from real books; phonics instruction offered only in close conjunction with the reading of actual texts; and dictation by the children of stories—used subsequently as reading material—based on their own experiences. In June, all 225 children were able to read their own dictated stories and simple books. Some read on second-grade level. "Best of all," writes Larrick (1987) "they loved to read stories and were proud to be readers" (p. 189). Follow-up studies indicate that these children continued to do well, 60% of them reading on or above grade level at the end of first grade, and this on tests that stress phonics, not comprehension.

Carol Chomsky (1978) worked with third graders, remedial readers since first grade, who "hated" reading, decoded painfully, but could not read—readers whose progress had come to a standstill. The children listened individually to self-selected tape-recorded stories while following along in the printed text. Gradually, after a month in which they completed up to 20 readings, they achieved fluency and began to transfer their new skills to other material. Comprehension and word knowledge increased by one to two grade levels on subsequent standardized tests. Writing ability improved. Most significant was the change from a negative to a highly positive attitude toward reading and writing.

In an earlier study, Chomsky (1972) had found that reading aloud to children ages 6 to 10 a variety of literary materials at different complexity levels strongly influenced linguistic development at all ages. Prereaders at high linguistic stages heard more books of greater linguistic complexity each week than did prereaders at lower linguistic stages. Far from confusing the prereader and beginning reader, hearing the authentic language of folktales strengthened vocabulary and comprehension. Chomsky comments:

> The written language is potentially of a more complex nature than speech, both in vocabulary and syntax. The child who reads (or listens to) a variety of rich and complex materials benefits from a range of linguistic inputs that is unavailable to the nonliterary child. (p. 23)

Michael Tunnell (1986) describes outstanding success with an individualized reading and writing program with fifth graders. Children read daily books of their own choosing and heard books read aloud by the teacher. Response to the books was made through a variety of reading and writing activities: sharing books, writing reviews, and developing displays. An effort was made to use actual books in all curriculum areas. Skill practice was based on individual and group need as demonstrated by actual reading and writing. After 7 months, the average gain, as measured by a standardized reading test, was one grade level. Even more important, surveys, administered before and after the treatment, showed dramatic positive change in attitude toward reading.

I obtained pre- and post-treatment data from six inner-city and suburban classrooms where literacy development was partially literature-based (Sloan, 1988). In these classrooms, reading instruction included mandated directed reading from basal readers and other reading systems, skills development, reading of self-selected trade (library) books, and listening to books read aloud. For all cases studied, standardized reading scores measuring comprehension and vocabulary showed an average gain of one-and-a-half grade levels. Examination of pre- and post-treatment writing samples showed growth in syntactical complexity and vocabulary range in 68% of the cases. While these gains may, in part, be attributed to other variables, it is interesting to note that the gains were consistent for all six classes. Constants in these classes were daily sessions of reading aloud by the teacher from fine prose and verse and periods of independent reading from self-selected books with literary and interest value.

Rick Traw (1998) describes the success of two large-scale literature-based programs in Iowa in which trade books were favored over textbooks and the emphasis was on holistic literacy development through oral and written response to engaging literature. Authentic literacy events replaced lock-step study of basal texts. The old curriculum, with its skills approach, was replaced by one more attuned to children's interests that offered more opportunities to read and write for a purpose. Even when the programs were evaluated by standardized tests "essentially unfriendly to the theory base" (p. 149), literature-based, holistic programs to develop literacy emerged successful. Besides using standardized tests, teachers gauged success by what they observed: "Students who have been in a whole-language program and have developed a love of reading are not excited about basal texts" (p. 141).

Millions of words have been written by educators and researchers about literacy: what it is, how to achieve it, how to measure it. Until the trend toward literature-based reading programs began, the words of advocates for these programs went unheeded. Perhaps we need to hear what children have to say on the subject of reading real books in school. These comments were written by seventh graders who participated with me in a reading program that consisted in large part of reading in class self-selected trade books with no strings of questions attached. Conferences with the teacher and oral reports to the class were all that were required of these independent readers.

"It was sure different getting to read real books in school."
"What I like best about special reading [the name given to the program] was getting to pick out what I read."

"I never knew reading in school could be this fun."
"I read all the books I wanted to because you didn't have to
    write a book report after every book."
"Special reading is nothing like regular reading [using a basal
    or "skill-building" booklet]; that's the best thing about it."

The last word (for many educators) on the subject: All seventh graders in the special reading program gained one to two grade levels during the year, as measured by standardized tests of comprehension and vocabulary. For other equally important gains—interest, enthusiasm, joy in reading—there were no formal measures, only the children's changed reading behavior (enthusiastic oral sharing of books, more requests to take home books from the classroom library, increased use of the public library) and their own words in praise of "special reading."

PART II

The Unifying Principles of Literature

3

On Teaching Literature

Thinking about readers and the way they make sense of literature has led to what has been called "reader-response criticism," which claims that the meaning of the text is the experience of the reader (an experience that includes hesitations, conjectures, and self-corrections). If a literary work is conceived as a succession of actions upon the understanding of a reader, then an interpretation of the work can be a story of that encounter, with its ups and downs: various conventions or expectations are brought into play, connections are posited, and expectations defeated or confirmed. To interpret a work is to tell a story of reading.

—Jonathan Culler (1997, p. 63)

A discussion of teaching literature properly begins with an attempt to explain what is meant by the slippery word *literature*. In Chapter 1, I defined literature as "unique writings that demonstrate excellence of form and expression." While I stand by that definition, I acknowledge that it may be open to question and probably is in need of emendation. *Literature* has multiple connotations. We are likely to use the term for critical or imaginative writings in prose or verse as distinguished from news reports and entries in the encyclopedia. It is associated with works considered to be of lasting value because of marked originality, significance of content, or excellence of form and style. But even these descriptions are far from definitive. In the second edition of *Literary Theory*, Terry Eagleton (1996) exposes the flaws in typical definitions of literature.

QUESTIONS OF DEFINITION

If literature is defined as "imaginative" or "fictional" writing, must essays, memoirs, and historical accounts of obvious literary quality be excluded? If I claim that literature is literature because it contains the generally acknowledged beliefs and traditions of a society, can I be certain that these ideas are shared by all people over time? Critics today question the value of the established canon of works taught in colleges and schools. Feminists demand equal time in the curriculum for consideration of works by women writers and writings that address women's issues. In a society so diverse, many ask how it can be appropriate to study in schools a predominance of literary works written by dead, white, European males.

If I say that literary language is different from ordinary language, that it draws attention to itself, then I must not describe as literature writings of notable beauty executed in simple, straightforward style. In the 1920s, a group of Russian critics known as "formalists," of whose work Roman Jakobson (1972) is representative, did offer such a definition, one that focused not on a work's social and historical setting, nor on the author's noble intentions or distinguished biography, but on the text itself.

For them, language was recognized as "literary" by its deviations from the normal. However, this definition proves as unsatisfactory as others, since "strange" and "normal," two highly relative terms, are designations—when applied to language or, for that matter, anything else—on which few listeners and readers would agree absolutely.

Any additional definition of literature one might propose is certain, on examination, to reveal similar flaws. For instance, the notion that literature, unlike a textbook on, say, biology, has no *practical use* is of course fallacious. As Louise Rosenblatt (1978) has taught us, even the most literary of texts may be read both aesthetically, for the lived-through experience with the work, and efferently, for the purpose of carrying away information about a work or factual information found within it.

Most of us have in mind a personal definition of literature like the one I offered above. Yet, as we see, the term is a slippery one. Now that we've given the matter some thought, we are ready to hear critic Terry Eagleton's postmodern comment: "Literature, in the sense of a set of works of assured and unalterable value, distinguished by certain shared inherent properties, does not exist" (1996, p. 9). Whether one agrees or not depends on how easily traditional views can be set aside.

Disagreements about what literature is are nothing compared to differences of opinion regarding approaches to literary criticism, the process of studying literary works. Early study, as we shall see, focused on the historical background of the work. Next came emphasis on the work itself as the repository of meaning. Then, new insights into the nature of language radically changed the way scholars regarded the relationship between texts and readers. At this writing, the focus is on readers and how they *make* meaning, not by extracting it from the work—where, according to deconstructionists, no meaning resides anyway—but through *transactions* with the text. Educators are notorious for embracing one instructional approach to the exclusion of all others (the ongoing yes–no debate about phonics is a case in point). Passionate attachment to an approach almost certainly signals an eventual pendulum swing away from it. But for now, reader response is the critical approach *du jour*.

However, Richard Beach (1993) points out that even within reader response theory there is plurality of approach: vestiges of an earlier structuralist emphasis, inroads from later deconstruction theory, and inclusion of the psychological and social emphases of Marxist and feminist criticism. Indeed, today works are examined *primarily* from psychological, cultural, and social viewpoints (Soter, 1999) and seldom from the perspective of the literary work as art. Entrepreneurial critics from the golden age of reader response, the 1970s and early 1980s, spun theories that celebrate reading and readers (Barthes, 1977; Bleich, 1978; de Man, 1979; Fish, 1980; Holland, 1975; Ingarden, 1973; Iser, 1978; Jauss, 1982; Rabinowitz, 1987; Rosenblatt, 1938, 1978).

Critical theories formulated in the 1970s and 1980s slowly trickled down to inform elementary and middle school practice. Today we read scholarly treatises containing references to Barthes' "jouissance" (Tuleja, 1998), another way of talking about Rosenblatt's "lived-through" encounter with a text; Iser's "implied reader" filling in "gaps" in a text (Daley, 2002); and Ingarden's "concretization" (Nodelman, 1996). When talking about this process of bringing concepts in the text to life, Judith Langer (1995) uses the term "envisionment." Iser prefers "realization." Discussing from a perspective of cultural criticism, Soter (1999) invokes Jauss's (1982) "horizons of expectations."

In today's literature on literary studies we can find statements that are interesting and enlightening, others that seem obvious and simplistic, and still others that appear to be the old theories cloaked in new jargon—for "the problems of literary criticism have a way of returning in glamorous new disguises" (Adams & Searle, 1986, p. 22). The comment that literary theory is a field in which "there is much endeavor and little attempt at perspective" (Frye, 1957, p. 3) is as valid today as it was a half century ago.

The following brief history of the growth of literary studies is intended to provide perspective on this volatile field, characterized by Jonathan Culler as "contentiously constituted by apparently incompatible activities" (1982, p. 17).

THE GROWTH AND DEVELOPMENT OF LITERARY STUDIES

The Early Days of "English" Studies

Literature as a subject of study is a relatively new concept. It was introduced in the Victorian period by educators such as Matthew Arnold (1822–1888) primarily as a means of edifying the burgeoning middle class and indoctrinating its members with the moral and ethical understandings they formerly received from organized religion. The "masses" were, in Arnold's experience, "losing the Bible and its religion" (1896a, p. 282).

Arnold argued in his lectures and writings that what he considered to be "great literature" possessed as much or more potential as religion to counter for readers and listeners the dehumanizing effects of the industrial revolution. Systematic study of poetry, "nothing less than the most perfect speech of man, that in which he comes nearest to being able to utter truth" (1896b, p. 128), would, he believed, result in the attainment of *culture*, a state of sensitivity and refined enlightenment.

"English was literally the poor man's Classics—a way of providing a cheapish 'liberal' education for those beyond the charmed circles of public school and Oxbridge" (Eagleton, 1996, p. 23). Early study of literature centered on selected literary works as potential developers of moral values and aesthetic sensibility as well as a means of endowing the masses with the social and religious ideology their "betters" found good for them. The means to these ends were to be found in select "great works" of "great men" (those were sexist times)—works that were identified as the touchstones of English literature. These included the work of Milton, Donne,

Bunyan, and Wordsworth. Shakespeare's work did not often meet Matthew Arnold's exacting criteria for a literary touchstone: "sustained high seriousness, clarity of language, evidence of morality, and the exercise of the grand style" (Eells, 1955, p. 143).

Then, even as now, there was disagreement as to *how* and *why* literature should be taught. Some scholarly detractors, who saw the new study as intellectually "soft," questioned the point of teaching novels, plays, and poetry that people could read on their own. For the most part, interpretive emphasis in early literary studies was primarily on the content and emotional appeal of the text, engendered by beauty of language and nobility of moral tone. The lives, times, and intention of the "great men" who composed the works were also incorporated into the study. *Appreciation* and *reverence* are key words in describing the criticism that prevailed in these early days of literary studies. Robert Louis Stevenson (1850–1894) aptly echoed the sentiments of the time when he wrote in *Songs of Travel*: "Bright is the ring of words/ When the right man rings them."

Intellectuals in these early days of literary study worried that literature lacked its own body of knowledge. Edward A. Freeman, the Regius Professor of History at Oxford, feared that the study of literature would degenerate into gossip: "chatter about Shelley, or worse, chatter about Harriet [Shelley's first wife]" (1887, p. 566). However, language, when joined with literature, became a body of knowledge that helped to bring justification to literary study. Hard facts about early Anglo-Saxon verb forms and phonetic laws were testable knowledge that students had to struggle sufficiently to learn. History supplied the other major body of knowledge for literary studies. Requiring students to know facts about the historical and social background of literary works appeared to make their study more solid and tangible.

The New Critics

Frank Raymond Leavis (1895–1978), Sir Arthur Quiller-Couch (1863–1944), and Ivor Armstrong Richards (1893–1979) were leaders in efforts to systematize and bring purpose and prestige to literary studies. They advocated a disciplined critical analysis or "close reading" of literature. This meant scrutinizing the devices of a text while setting aside subjective emotional response to it and paying less attention to its author's biography and times. *Scrutiny* was the apt title of a critical journal founded by Leavis in the 1930s. Previously, criticism had consisted largely of treatises appreciative of the delights of instructive texts. The "practical criticism" of men such as Leavis, Quiller-Couch, and Richards maintained that a text was an entity in itself, set apart from writer, reader, and historical or social context. These ideas were set forth in New Critical texts, among them *The Verbal Icon* (Wimsatt & Beardsley, 1954) and *The Well-wrought Urn* (Brooks, 1947/1968).

Referring to it as the "Intentional Fallacy," the New Critics blasted the notion that the author's intention, even if it could be determined, was relevant in interpreting a text. Equally irrelevant to interpretation, they insisted, was the emotional response of a reader to the text. Denigrated by influential New Critics, among them Cleanth Brooks, W. K. Wimsatt, Allen Tate, and Monroe Beardsley, this response was dubbed the "Affective Fallacy." The New Critics sought objectivity in their approach to a literary text. Their study concentrated on how language works to create the tensions, ambivalences, and paradoxes discoverable in a work.

Flourishing in America from the 1930s to the 1950s, New Criticism functioned in part as a means to provide literary criticism with a pseudo-scientific approach that would endow the study with rigor, ultimately bringing respectability to the discipline. The exact meaning of a work was thought to be within the language of the text and completely explicable; an erudite professor or teacher, who—through study and experience—already knew the "correct" meaning, refereed students' attempts to ferret it out.

Close textual analysis was an approach easily replicated that gave specificity and structure to literary study, and in particular to the study of poetry, where techniques and devices such as point of view, figurative language, meter, and rhyme were more readily apparent and more immediately accessible than in longer prose forms. In addition, through their use of terms such as *paradox*, *ambiguity*, *tension*, and *dramatic structure*, the New Critics provided literary studies with its own language.

New Criticism and earlier approaches to literary study are by no means extinct. Reverence for certain "classic" works as well as a preoccupation with their historical background are still common today in classrooms. Nor is New Criticism's focus on close analysis of the text a mere relic of the past. While teachers may give lip service and a certain amount of time to the reader response approaches in fashion today, in the end close reading of texts becomes the central feature of study in many classrooms (Applebee, 1992).

THEORIES OF READING AND THE READER

In the 1960s, theorists began to apply the ideas of the Swiss structural linguist, Ferdinand de Sassure (1857–1913). Language, he declared, is a system of signs with underlying rules that allow the signs to combine into meanings. The sign system is a code whose conventions are agreed upon by a society to make communication possible. As we grow, we are socialized into our native language, which dictates how we perceive the world.

Meaning is therefore not a function of an author's intentionality but of language itself. Therefore, formalists and structuralists insisted, study of a text's formal linguistic properties or structures was the only valid critical approach.

Sassure made a distinction between what people said (parole) and the linguistic deep-structure that allowed them to say it (langue). Each sign is made up of a signifier (a sound or its graphic representation) and a signified (its meaning or concept). What is signified by a signifier is by no means identical for each reader or listener. Furthermore, signifying systems undergo change. A literary work, therefore, cannot be an objective entity with its "meaning" existing apart from the experience of the reader. This notion is at the center of reader response theory.

The validity of a reader response approach to literature is without question, although scholars warn against carrying its notions to extremes. Alvin Kernan notes:

> It seems to me that the theories of recent years declaring the emptiness of literary language and the total dependence of a text for its meaning on the reader have earned literature a foolish name in the world. . . . Deconstruction exposed the excesses of the old formalist New Criticism that located its own super-refined meanings in the text itself, and various kinds of reader response criticism have made clear the involvement of readers in the construction of meaning. But to accept in practice that there is no meaning in literature's words except what we impute to them is not really a tenable working position. (1993, p. 16)

Louise Rosenblatt's Theory of Reading

In a historical look at trends and theories in reading and literary studies, Louise Rosenblatt holds a special place. It is she who has articulated literary theory for practical application by elementary and secondary school educators. Even though they may not have read her works, Louise Rosenblatt's name is well known to teachers in elementary and middle schools. Of the 72 teachers I surveyed (Sloan, 1995) on the subject of literature-based reading and related matters, only a handful had actually read Rosenblatt's own words; what they knew of her ideas was second-hand. Still, most could repeat a familiar litany that they attributed to Rosenblatt: "The aesthetic response to a literary work is primary and inviolable"; "There are no right, wrong, or definitive interpretations of a text"; "Each reader makes meaning from the text through his or her unique transaction, because each brings to the process particular experience of life and other texts."

Rosenblatt advocated a reader-centered approach to literary studies as far back as 1938, but at that time and for a long time afterward, New Criticism ruled in all but the most "progressive" classrooms. Hers was a voice of reform raised against what she perceived as the one-note extremes of New Criticism. She believed that "a philosophy of teaching based on a balanced recognition of the many complex elements that make up the literary experience can foster the development of more fruitful understanding and appreciation of literature" (1938, p. 24).

While Rosenblatt insisted on the primacy of the aesthetic experience of literature, she never advocated, as some interpreters of her particular version of reader response theory ("transactional theory" is her preferred term) seem to suggest, that response end there. A closer look at her work reveals a deep concern for rigorous, reflective study:

> The literary critic draws on the results of efferent analysis or study in order to illuminate, to reinforce or enrich, to place in context, that aesthetic event. *In the basic paradigm for literary criticism, then, the movement is from an intensely realized aesthetic transaction with the text to reflection on semantic or technical or other details in order to return to, and correlate them with, that particular personally apprehended aesthetic reading.* (1978, p. 162. Emphasis in original.)

This position, representing a balance between initial aesthetic response to a work and subsequent critical study of it, is the approach to literary study advocated in this and previous editions of *The Child as Critic*. For me, as for Rosenblatt and others (Apol, 1998; Cai & Traw, 1997), literary study implies interpretation through analysis and reflection. In Rosenblatt's own words: "To do full justice to the literary transaction, we want not only to depict the work as we envision it but also to characterize it in terms of the second stream of responses that contributed so much to its texture and import" (1978, p. 136). This is not to suggest that there cannot be occasions, as when reading simple fare to pass the time, that one is "satisfied simply with the evocation and response dimension of the reading process" (Rosenblatt, 1978, p. 70). However, lacking the element of interpretation, this reading experience should not be construed as study or criticism.

Rosenblatt left teachers to interpret and implement her instructional ideas on their own, with only a few instances from her own teaching as examples of procedure. Unfortunately, this has often resulted—at least in my experience observing in classrooms—in "study" that is little more than superficial chat about readers' aesthetic responses to a work. For this practice to be rectified, teachers need to know first-hand Rosenblatt's sound educational ideas. To clarify the role of the teacher, as Rosenblatt describes it, Robert Probst provides a useful extrapolation of Rosenblatt's "Principles of Instruction" from her book *Literature as Exploration* (1938):

- Students must be free to deal with their own reactions to the text (p. 66);
- The classroom situation and the relationship with the teacher should create a feeling of security (p. 66);
- Teachers must provide time and opportunity for "an initial crystallization of a personal sense of the work" (p. 69);
- Teachers must avoid undue emphasis upon the form in which the students' reactions are couched (p. 67);
- Teachers must try to find points of contact among the opinions of students (p. 71);
- The teacher's influence should be "the elaboration of the vital influence inherent in literature itself" (p. 74);
- Although free response is necessary, it is not sufficient—students must still be led to reflection and analysis (p. 75).

(Probst, 1990, pp. 31–35. Page numbers in parentheses refer to corresponding pages in Rosenblatt's text.)

Variations Within Reader Response

In his discussion of reader response theories, Richard Beach notes that "theorists and teachers may adopt quite different conceptions of readers' roles, purposes, texts, and contexts, suggesting there is no single 'reader response' theory" (1993, p. 5). Nor is there a single reader. Elizabeth Freund (1987) reviews some of the characterizations theorists have applied to readers: Iser's "implied reader," Eco's "model reader," Culler's "competent reader," and Fish's "informed reader in the interpretive community."

Beach (1993), like Soter (1999), divides reader response by various perspectives that are not mutually exclusive nor ordered linearly. Beach advocates the use of many lenses to examine texts in the meaning-making process. To focus only on the reader is unrealistic. In good practice, talk about a text ranges over a multiplicity of approaches. Some possible approaches might be:

> *Textual*. Theorists focus on how readers draw on and deploy their knowledge of text and/or genre conventions to respond to specific text features. For example, in responding to a mystery story, a reader might apply her knowledge of mystery genre conventions to predict the story outcome.
>
> *Experiential*. Theorists focus on the nature of readers' engagement or experiences with texts—for example, the ways in which readers identify with characters, visualize images, relate personal experiences to the text, or construct the world of the text.
>
> *Psychological*. Theorists focus on readers' cognitive or subconscious processes and how those processes vary according to both unique individual personality and developmental level.
>
> *Social*. Theorists focus on the influence of social context on the reader/text transaction—for example, the ways that a book-club context serves to encourage a lot of open-ended responses.
>
> *Cultural*. Theorists focus on how readers' cultural roles, attitudes, and values, as well as the larger cultural and historical contexts in which the text was written, shape readers' responses. For example, members of a religious sect are socialized to respond to sacred texts according to the cultural values of that sect.

Seldom, in good practice, will response center on one approach to the exclusion of the others. Predominantly oral for younger students, but also written or in art forms such as painting, crafts, drama, and dance, response involves a rich mix of transactions with a text. Interpretations of a story, an informational piece, or a poem spread outward from the text under study like ripples, ever widening from the initial close encounter.

Theories of reading move us toward a better understanding of an activity that has always held mystery. No matter how interesting and informative these approaches and theories may be, however, they do not form a comprehensive schema capable of bringing a sense of coherence to literary studies.

THE NEED FOR A UNIFYING LITERARY THEORY

While the study of literature does not lack for theory, it has, since its beginnings, lacked an *encompassing* theory. Whether the vogue is to approach a text from either a New Critical or a reader response stance, there is no approach to literary study that provides any real sense of how separate texts relate. Attempts to provide an overarching, systematic study plan for Western literature may have begun with Aristotle, but we must concede that there has been little progress toward achieving it. René Wellek and Austin Warren (1949) acknowledged the need for a comprehensive literary theory to inform scholarship, but their attempts to provide it failed due to lack of agreement among the various and divisive viewpoints of the differing schools of criticism.

The Frye Vision

In 1957 the Canadian scholar and literary critic Northrop Frye published a thoroughly original, groundbreaking book, *Anatomy of Criticism,* in which he described a unique vision of a synoptic theory of literature that he believed was capable of containing *all* valid critical methods and providing for the field of literary studies a much-needed unifying perspective. His theory does not supplant other critical methods; it simply supplies an umbrella for them. Under the umbrella is room for any approach one chooses to take in literary studies. As Peter Yan states, "Frye's writing is the operating system adaptable to any platform, the ultimate shareware, the great code which builds on old programs and allows you to write new ones" (2002, p. 31).

Frye's view of the fundamental unity in literature may be compared to a giant jigsaw puzzle. When it is completed and you stand back from it, you see the picture as a whole. But you are simultaneously aware that the picture is composed of interlocking pieces.

Frye embraced no "school" or specific critical approach. His intent was to articulate a number of the central problems of critical theory (Frye, 1976b, p. 23). These he set forth in the "Polemical Introduction" to *Anatomy of Criticism* (1957).

> "The axioms and postulates of criticism . . . have to grow out of the art it deals with." (pp. 6–7)
> "Criticism . . . must be an examination of literature in terms of a conceptual framework derivable from an inductive survey of the literary field." (p. 7)
> "Art, like nature, has to be distinguished from the systematic study of it, which is criticism." (p. 11)
> "Criticism seems to be badly in need of a coordinating principle, a central hypothesis which, like the theory of evolution in biology, will see the phenomena it deals with as parts of a whole." (p. 16)
> "Criticism cannot be a systematic study unless there is a quality in literature which enables it to be so." (p. 17)

In *Anatomy of Criticism*, Frye presents a metaphoric vision of literature (described in Chapters 4 and 5 of this book) as forming a total schematic order, interconnected by conventional plot structures, characters, themes, and patterns of imagery that he called *archetypes*. These recurring patterns or motifs, expanding from myth and especially from folk tales into the rest of literature, are the elements that build the repetitive quality of literature, or its allusiveness. Frye believes that "certain themes, situations, and character types have persisted with very little change from Aristophanes to our own time" (1982, p. 48).

In his study of the symbolism in the art and poetry of the eighteenth-century poet/painter William Blake, Frye found evidence of the existence of recurring patterns or archetypes as well as other organizing principles for the whole of Western literature. For example, he traces the development of stories as "displacements" from myth and folktale, always moving toward verisimilitude or reality. He suggests four basic narrative patterns, a circle of stories, that encompass all forms of story: comedy, romance, tragedy, and irony-satire. (See Chapter 5, "The Circle of Stories," for more on these narrative patterns.)

Theory as Metaphor

Frye's vision of literature as an "order of words" is held out for us to take from it what we will, but he never suggests that the

vision is anything more than a metaphor. The schematic overview he proposes (he preferred "schema" to "system") is intended
to be "a scaffolding to be knocked away when the building [liter-
ary criticism] is in better shape" (1993, p. 14).

Literary criticism is certainly no closer now than it ever was
to assuming a single shape, and "better" is by far too relative a
term to apply to it. This poststructuralist, deconstructionist era
has been dominated by ideological critical approaches such as
Marxism, feminism, arcane psychoanalytical analyses, and reader
response theory, all of which have been variously interpreted and
implemented. Archetypal criticism has gone out of fashion in a
milieu that rejects "the very possibility of a 'totally intelligible'
criticism" (Willard, 1994, p. 20).

However, in a time when poststructuralist movements dis-
appoint and wane Frye's theories are starting to make a resur-
gence. Leading Frye scholar Robert D. Denham of Roanoke College notes that "more than half of the translations of [Frye's]
works into 21 languages have occurred during the past decade"
(personal communication, March, 2002). Also, during this period
there have been a dozen or so international conferences and two
dozen books devoted wholly to Frye's work.

LITERARY STUDY IN THE NEW MILLENNIUM

If we plan to teach criticism in schools we need a curriculum that serves as a deductive framework to facilitate an inquiry-
based, inductive learning process for young students. Frye's
"order of words" provides the basis for an understanding of what
literature, as a whole, is about. Whether a reader responds to literary works aesthetically, efferently, as a woman, as a Marxist,
or from any other critical stance, the discovery of the unifying
principles that unite both the literary and the nonliterary will
enrich his or her response.

Frye on Teaching Literature

Frye declared that "the only guarantee that a subject is theo-
retically coherent is its ability to have its elementary principles
taught to children" (1963c, p. 33). The comment was repeated in
Frye's foreword to the first edition of *The Child as Critic*, which
is included at the beginning of this book. As if in support of Frye's

statement, Jerome Bruner published *The Process of Education*, an educationally influential report in which Bruner writes that "we begin with the hypothesis that any subject can be taught effectively in some intellectually honest form to any child at any stage of development" (1960, p. 13).

Frye presented a detailed argument for a curriculum that provided a sense of the structure of the subject to be studied. Famously known as "the spiral curriculum," this concept of sequence suggested that central ideas of a discipline would be revisited at different grade levels, each time at successively higher levels of complexity. Learning would proceed inductively, through a process of inquiry.

To Frye, the concepts of the spiral curriculum and inductive, inquiry-based learning were educationally sound and he offered an order of literary studies in keeping with it. He believed that reading and listening to stories, particularly those of the Bible and of classical mythology, should have a central place in early literary study (Frye, 1970, p. 101). Through familiarity with many stories, a child discovers that there are a limited number of ways of telling a story. The child therefore has a "structure of storytelling implanted in his mind, and a critical standard as well, which he badly needs in a world of sub-literary entertainment" (Frye, 1988, p. 54).

Frye (1963b, 1970) considered it essential that poetry be at the center in literacy education. However, we know that in elementary and middle school classrooms it is typically at the periphery of the curriculum, if it is in sight at all (Sloan, 1998, 2001b). In Chapter 6 of this book, "Poetry and Literacy," Frye's views on poetry are applied. More than 20 years worth of classroom research conducted by my graduate students suggests that poetry and verse does, indeed, promote literacy by fostering word awareness and an interest in words (Sloan, 2003).

The Goals of Literary Study

In deciding how to teach literature (or, more properly, how to teach *criticism*, since literature, like architecture, cannot be directly taught) it is important to have clearly-defined goals as well as an informing theory. Goals determine how and what we teach.

Reading for Connections. Intertextual insight seems to me to be a primary goal of literary study. Works relate to each other like members of a large, extended family, with a family tree traceable to the earliest times. Relationship among texts, or intertextuality, can take many forms (Adams & Searle, 1986; Childers & Hentzi, 1995, p. 159; Makaryk, 1993, p. 568). Essentially, it refers to how texts echo, or are linked to, other texts. This linkage may be through either overt or covert allusions and citations, through use of common literary conventions such as stock characters or recurrent plot patterns, and by the repetition of various features and motifs. The quest, for instance, whether psychological or in the form of a journey, is one example of a ubiquitous literary motif.

The notion of intertextuality fits well with Frye's belief that a true critic, in order to ultimately understand what literature as a whole is about, must "interpret every work of literature in the light of all the literature he knows" (Frye, 1963a, p. 44).

We learn all things by making connections, by constructing new knowledge from what we already know. All imaginative verbal constructs, whether literary or subliterary (advertisements, comics, pop songs) interrelate. Thus, literature may be considered not merely as discrete works but an "order of words." Whether a text is approached from a New Critical stance or from some aspect of reader response theory, "we need to help [our students] to see that every poem, play, and story is a text related to others, both verbal pre-texts, and all manner of post-texts including their own responses, whether in speech, writing, or action" (Scholes, 1985, p. 20).

An awareness of relationships among works of literature brings with it a sense of literature as the continuous journal of the human imagination, an interrelated body of imaginative verbal structures that examine every aspect of human experience. This awareness brings to the study of literature a sense of its significance in our lives, an understanding that does not come to students who see each literary work only as a separate entity, never exploring its connection to all other works.

Reading to Educate the Imagination. An important reason for studying literature is to effect a transfer of its imaginative energy and vision to the reader or listener—in other words, to educate the imagination and to engage the emotions. Plato, recognizing the power that language can exert, excluded poets from his ideal state. For him, the "literary work is not so much an object as a unit of force whose power is exerted on the world" (Tompkins, 1980,

p. 204). To experience this force is to motivate the desire to read. The initial lived-through experience of a work that raises goose bumps or causes belly laughs in the young can make them life-long readers. Children need to experience literature that awakens their emotions and piques their sense of wonder.

Reading for Fluency.   Another goal of the elementary and middle school reading program is to develop fluent, independent readers who turn readily to books for information and enjoyment. This goal can never be achieved through the minute dissection of poems and stories. As works of art they should be experienced first as entities. Young students deserve the chance to savor much of the literature they read and hear, with no strings of questions attached. When they move on to critical study, it should be undertaken as exploration, not plunder.

Good questions and prompts are, of course, both necessary and possible. Responding to literature through discussion, preferably in small groups, is a time-honored way to promote literary growth through reading, reflecting, and reevaluating one's response in light of the responses of others (Sloan, 1975, 1991). The best questions on literary works, unlike those directed to arithmetic problems, seldom have a single "correct" answer. Here are some prompts teachers in my classes have found useful:

> "You were listening hard to that story, or you seemed interested in the story. Why was that?"
> "You read the whole book," or "You didn't finish the book." "Why?"
> "What other literature that you have read, heard, or viewed was brought to mind by this story or poem?"
> "Did the story leave you feeling satisfied, with a feeling of completeness? Why or why not?"
> "Why would you like to hear the story (or poem) again?"
> "Why was this a good story for you especially?"

Depending on the focus of study, questions to guide discussion will vary. For example, a question like the following focuses on textual elements: "Suppose you thought of a new ending for the story. How would you have to change the rest of the story to fit the new ending?" From a perspective of cultural criticism, Laura Apol asks a question designed to identify and clarify ideology: "Think not only about what the text says, but about what it does not say as well. Whose voices are given prominence? Whose voices are not heard?"(1998, p. 38).

Reading to Interpret.   Interpretation is an accepted goal of literary study, with a distinction always made between making meaning for oneself and trying to ferret out the *true* meaning of a work. If a poem or story is richly textured, genuine literature of substance, the latter will be impossible to do. Meaning is subject to change; it is affected by new information, the opinions of others, or new insights from other reading or viewing.

Talk about literature needs to go beyond chatter and gossip, needs to be grounded in theory, and needs to be purposeful. Cai and Traw insist that literary study worthy of the name helps students "achieve a more active, competent literary transaction with literature, arriving at a fuller, richer reading that does justice to its artistic complexity" (1997, p. 24). Arguing for a holistic approach to teaching literature, they advocate cultivating a response that combines the transactional and the textual. In classroom instruction, personal responses to literature should and can "be combined and enhanced with the learning of literary conventions" (p. 30). Others agree that literary conventions, the study of how the *art* of literature works, need to be an integral part of literary study (Sloan, 1991, 1997; Soter & Letcher, 1998).

Reading to Become Articulate.   Articulateness is another goal of literary study. Attempting to express, whether orally in a book club session or through writing in a journal entry, one's personal experience of a literary work and trying to explain what an author did to make a story or poem work are both exercises in becoming articulate. Oral reader response is a developmental skill, growing with patience and skilled guidance under the influence of the ultimate language art, literature.

Reading Critically.   Above all, children need to know that the unexamined response is not worth having. They must be taught to critique their response to all they read, hear, or view, whether it be literary or subliterary, such as pop songs, advertisements, and situation comedies. Each child needs to learn to ask: Is my response to this story truly the product of my own thinking or is it simply a parroting of ideas imbedded in my culture and society and taken for granted by me? Do I read as an activist, constantly confronting a text and its premises, always questioning, and struggling to deconstruct the text by uncovering discrepancies, misconceptions, or contradictions in it? Am I vigilant, watchful for manipulative texts that perpetuate stereotypes or racist and sexist beliefs? Positive answers to these questions indicate that an essential goal of literary study has been met. Only critical thinkers can take a free and independent part in society.

CONCLUSION

Growth in criticism is based on knowledge. Experiencing literature is therefore the first step toward becoming a critic of it. However, just as experiencing a city full of buildings is not studying architecture, experiencing poems and stories is not studying literature. Its study involves a number of things, including both free response and guided response from various perspectives, the objective of the latter being to heighten and illuminate personal experience. It is a systematic study that proceeds from a teacher's deductive framework to an inductive process of inquiry on the part of students in order to discover for themselves how the human imagination works as it creates art from words and to examine its effect on their mind and emotions.

A growing sense of the continuity of literature, of one step leading to another, of details fitting into a larger design, is essential to criticism. By emphasizing the explorative part of the mind, teachers help students to discover that literature is even more than good stories, poems, and books of useful information. The next two chapters present the unifying principles that are the basis for a comprehensive look at literature.

4

Likenesses Unify Literature

The order of words is there. . . . The fact that literature is based on unifying principles as schematic as those of music is concealed by many things, most of them psychological blocks, but the unity exists and can be shown and taught to others, including children.

—Northrop Frye (1976b, p. 118)

Without its own conceptual framework to contain and inform it, literary study—criticism—moves outside itself, typically utilizing concepts from other studies in the humanities, like history and philosophy. For example, literary works are frequently considered chronologically, a concept borrowed from history. Another common approach to literary study, which focuses on content, leans toward philosophy; here certain stories, poems, and plays are considered as repositories of moral and social ideals, and study consists mainly of gleaning from them profound axioms of the human situation. New literary theories examine a text from either cultural, ideological, or new-historicist viewpoints (Soter, 1999). These approaches, however valid, provide no sense of the unity and coherence of literature as a whole or insight into what literature is and how it works.

Criticism has to be based in literature itself. A conceptual framework within which study may be systematic and developmental needs to come from organizing principles actually present in literary works. Literature grows out of itself; new works are recognizably related to old, just as a baby is a new and unique individual as well as an example of a human being, a descendant of a long line of other humans. Literature does have a context of its own; the context of each work is its place with regard to other works.

51

Literary works relate through their likenesses. These likenesses—similarities recurring throughout all literature—are discussed in this and the next chapter; through them literature is unified. Their delineation provides a conceptual scheme that allows us to see each work as a part of a whole.

HOW LITERARY WORKS INTERRELATE

Literature is more than a collection of unrelated poems and stories; the more we read the more obvious this becomes. Hercules and Superman were created centuries apart but they are recognizable as the same character type: the hero with magical powers. We find images like gardens and wastelands in the Old Testament and in the ballads of folksingers. That love is more powerful than any evil or even death itself is a theme of stories as different as the old tale *Beauty and the Beast* and the more recent *Charlotte's Web* (White, 1952). We recognize the shape of the romance story—the adventurous quest—in ancient epics, westerns, space odysseys, and the countless cops and robbers shows of television. In the latter, a crusading attorney or police officer, like the dragon-slaying knight of old, sets out to confront and capture modern-day dragons who may appear in the shape of corrupt politicians, drug dealers, murderers, or child molesters.

Archetypes

In literature, as well as in other verbal structures such as advertisements, certain elements and structural patterns are recurrent; this is evident in works both old and new, classical and pop. These patterns or models—fundamental and ancient—recur often enough to be recognizable as aspects of all literary experience; as such, they are archetypal.

Archetypes can be characters (wise old men or women); events (rites of initiation); symbols (innocence equated with youth); plots (the Cinderella story, the quest); themes (love is more powerful than evil); images (wastelands and gardens); or motifs (transformations, patterns of three). Archetypes are repeated patterns that recur in the literature of every age. They are found in the Bible, in mythology, and in folk literature. Nor are these units of imaginative thought common only to the main body of literature; they turn up in comics, films, song lyrics, and children's drawings. Archetypes are forms of imaginative thought, present in both primitive and sophisticated art. These repeatable units of imaginative experience occur constantly and unpredictably. Their existence makes it possible to connect one literary work with another.

Convention and Genre

The word *convention* expresses another kind of similarity found in literature. If we read a detective story, for instance, we expect to find certain elements in it—a crime, someone to solve it, a criminal who is apprehended. Each detective story, like each game of chess or checkers, is different enough from others to make it a distinct experience, yet similar enough to make us recognize it as one of a type.

In addition, we find that literary works fall into categories or genres. Most of these genres or forms have long histories. Primitive rituals and dances, for example, are known to be the antecedents of drama.

The primary literary categories are drama, prose fiction, lyrics, epics, and nonfiction forms like the essay and autobiography. Genres may change over time; new forms may evolve. However, literature derives its forms from itself, and every form may be traced back to the earliest times. *Huckleberry Finn* and *Moby Dick* are epics of a new country, the United States, but even so they have elements in common with the *Iliad* and the *Odyssey*, epics of ancient Greece—among them disguises, clever lies to ensure survival, and the idea that human friendships can be stronger than disaster. It is a fact that writers write out of their experience with literature, no matter how innovative we may consider their new works to be.

LITERARY PATTERNS FROM MYTHOLOGY

From its beginnings, literature has been people's imaginative attempt to give shape, order, and structure to their experience. Literature's roots are with myth and ritual, myth being the spoken part of a ritual, the story that the ritual enacts. Early religious rituals aimed at securing the well-being of a group of people, and most shared the same general pattern: They depicted the death and resurrection of a god-king in a series of episodes that typically included a battle in which the god-king was victorious, a triumphal procession, an enthronement, a ceremony to ensure the destinies of the people for the coming year, and a sacred marriage.

Confronted with an alien universe, people—the storytelling animals—described natural phenomena in human terms. Occurrences in nature that frightened and bewildered them were given human shapes and "controlled" through story by means of analogy and metaphor. The clearest forms of such associations are in mythical images where we have "gods" who are human in shape and character, yet identified with something in nature like the sun or the seasons. These myths are metaphors in action, stories about sun gods or fire gods who are human yet totally identified with some force in nature. (Apollo is the sun god and the sun itself.) Simile and metaphor—the primitive and archaic forms of thought used to identify the inner with the outer world—are still used by imaginative writers to suggest an identity between the human mind and the world outside it. In these literary devices, we have another kind of likeness found in literature.

Feeling lost and helpless against the forces of nature, early people told stories of a time when they and nature were in harmony. The story of the Garden of Eden is one such story, but similar ones are found in the mythology of many cultures. The story tells how humans lost their perfect home and became alienated from the rest of the universe and subject to time and death. By the power of imagination, people seek to regain the lost perfect world. In later stories—legends and folktales—the gods take on more human characteristics and have less divine power. Eventually they disappear from stories, and characters become more and more recognizable as limited human beings. Even so, there always exists the desire, expressed implicitly or explicitly in poems, stories, and the lyrics of popular songs, to "get back to the garden." Our literature is a continuous journal of people's search for identity, a metaphorical quest to rediscover a lost perfection, a truly human identity. In modern literature nature is no longer a threat, but the world often seems an alien place, and stories still tell of the individual's efforts to find a place in it. Poet and artist William Blake said, "The nature of my work is visionary and imaginative; it is an attempt to restore what the ancients called the Golden Age."

The Two Rhythms of Literature

For constructing any work of art, we need some principle of repetition or recurrence, like rhythm in music and pattern in painting. In the early development of literature from myth, the storytellers took for their recurring pattern the cycles of nature and eventually made analogies between the natural cycles and the human life cycle.

Mythologies are filled with tales of young gods or heroes—Perseus, Theseus, Jason—who go through various successful adventures, endure great dangers, and are deserted, betrayed, even killed, but who usually emerge safely in the end. The movement of the stories is analogous to the progression of the seasons. The merging of the natural cycle with mythology provided myths with two opposing movements: the rising movement that we find in myths of birth, marriage, and resurrection; and the falling movement in myths of death, metamorphosis, or sacrifice. Later, in stories, they appear as the rising movement of comedy and the falling movement of tragedy.

These early stories reveal another aspect of the human imagination. The hero's quest involves a dialectical or philosophical way of looking at life, reflecting at one limit what people most desire and at the other what they most hate and fear. Myths project a paradise above the world of experience, a place of wish fulfillment in which all obstacles are overcome. Below it, they project a hell, a world of nightmare and bondage. To the quest for identity is added this goal: to reach a state where people are released from an indifferent world into the upper world of their dreams and desires, a world that is the opposite of their nightmares. These two opposing worlds appear in literature as the idealized world of innocence and the absurd, suffering, frustrated world of experience (as illustrated in Figure 4.1).

Out of the cycle of death and renewal and human emotional response to it, there gradually emerged four fundamental patterns of imaginative experience: (1) romance, (2) tragedy, (3) irony-satire, and (4) comedy.

In romance we see how strong and beautiful heroes and heroines set out in search of the ideal green and golden world, the world of forever-summer. Tragedy tells how people, although capable of great things, have limited powers. They are sometimes victims of forces they do not understand and cannot control. Just as the autumn leaves must fall, so they must inevitably move toward death. Irony and satire present the wintry world of experience where life is often as harsh and cruel as the winter winds. In comedy, we find hopeful stories of the renewal of the human spirit. New life springs up as new growth comes again in the

FIGURE 4.1. Literary Imagery

spring. Just as the seasons may be considered as distinct though related, so the four imaginative patterns may be seen as aspects of the "one story," people's collective imaginative efforts to give shape to all of human experience. (These four patterns are discussed in detail in Chapter 5.)

John Keats' "The Human Seasons" (1956) is one of many literary works in which the cycles of nature are related to life:

> Four seasons fill the measure of the year;
> There are four seasons in the mind of man:

He has his lusty Spring, when fancy clear
　Takes in all beauty with an easy span:
He has his Summer, when luxuriously
　Spring's honied cud of youthful thought he loves
To ruminate, and by such dreaming high
　Is nearest unto heaven: quiet coves
His soul has in its Autumn, when his wings
　He furleth close; contented so to look
On mists in idleness—to let fair things
　Pass by unheeded as a threshold brook.
He has his Winter too of pale misfeature,
Or else he would forego his mortal nature.

These two thought constructs (the cycle, together with the image of an upper ideal world and its opposite) underlie all literature. Even a brief lyric poem, although it does not tell a "story," may express the emotions connected with the comic, spring part of the cycle or those related to the wintry world of irony. Because it is so structured, literature is in itself a coherent unity. Within this essentially simple structure one can fit all one's literary experiences. Each poem or story takes on a greater significance when it is seen as part of a whole. The whole is the art of literature, people's imaginative attempt to make sense of the world and their existence in it.

The literature of every culture is shaped by its mythology. Besides being the source of countless allusions in later literature, the Bible and classical mythology supply Western literature with the structure that informs it. The Old and New Testaments of the Bible together provide us with the most complete form we have of the archetypal story of the loss and recovery of identity, the story that is the framework of our literature. The Old Testament begins with the story of the creation of man and woman (Adam and Eve) in paradise, then goes on to tell of their fall from innocence and the loss of their original home. Eventually the story of Adam and Eve becomes the story of Israel, a people who endure a long exile in a wilderness where they cannot feel at home, and who quest to reestablish the ideal world—the rightful kingdom— they once knew here on earth. The New Testament tells of the coming of the second Adam (Christ), who rescues the human race from the wilderness and restores the lost paradise where people are one with themselves and God.

The classical myths give us—more clearly than does the Bible—the main episode of the central myth of the hero whose mysterious birth, triumph, betrayal, death, and rebirth follow the rhythm of the seasons. All stories in literature are developments of fundamental shapes that are seen most clearly in myths, particularly the myth that tells of the quest of the hero.

Displacements from Mythology

Viewed historically, our literature is actually a series of "displacements" from the level of pure myth (religion) to naturalism or realism, the mode of most serious fiction in Western literature for the past 100 years. (Interestingly, literature for children, until recently comic or romantic, is now increasingly written in the "realistic" ironic-satiric mode while much printed or filmed fiction for adults is fantasy.) The images, themes, characters, and plots are "displaced" to make them rationally credible and acceptable to the audience of a particular period, a point that becomes clear when we consider literature both historically and in terms of the principal characters' power in relation to their natural and social worlds.

At the level of pure myth, we have characters who are divine, supernatural figures superior to people and nature. Next come the heroes of epics, who are superior in degree to others and to their environments, moving in a world where the ordinary laws of nature are suspended, and often in close touch with the gods themselves. The next level features princes, kings, and queens, who are portrayed as superior to others but not to their environment. At the next remove, the hero has powers similar to our own. The farthest displacement from myth is a phase of the ironic-satiric mode where we have the anti-hero, who is inferior in power even to ordinary people, a victim of others and the powers of nature.

These levels may be traced through a linear progression in history, one mode dominating in a given period, though not to the exclusion of all other modes. Myth, for instance, prevailed from prehistory to the Middle Ages. Here we have Greek and Roman myths and later those of the Christians. Romance, featuring towering figures like King Arthur and his knights, dominated from the Middle Ages to the Renaissance. The high mimetic mode was dominant from the Renaissance to about 1700, a period that included Shakespeare's great tragic plays about the lives of kings and princes like Lear and Hamlet. Dominant from 1700 to about

1900 was the low mimetic mode, most clearly seen in novels like those of Charles Dickens, which feature ordinary people who cope, mostly satisfactorily, with the problems of ordinary life. Although recently incursions have been made into fantasy, since 1900 the ironic mode, exemplified by the novels of Thomas Hardy, has dominated adult fiction.

In children's literature, which began to appear as separate and distinct from adult literature toward the end of the nineteenth century, the low mimetic mode prevailed until after 1950. Examples of the mode are stories of everyday experiences of ordinary folk by such authors as Louisa May Alcott and Lucy M. Montgomery, followed by Laura Ingalls Wilder, Elizabeth Enright, and Eleanor Estes.

Since 1950, realistic stories for children increasingly have incorporated many of the ironic-satiric elements common to adult fiction. Themes and subjects previously thought unsuitable for children's books are presented with candor—abduction: *The Girl in the Box* (Sebestyen, 1988); rape: *Are You in the House Alone?* (Peck, 1977); racism: *The Land* (Taylor, 2001); racism and sexual abuse: *Dangerous Skies* (Staples, 1996); divorce: *Holding Me Here* (Conrad, 1986); the devastation of war: *The Bomb* (Taylor, 1995) and *Parvana's Journey* (Ellis, 2002); and slavery with its attendant atrocities: *Nightjohn* (Paulsen, 1993).

Besides ironic realism, contemporary literature for children features historical fiction like *The Sign of the Beaver* (Speare, 1983); *Catherine Called Birdy* (Cushman, 1994), *The Midwife's Apprentice* (Cushman, 1995), and works of fantasy, which include *The Hero and the Crown* (McKinley, 1985) and *The Crown of Dalemark* (Jones, 1995), the final book of Diana Wynne Jones' *Dalemark Quartet* (*Cart and Quidder, Drowned Ammet, The Spellcoats*). Both forms permit protagonists the positive heroic action associated with romance and comedy. In stories set in the far past or the faraway future (as in science fantasy like *A Dusk of Demons*, John Christopher's 1994 tale of future Britain), the power of the protagonist is likely to be similar to that of heroes and heroines in the romance and high mimetic modes.

Fantasy may show a dual modality. Child protagonists in the realistic portions of a tale like the modern classic *The Dark is Rising* (Cooper, 1973) assume the child's role in society, which in general might be characterized as inferior in power to that of adults. However, transported to the fantasy setting of the same story, child protagonists are capable of heroic action. This is equally true of a picture-book hero like Max in *Where the Wild Things Are* (Sendak, 1963).

In fantasy that uses diminutive human beings or small animals as characters, the heroic and ironic modes are combined in a single story through manipulation of point of view. Such characters are inferior in power and therefore ironic when seen from the point of view of a human of ordinary size. However, the characters do not perceive themselves as inferior. Since this is so, they may be presented in their story as heroes in the romantic mode. This is true of the child in an early, interesting work of Russell Hoban (1967/2001), *The Mouse and His Child*. Although the child is a windup toy that is cast away in a garbage dump, he has heroic aspirations and is portrayed as having the courage and persistence to achieve them.

Use of diminutive characters and animals provides scope for authors in presenting a child's world. Tiny people and small animals function as metaphors for the child's status in the adult world (Fleming, 1981). But these characters need not be portrayed as victims; through fantasy and manipulation of point of view (the readers' view of the characters and the characters' different view of themselves), they become the take-charge heroes and heroines of romance or the successful survivors of comedy.

Most writers for children, and their publishers, appear unwilling to rob children's literature of its role in educating the young in the positive social and moral ideals of society. In the main, literature for children continues to portray romantic and comic visions of life, where hope and optimism prevail.

CYCLICAL AND DIALECTICAL IMAGERY

As stated in the previous section, the archetypal structures that underlie literary imagery are of two kinds: cyclical (imagery based on natural cycles) and dialectical (images that present contrasting worlds).

Over and over in literature, images of the cycles of nature recur. Countless stories involve a cyclical journey, the hero or heroine returning in the end to the point of departure upon completion of a quest. The pattern of the cyclical journey is common to tales old and new: Odysseus' story shows it, as do *The Tale of Peter Rabbit* (Potter, 1902) and modern fantasies like *Where the Wild Things Are* (Sendak, 1963).

I referred earlier to associations often made in literature between human and animal life and the daily or seasonal cycles. The rejected Ugly Duckling suffers his greatest loneliness in the winter when the ground is frozen and barren. He finds his identity in the springtime in a garden where apple trees are in bloom and the scent of lilac is in the air. When the Norse god Balder lies dead in Asgard, darkness spreads over heaven and earth, the "night of death." Johnny Appleseed dies, but he is memorialized each spring when the apple tree blooms.

In Robert Frost's "Stopping by Woods on a Snowy Evening" (1978), the temptation to give up is associated with winter and the darkest evening of the year. In "Old Man and the Beginning of the World," a myth of the Blackfeet Indians, Old Man promises to return like the sun as he disappears into the west. In more westerns than we can count, the hero rides off into the sunset, not to die but to be reborn in yet another episode of his endless story. The epic hero Gilgamesh, in his quest to find the secret of life and death, follows the "way of the sun" to the Eastern Garden, the sun's dwelling.

Spring and summer are associated frequently with new beginnings, with joy and hope, youth and the prime of life. Autumn and winter are as often associated with old age, death, decay, and loss.

The second major organizing pattern of imagery is revealed through pairs of opposite categories. Above and below the world of human experience, myth projects an upper, desirable ideal world (the heaven of religion) and its opposite, an undesirable nightmare state (hell). The main body of literature is not religious, however, and does not deal with heaven and hell. Instead, the human experience is seen as analogous to these contrasting worlds. William Blake called these human worlds innocence and experience. The imagery of the heavenly world reaches down into the world of innocence; that of the demonic, up into the world of experience (refer to Figure 4.1).

Archetypal Patterns of Imagery

Some important images and their correspondences are presented in Tables 4.1 and 4.2. Table 4.1 shows correspondences between heavenly and demonic images; Table 4.2, between the world of innocence and the world of experience. Table 4.2 relates to Table 4.1, but shows the same images displaced from the heav-

TABLE 4.1. Images of Heaven and Hell

	Heavenly	*Demonic*
Divine images	Benevolent gods "above" Luck Angels	Malicious gods "below" Blind fate Devils
Sky images	Sunlight Angels Promethean fire	Darkness Demons and pestilence (as released from Pandora's box)
Human images	Humans as community, members of one body The Good Shepherd	Humans as mindless mob The tyrant
Animal images	Lamb, dove	Monsters, birds and beasts of prey
Vegetable images	Garden of Paradise Tree of Life	Wilderness Gallows
Water images	Water of Life	Flood
Mineral images	Temple Jacob's ladder The One Way	Wasteland Tower of Babel The labyrinth

enly and demonic toward the fantasy world of innocence and the more realistic, human world of experience.

Divine and Demonic Imagery.   The heavenly world gives us images of gods like Zeus and the Olympians, a sky-father like Odin, and the three-in-one god of the Christian religion. Its opposite, the demonic world, features malicious gods like Satan or mindless forces that are revealed through images of menacing natural forces, like the sea in the classic, *Call It Courage* (Sperry, 1940). This world may also be represented by a blind, cruel, or capricious fate against which people and animals have no defenses. Examples of imagery of the latter type are found in *Faithful Elephants* (Tsuchiya, 1988), a story based on the killing of the animals in Tokyo's Ueno Zoo during World War II, and *Dangerous Skies* (Staples, 1996), where children are caught up in the injustices of racial prejudice.

The innocent world is one of romance or of stories and poems with a comic or upward movement. The young themselves symbolize innocence. Good parents, wise old men, and benevolent fairy godmothers are analogous to the divinities of the heavenly world; false fathers, wicked stepmothers, and ambitious kings, to the undesirable gods of the demonic world. King Arthur's mentor—Merlin—and Chiron, instructor of Greek heroes like Achilles and Jason, are good examples of the wise old men who counsel the young. The cruel stepmother of "Snow White" and the vicious witch who captures Hansel and Gretel are typical of the heartless hags and other varieties of horrible women whose images haunt the tragic, ironic, sad visions of life.

In *Dorp Dead* (Cunningham, 1965), the evil Kobalt is a literary relative once removed from the wicked sorcerers and wizards of old fairy tales who are themselves one step away from the gods of the underworld. The hunter in the same book who befriends young Gilly provides an opposite image: that of counselor and

TABLE 4.2. Images of Innocence and Experience

	Innocence	*Experience*
Divine images	Good parents	False fathers and wicked stepmothers
	Wise old men	Wizards and sorcerers
	Fairy godmothers	Witches and hags
Sky images	Staff, wand	Fiery sword, bombs
	Moon and stars	Jewels and other treasure
	Spirits and fairies	Hobgoblins
Human images	Loving siblings	Wicked stepsisters and stepbrothers
	Wise and helpful men and women	Witches, wizards, temptresses
Animal images	Domesticated animals: dogs, sheep, horses	Birds and beasts of prey
	Unicorns and dolphins	Lions and eagles
Vegetable images	Blossoming tree	Dead tree
	Magician's wand or staff	King's scepter
	Meadows	Gardens and parks
Water images	Warm rain	Sleet
	Water as purifier	Water as destroyer
Mineral images	Paths	Highways
	Country	City
	Mountaintop	Subterranean tunnel

benefactor. The story takes place in the human sphere but in the character of the hunter is an image that resembles the benevolent deity of the heavenly world.

Sky and Fire Imagery.   Sky and fire images come "down" and "up" from the heavenly and demonic worlds into the literary worlds that deal with human concerns. (It becomes clear that knowledge of biblical and classical imagery will make the reading of all subsequent literature more richly meaningful.) In the heavenly sphere we have the sun and the angels, the thunder of Zeus, and Prometheus' gift of the gods' fire to man. There are saints' halos, seraphim and cherubim, ritual sacrifice by fire, and burning bushes.

At the opposite pole is Lucifer and images of consuming fire and brimstone. In between, the world of fire may be represented by malignant demons, will-o'-the-wisps, and burning homes or cities.

In the innocent world fire is usually a purifying symbol, flames that none but the pure may pass through. Sigurd, alone of all the Volsungs, is able to penetrate the wall of fire that surrounds Brynhild. In the story of Sleeping Beauty, the wall of fire is replaced by one of thorns and brambles, but the images are closely related. In the world of experience the heavenly fire blazes in the jewels of the king's crown and the flashing eyes of the beautiful lady.

Human Imagery.   Human images in the heavenly world are those of mankind as members of one body, united in God. At the beginning of the eighth book of the *Iliad*, Zeus remarks that, should he desire to do so, he can pull up the whole chain of being, both gods and humans, into himself, the supreme divine will. There are also images of the Good Shepherd, pastor of a human flock.

In the demonic world the human images indicate disorder and ruthlessness. Among them are cruel tyrants who demand human sacrifices, bloodthirsty mobs, and sirens like those in the *Odyssey* who tempt others to forget their humanity.

In the world of innocence that we see in romance, kings and lords abound, analogous to the gods of heaven. Here the peasant and commoner are idealized, with poor but worthy lads like Boots meeting success against all odds.

In more "realistic" stories in the world of experience there is a closer relationship of imagery to the demonic world. Order and reason and justice do not prevail as in the innocent worlds of comedy and romance. Characters are common and typical men, women, and children subject to all the ills that beset humans. Here characters are more likely to be victims than triumphant heroes. Examples are the girl and her family in *Out of the Dust* (Hesse, 1997), the young escapee from the concentration camp in *North to Freedom* (Holm, 1965/1984), the abducted child in *Where It Stops Nobody Knows* (Ehrlich, 1988), and victims of war such as the young men in Patricia Polacco's *Pink and Say* (1994).

Animal Imagery. Imagery in the innocent world strongly reflects the biblical and classical. Domesticated animals, notably sheep, are symbols of devotion and loyalty analogous to the Lamb of God. The dove and other gentle birds provide images of peace and love. Unicorns and dolphins contrast with the dragons and monsters of the demonic world. In the Bible we have the monster Leviathan, symbolic of the whole fallen world of sin, tyranny, and death in which man lives. Traditional tales like those of St. George and Beowulf commonly show the heroes fighting evil in the form of dragons and monsters.

Vegetable Imagery. Vegetable imagery in the heavenly world is well known to us. Both the Bible and classical mythology tell of gardens of paradise. The rose and the lotus are associated with the heavenly world. The tree of life contrasts with the demonic cross. In the human world of innocence, the natural meadow is once removed from the heavenly garden; the more sophisticated cultivated gardens and beautiful parks are associated with the world of experience. In romance, pastoral settings like Sherwood Forest are desirable images. Many modern realistic stories with harsh, bleak urban settings show by contrast that the rural setting is still seen as closer to people's vision of the ideal. A romantic counterpart to the tree of life appears in the wand of the magician and the fairy godmother, which can give life and cause miraculous change.

Demonic imagery is lacking entirely in lush vegetation. Hell is a rocky wasteland where no trees and plants grow or, when they do, their appearance and intent are sinister (the tree of forbidden knowledge, for example). Its counterpart in modern stories of human experience is the concrete and glass city, often depicted as a place of alienation and despair, as in the recent works of Walter Dean Myers, set in the mean streets of the inner city.

Water Imagery.   Water imagery extends all the way from the water of life to the Deluge. In romance literature the hero often descends into or under water, just as the soul of biblical imagery sinks into it at death. For the hero of romance a descent into water may be a kind of ritual death. Mafatu in *Call It Courage* (Sperry, 1940) emerges from submersion in the sea reborn with a new identity.

Water in the world of innocence may be symbolic of growth and fertility or seen, like the biblical ritual of baptism, as a purifier. King Midas must bathe himself in a pool to remove the stigma of the golden touch.

In realistic stories the sea is an adversary to be feared and respected. Water can be shown as the blessing of rain for crops or the destruction of life and property through flooding.

Mineral Imagery.   In the Bible, the mineral world is represented by images of temples and jeweled cities paved with gold. These are reflected in the enchanted towers, castles, courts, and capital cities of romance, and are frequently the goal of young travelers who journey on the highroad in search of treasure or a better life. The highroad itself may be seen as the counterpart of "the one way" of biblical imagery. Demonic mineral images are of deserts, wasteland, swamp, and rocks.

Archetypal Imagery

Archetypes, the building blocks of literature, are most evident in folktales, fantasy, and formulaic fiction. In the folktale, the romance form—a journey or quest—is typically exemplified. Romance, directly descended from folktale, may be considered the structural core of all fiction. In it we have the fundamental "story" of all literature: the human vision of life as a quest for identity. (See Chapter 5 for a full discussion of the romance structure.) In the quest-romance, the cyclical and particularly the dialectical principles discussed above are evident in all aspects of the tale. The quest is "good," undertaken by one who is worthy. Any person or event that conspires against the success of the quest is "bad." The archetypes recurrent in the tales—and discoverable in the fiction that follows them—reflect this dichotomy. A selection of examples of these patterns follows.

Folktales.   Tales typically feature courageous, innocent protagonists with inherent positive energy or luck, who are often underdogs. Their origins may be humble or mysterious. Pitted against the protagonist are evil villains who block the successful completion of the protagonist's quest. Many tales contain contrasting pairs—usually female—of characters: one good, the other bad. (Films portraying these "light" and "dark" character pairs, it is interesting to note, frequently cast blondes as the good girls and brunettes as the scheming temptresses.) Often present are wise men or women who watch over or control the action in a positive way, frequently providing a talisman or amulet to aid in the quest. Another archetypal character is one who speaks for the practical and realistic side of things, like Sancho Panza. Common in folktales are helpful animals, spirits, green men, kind daughter figures, creatures of mysterious origin, and the like, who come to the protagonist's aid. In the protagonist's darkest hour, a strange being may materialize, uttering prophecies and oracular sayings.

As for plot, countless folktales (and their descendents in fantasy fiction) feature a series—typically 3, 5, or 7—of combats or tests in which the protagonist is ultimately successful. Parallel plots are common, in which a bad brother or sister may try—without success—to repeat the actions of the good hero or heroine. Common plot devices involve loss and recovery, rescue from evil, twists and reversals of fortune, temptations, and exchanges of various kinds. A final or climactic test of the protagonist often involves a descent into the demonic world, with an eventual ascent that retraces the journey and ends in triumphal completion of the quest. Goodness is rewarded; evil is punished.

Contemporary Novels. *The Mouse and His Child* (Hoban, 1967/2001) is a complex example of the romance structure, with that structure's corresponding patterns of imagery and characterization.

The Mouse and his Child, joined together as a windup toy, journey from the harmonious perfection of their early life in the toy shop and the dolls' house down into the demonic world of the garbage dump, which is controlled by satanic Manny Rat, and undergo a further descent into the underworld below the pond before they return to the goal of their quest: to live as a family in the dolls' house with their lost loved ones restored to them.

Despite their misfortunes, the Child is steadfastly optimistic and hopeful for their future. The father Mouse, although supportive, plays the role of realistic advisor when the innocent Child is likely to be disappointed in his hopes.

In the mud below the pond, the Mouse and his Child acquire insight from the oracular wisdom of the turtle, C. Serpentina, and from the Child's own contemplation of infinity in the form of dog food labels on which is printed a picture of a black and white spotted dog in a chef's cap and apron, walking on its hind legs and carrying a tray on which there is another can of Bonzo Dog Food, on the label of which another dog, exactly like the first, may be seen, and so on and on to the last visible dog.

C. Serpentina informs the young mouse that "Nothing is the ultimate truth" (p. 178) but the Child—naively innocent and optimistic like the typical romance hero he is—refuses to accept this. He discovers that he is on the other side of nothing and must help himself; in true heroic fashion, he does. "Nobody can get us out of here but us" (p. 181). Both the Mouse and his Child get out of the mud through the Child's efforts. Images of flying accompany the ascent. The mice fly out of the pond using an invention devised by the Child. Returned to the world of experience, they fly with the hawk to safety.

Helped by gentle animals and birds—a kingfisher, a frog, a bittern—they eventually find their way to the dump and their goal, the dolls' house. Now appropriately painted black, the burnt-out remains of the house are occupied by the monster, Manny Rat. The romantic image of home and haven is replaced by a demonic one of the monster's ugly lair. The protagonists must retrieve the house and restore it. The hero and his helpers battle for the dolls' house, achieving victory—significantly—at dawn.

In the end, the Mouse and his Child, their trials and struggles ended, walk beside the renovated dolls' house, ablaze with electric light, admiring the stars that seem so close to them now that their house is secure on its pole high above the dump. The tramp, the wise old man figure who, at the beginning of the story, mends the Mouse and his Child, appears again at the end, the moment of epiphany, to bless them. The Mouse and his Child have climbed from the depths to the heights to achieve their dream.

The imagery of the dump is demonic imagery of the ironic mode. The divine world, represented throughout by the stars, seems menacing to the evil Manny Rat who "liked dark nights best" (p. 29). Reference frequently is made to Sirius the Dog Star, sacred both to Isis, consort of Osiris, and in Egyptian agricultural rites. References to Sirius suggest that the god is protecting the Mouse and his Child.

The demonic fire world is manifest in the hellish glow arising from the many fires of the dump and from Manny Rat's attempts to blow up the dolls' house. It is also represented positively by the blaze of electricity from the renovated dolls' house. The human world is parodied by the rat society. It is one in which the individual is subordinated to the ruthless power of the leader. Loyalty stems from fear rather than respect. The friends and extended family of the Mouse and his Child present the opposite image of the power of love and mutual aid in overcoming adversity.

The demonic animal world is characterized by monsters and beasts of prey: shrews, weasels, an owl. The ideal animal world features a wise fortune-telling frog, a clever crow who directs the Caws of Art Experimental Theatre Group, a philosophizing muskrat, and a bluejay journalist. The demonic vegetable world is seen in the wasteland and in the symbolic tree of death, here not a gallows but the pole on which the ruined dolls' house perches unsteadily. In their fight to recover the dolls' house from the rats, the animals and birds mount their offensive from an oak tree, which is sacred in folklore as symbol of life and power.

Demonic water images are of death; a flooding dam sweeps the Mouse and his Child into the underworld of the pond. But it is also water that cleanses the dolls' house so the process of restoration can begin.

Only a reading of this intriguing tale can give a full picture of the richness of its contrasting patterns of archetypal imagery, which move from ironic to heroic as the Mouse and his Child are successful in their quest for a home and family.

Dominic (Steig, 1972) shows how another contemporary writer for children makes use of conventional imagery. The hero is Dominic, a cheerful, gregarious mutt who, like countless adventurers, leaves home to seek his fortune: to find adventure and a more satisfying life. Along the way he encounters adversaries, the evil Doomsday Gang: foxes, weasels, ferrets, a wildcat, a wolf, tomcats, dingoes, and rats. The hero and those he befriends in the course of his travels are gentler animals, friendly to people and not given to preying on each other.

Another friend is the archetypal character of the old wise woman, here in the form of an alligator witch. She shares her magic powers with Dominic by giving him her magic wand— wands are fragments of the tree of life—in the shape of a sword that will make him invincible in combat.

Dominic sets out on his adventures along a springtime road strewn with leafy trees and flowers. In this story the forest is sinister, the setting for the hero's greatest trials, confusion, and despair. It is only with great difficulty that Dominic is able to "get out of the woods" to safety. He finds treasure both in the form of diamonds, rubies, and emeralds and in someone to love. His love he discovers in a miniature palace in a beautiful enchanted garden where it is always summer. His dreams of a new and more fulfilling life have come true.

CONCLUSION

Taken together, the patterns of imagery and the archetypal narrative plots—described in the next chapter—provide a description of the total schematic order found in literature itself. An awareness of the interconnectedness of literary works through recurring and conventional patterns—archetypes—conveys a sense of literature as a unified order of words. This knowledge is crucial to an understanding of the significance of the total body of literature as an imaginative journal of all human experience.

5

The Circle of Stories

> We may feel that this "circle of stories" considerably simplifies
> the facts of literary experience. Three points in this connection
> are important. First, the simplification may be valuable for teach-
> ing purposes, giving shape and coherence to an inexperienced
> student's reading. Second, no boundary lines exist, except in
> diagrams: no classifying or pigeonholing is involved; literary
> works are simply seen as being in different areas, where they can
> be both distinguished from and related to one another. Third, and
> most important, this is not a schematism to be imposed on stu-
> dents. The teacher should have it in mind, but as a principle to
> give form to his teaching, not as something for the student to
> memorize and present as a substitute for literary experience.
> —Northrop Frye (1988, p. 118)

The content of each story we read in a book or watch on a
screen may be different: The possible combinations of characters and incidents are infinite. What is limited is the number of
ways in which stories may be told. In the model he developed to
provide a theoretical structure for literature, Northrop Frye (1957)
describes four basic narrative patterns—romance, tragedy, irony-
satire, and comedy—that remain constant as the constructive
principles used to shape story content.

The four "stories" or plots form a ring or circle of stories (see
Figure 5.1). They merge into one another at their limits. Where
they overlap we have romantic comedies, for instance, or ironic
tragedies.

Within each plot, Frye identifies six separate phases or variations of a central or typical structure—like the quest of romance.
However, few works exist in this "pure" form. "The forms of prose

71

FIGURE 5.1. The Circle of Stories.

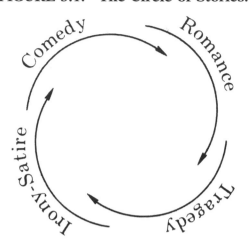

fiction are mixed, like racial strains in human beings, not separable like the sexes" (Frye, 1957, p. 305).

All four plots grow out of the fundamental story of the quest of the hero, as explained in Chapter 4. The circle of stories begins with romance, which develops out of the mythical story of the hero's adventures. His sufferings and trials, his brushes with death, are the focal points of tragedy and irony-satire. The circle ends with comedy, which develops out of the hero's triumph after a successful quest. Taken together, the four basic stories provide an imaginative shape for each aspect of human experience. No one story is the whole. All the stories together are part of the one story: people's quest for their human identity.

ROMANCE

Characteristics

Frye sees romance, considered in formal terms, as the most inclusive literary type. "Romance is the structural core of all fiction: being directly descended from folktale, it brings us closer than any other aspect of literature to the sense of fiction, considered as a whole, as the epic of the creature, man's vision of his own life as a quest" (Frye, 1976a, p. 15). The romance story is one of the great creations devised by the imagination, a form in which wishes come true, goodness always triumphs over evil, and heroes and heroines "live happily ever after" in peace and plenty.

Although there are variations within the romance pattern, the central form follows a cyclical pattern involving three principal stages: a dangerous or marvelous journey with attendant preliminary minor adventures (conflict); a central struggle, test, or ordeal (death-struggle); and successful completion of a quest, typically followed by a return to the point from which the journey began (recognition). This complete form is most clearly seen in the stories of the epic heroes: Perseus, Theseus, Jason, Sigurd, Beowulf, Odysseus.

Other stories, actually episodes within the romance form, may tell of the birth of the hero and his early days. His birth, like that of Moses, is often shrouded in mystery and secrecy. Stories of his early life tell of extraordinary powers: Paul Bunyan wields his axe in babyhood; Hercules is still an infant when he strangles the serpents sent by Hera to kill him.

There may be false "fathers" or "mothers" who seek the child's death; Pharaoh, Herod, and the wicked stepmothers of folktales are examples. Often the child is prepared for the illustrious life he will lead by kindly foster parents or wise teachers like Merlin in King Arthur's story.

In variations of the basic romance form, there are stories of innocence pressing toward experience; contemporary examples are *Dicey's Song* (Voight, 1982) and *Homeless Bird* (Whelan, 2000). In other romance stories, the power of innocence overcomes evil or ugliness, as in *Beauty and the Beast* (Osborne, 1987) or "Soldier Jack" (Chase, 1943).

Since romance is a wish-fulfillment dream, it may also—in some of its forms—show the shadow side of romance: the world we most want to avoid. Here fantasy descends to horror, the principal character doing battle with horrible monsters and giants, perhaps even with death. Romance literature in its demonic vein contains the sinister and horrible images associated with nightmares. Here are tales of the supernatural or of magic powers that operate on the side of evil. Frankenstein is like the scary giants and ogres of fairytales, a dream turned into a nightmare.

On its simplest level the quest is a search for adventure. However, because of its association with the good and the ideal, the quest always has a deeper significance. It is more than adventure for its own sake. Beowulf goes to slay a monster who is lay-ing waste a kingdom; Theseus' goal is to kill the minotaur and put an end to tyranny; Perseus' aim is to destroy the gorgon Medusa whose terrifying visage turns all who look upon her to stone. Countless youngest sons and daughters go forth in folktales to seek their fortunes or a better life. The object of the quest determines the seriousness of the story's tone.

Questers may be rewarded with something tangible: a treasure, a bride, a husband, lands, or a kingdom. They may gain wisdom or magical powers. Whatever the reward, the questing itself is symbolically significant. It represents a journey into the darker regions of experience where the heroes and heroines confront evil and risk annihilation in performing tasks and facing tests that reveal their true relationship to nature, to other people, or to their own selves. Although tangible treasures may result from the quest, perhaps the greatest benefit is the questing character's discovery of self. In its deepest sense, the quest seems to be a search for the knowledge of what it means to be human, of what is involved in taking one's place in the pattern of human civilization as a fully functioning member of society.

The quest may be compared with the rites-of-passage rituals of primitive tribes. Typically the initiates are isolated, given instruction, and made to undergo some ordeal to test strength or wit. When they survive the ordeal, they are reunited with the tribe amid feasting and rejoicing. They may be given new names to symbolize their rebirth as mature members of the society.

The archetype of a questing character is common to all civilizations, from the ancient Babylonians to contemporary primitive tribes. Its ubiquity suggests that the central pattern of romance—the quest—embodies a fundamental pattern of human experience. It has an essential function in the development of the individual's awareness of personal strengths and weaknesses, with psychological as well as ritual or tribal significance.

The two central characters of the romance are heroes or—in many contemporary versions of the form—heroines who are symbolically associated with spring, dawn, youth, and vigor, and their adversaries who are associated with winter, darkness, old age, and sterility. The principal characters of romance are often described as being larger-than-life. They are larger not so much because they are superhuman (though they may possess extraordinary powers) but rather in the sense that they have a vision of a world that is more perfect than the one we live in and a belief in their ability to make that world a reality.

The protagonists of romance are highly idealized figures, usually embodying the virtues held noblest by the societies from which their stories came. They are strong and steadfast, durable and self-controlled. They embody highly civilized virtues like courtesy, wit, and, above all, imagination and vision. Although they may not be gods or even the offspring of gods, they have a mysterious contact with a world beyond the world of experience, from which they seem to derive a power denied to ordinary mortals. Heroic figures radiate a kind of energy, a positive force that bears them forward through all adversity. They are leaders, people at the frontiers of experience. Their triumphs benefit all those around them; their powers lift others toward the heights they scale.

Typical romances move toward progress or fulfillment: victory, the acquisition of treasure, a better life. The achievement involves Herculean efforts on the part of the heroic character, with or without help from others. In the end his or her life is transformed through release from a threatening past or through the realization of some significant understanding. An example of this type of romance, displaced to realism in contemporary times, is *Red Midnight* (Mikaelsen, 2002), a story of the remarkable bravery of a boy named Santiago. The twelve-year-old flees from his home in Central America in order to escape the terrorist regime that killed his family. He sails to safety in the United States aboard an impossibly small boat accompanied by his four-year-old sister, the last remaining member of his family.

Most other characters in the romance are one-dimensional. They are either good or bad, for the protagonist or against. Good women in old romances are usually rescued maidens or brides or supporters of the hero; bad women are cast as evil stepmothers, witches, and temptresses. The people who inhabit the pages of romance are not particularly realistic, even in displacements of the form toward "realism." They are more like the desirable characters of our dreams and the undesirable characters of our nightmares.

Romance exhibits a clear up-and-down narrative movement, at times rising into dream or wish fulfillment, and again sinking into anxiety and nightmare. Themes of ascent and descent are common in romance. *Alice's Adventures in Wonderland* (Carroll, 1865/1988) is a case in point; besides Alice's own physical upward and downward movements, there are comings and goings beginning with the fall down the rabbit hole and ending in the eventual ascent into the world of reality. The emphasis on cards and card games relates to the elements of fate and chance in romance.

The settings of early romances—exemplified by folk- and fairytales—are generally idyllic or at least removed from the world of ordinary experience. There are possibilities of magic and miracles. Transformation and metamorphosis are common, as are mistaken identities, disguises, spells, and incantations. Things in nature, trees and animals, often have a mysterious rapport with the heroes or heroines and may provide them with help and advice. Birds warn Snow White of her danger; the Goosegirl has a talking horse as an advocate; Puss in Boots speaks for his master. Traditional tales are full of talking animals who aid the hero. We find this in "The Flea" (Sawyer, 1936), a Spanish folktale, and in the story of Drakestail (Neil, 1986).

Visions and revelations are common to romance. In stories that deal with moral opposites, it is not surprising to find some means of connecting the "heavenly" world with a "lower" one. The union is frequently achieved by a vision or (in more modern romances) an insight that takes place in a high or isolated place like a mountaintop, an island, or a tower. Jacob's ladder is an example of this enjoinment of the two worlds.

Examples of the Romance Form

The Tale of Peter Rabbit (Potter, 1902), durable and delightful, has been a source of literary satisfaction to generations of youngsters. A prime example of the well-constructed story, it exemplifies the romance form in miniature. The hero faces a perilous journey with minor adventures, a crucial struggle, and final exaltation or success, the whole expressing the passage from a point of ritual death to the "resurrection" of the recognition scene.

Peter sets out in defiance of his mother to seek identity, an identity undoubtedly associated with his father who had met an untimely death in Mr. McGregor's garden. The young adventurer undergoes a series of hairsbreadth escapes. He loses his jacket and shoes, is wet and frightened, and escapes only after he finds himself a vantage point that, together with his fleetness of foot, gives him an advantage over his enemy. In the end, as a result of his own efforts, he is safely home, undoubtedly a proven hero, although he has lost his clothes, is not feeling well, and is put to bed with a dose of camomile tea. His well-behaved siblings have bread and milk and blackberries for supper, but it is Peter who is most emphatically the hero of the piece since he is the one who has successfully completed a quest.

The characterization in Peter Rabbit follows the typical conflict pattern of romance. There are two main characters: Peter, the protagonist, and Mr. McGregor, the antagonist. At the lowest point of his trials, when he is imprisoned in the gooseberry net, Peter is encouraged by three friendly sparrows who "implored him to exert himself," characters with literary relatives among the children-of- nature figures common to romance, who are morally neutral and helpful to the hero. The proper siblings are foils for Peter, emphasizing by their docility the enormity of Peter's ambition and daring. The comforting figure of Mrs. Rabbit waiting at home until the hero finishes his wanderings is similar to wife-mother figures in more ambitious and lengthier works: Solveig of *Peer Gynt*, for example, and Penelope in the *Odyssey*.

For older children, the classic *Call It Courage* (Sperry, 1940) is another example of the romance plot. Mafatu, son of the chief of a Polynesian tribe, lives in fear of the sea, for as a young child he came perilously close to drowning when his mother lost her life as she rescued him. He is reduced to women's work on the island, scorned by his peers as a coward, and a disappointment to his father. The reason for Mafatu's quest is clear—he must find his identity in a face-to-face battle with his enemy, the sea.

Mafatu sets out on his perilous journey, weathering a storm and the destruction of his canoe on a reef. Finally he reaches a desolate island where he sets to work to make a shelter and replacements for the canoe and the weapons hc has lost. The sheltering island itself contains a threat, for it is the site of the holy place of sacrifice of a cannibal tribe who will surely return and destroy Mafatu when they know he has desecrated their sacred ground. Yet he sets out calmly to build his boat, gaining courage with every action of his own hand. He kills a wild boar with a weapon of his own making, saves his dog from a tiger shark, and kills an octopus in a daring underwater fight. Drums announce the arrival of the cannibals, but Mafatu's boat is ready and he eludes his pursuers with skill and daring, and sails in the direction of home. He cries out triumphantly to the threatening sea that he no longer fears it, even when there seems little chance of his reaching home again. Mafatu at this moment has won his personal battle and regained his identity. It remains, however, for him to be exalted in the eyes of others, and this happens when he lands safely home, a figure of mystery and magnificence.

In *Call It Courage* the sea is the antagonist, a personification of a being of unlimited strength, bent on destruction. Mafatu's only friends are misfits like himself: a nondescript yellow dog and a lame albatross. Like neutral nature spirits, they play a helping role: comforting the boy, giving him hope and companionship, and—in the case of Kivi the albatross—mysteriously offering guidance as Mafatu begins his quest and ends it.

The romance form is popular in children's literature. It is found in picture storybooks as different as *Where the Wild Things Are* (Sendak, 1963), the delightful melodrama *Brave Irene* (Steig, 1986), and Hardie Gramatky's venerable *Little Toot* (1939). The classical hero tales of Greece and Rome retold in splendid language suited to modern eyes and ears—as in retellings by Ian Serraillier, Roger Lancelyn Green, and Padriac Colum—are superb examples of this form.

Although it may appear with widely different subject matter and express a variety of values, the romance plot pattern has always been a favorite with children and those who write for them. Whether the romance is close to myth and magic like the old tales of heroes, a fantasy, or a realistic modern version of the form, there is no question about its power and importance in the development of the imagination.

Romance tells of dreams and how they are made to come true. It deals in hope. It tells of characters with the courage to prevail when difficulties threaten to engulf them. Romance brings a message from the imagination to the imagination that all children need if they are to slay their personal dragons.

TRAGEDY

Romance, as a story form, tells of wishes and dreams that come true. Poems and stories that explore the limits of people's ability to make their wishes and dreams come true belong to the literary form we call tragedy. Destruction of the innocent, beautiful, or virtuous is something we feel should not happen. Yet such destruction is a fact of the human experience, no matter how wasteful or unjust it may seem. Tragedy, leaving us feeling helpless and vulnerable, reminds us that humans are not omnipotent. Tragic stories sometimes suggest that heroes or heroines are destroyed because they have broken some natural law, even though they may have done so in all innocence. Tragedies are imaginative attempts to balance people's potential greatness with their perishable nature, to come to terms with powers that are greater than theirs.

Characteristics

The central idea of tragedy is catastrophe or death befalling a heroic character. A tragedy may be romantic or ironic and realistic, depending on whether it features idealized or more realistic heroes and heroines. Tragic figures typically endure their trials with the greatest possible dignity; that quality, together with their innocence and courage, claims our empathy for them. Hans Christian Andersen's Steadfast Tin Soldier is such a hero; Balder of Norse mythology is another, as is Barney, the doomed boy in Robert Cormier's contemporary novel, *The Bumblebee Flies Anyway* (1983).

Another form of heroic tragedy is the archetypal story of the loss of innocence, innocence being a lack of experience. Young people can be baffled and hurt by their first contacts with the harsh realities of the world, as is Lena whose life is scarred by racism in *Words by Heart* (Sebestyen, 1979). Such stories may tell of a youthful life cut off or of a child's coming to terms with the untimely death of a loved one.

Still another variation of the tragic story is that of the death, often a willing one, of the hero in support of some great cause. Beowulf deliberately gives his life to save his people. King Arthur knows that his whole life has been a sacrifice for a "dream of justice." This type of tragic story derives from the ancient ritual of the scapegoat: The evils of the tribe were ritualistically invested in an animal who was then driven into the wilderness to die. In the tragedy of sacrifice, the hero's society is purged of evil by his sacrifice, voluntarily made on behalf of his people.

The tragedy of sacrifice is a grave reminder of what it costs to be fully human in the noblest sense. The heroic characters accept fate and resist oppression, willing to risk or lose their lives for a great cause. Theirs is a sobering story but an exhilarating one, found in both epic tales like *Beowulf* and biographies of such men and women as Martin Luther King, Jr., Malcolm X, and the celebrated savior of slaves, Harriet Tubman.

Many tragic stories center around characters who are not of the world of innocence but of the world of experience. They are puzzling characters; they may be great leaders and in many respects heroic, but at the same time their character or outlook contains a flaw that leads them to make some disastrous mistake or choice. Their action appears to provoke a situation that causes their inevitable downfall, a sense of their having disturbed the natural order. Such stories seem to tell of a kind of revenge, a hostile reaction from some power that is beyond them. Great classical tragedies like *Antigone* and *King Lear* belong in this category.

As tragedy gets closer to irony in the circle of stories, heroes become more lifelike, no longer the larger-than-life figures just spoken of. Here are stories that reflect people's sense of being caught in a trap from which they cannot free themselves, of being victims of vast and overwhelming forces that immobilize and imprison. In ironic literature, we see the human spirit defeated under similar conditions. But in tragedy, even when all hope is lost, people retain their human dignity. By the very act of facing the realities and challenges of life, the characters triumph over them.

Elements of Tragedy in Children's Literature

William Armstrong's *Sounder* (1969) illustrates this last type of tragic story. The father, a black sharecropper in Louisiana during the Depression, is a victim of circumstances beyond his control. His opportunities are limited. Both nature and men are hostile. The land bears poor crops, and no one comes forward to help him feed his starving children; when he steals food for them, his captors are ruthless in their punishment. Yet he endures through agonies of pain when the posse's guns injure him and through the knowledge of his family's suffering when he is taken off to prison. He returns home, body broken but spirit intact, to die with dignity, leaving that and his courage as a legacy of hope to his children.

The full power of the tragic form is seldom experienced in children's literature, except perhaps in myths, legends, and epics. However, many modern children's stories contain elements of tragedy, notable among them Ouida Sebestyen's *Words by Heart* (1979) and *Dangerous Skies* (Staples, 1996).

Set in cotton country at the turn of the century, *Words by Heart* tells the story of Lena, a young black girl whose special talent is reciting scripture. Eager to earn her father's admiration and to make her white classmates notice her "Magic Mind," not her black skin, Lena sets out to win a Bible-quoting contest.

Lena wins, but winning does not bring her the expected acceptance and praise. Instead, her triumph forces her to acknowledge bitter truths: The people of the town begrudge her winning; worse, they resent her family's presence in the all-white town where her idealistic, pacifist father has settled them. Her father's ideals and good intentions cannot hold up against prejudice and bigotry. In the end Lena is left to reconcile herself to grief and bitterness at her father's murder.

Dangerous Skies tells the story of the sexual abuse of a young black girl by a politically powerful white man who is feared by the townsfolk where they both live. A shocking element in this tale of racism is the indifference of the "decent" people of the town, who are unwilling to confront racist and criminal issues because of their own deep-rooted fears and prejudices.

Tragedy, in contrast with irony, does not leave us with a sense of hopelessness. The tragic figure may suffer, even die, but he or she characteristically displays the highest of human attributes: nobility and dignity. In *The Bumblebee Flies Anyway* (Cormier, 1983), 16-year-old Barney, finally accepting—after a period of desperate denial—the bleak truth that his own death is imminent, forgets himself in his heroic efforts to bring happiness to a friend in the last moments of both their lives.

SATIRE AND IRONY

Satire and irony are literary forms set in the world of experience, reflecting the discrepancy between what is and what ideally ought to be. Satire attempts to change people and society for the better, often by using ridicule to expose follies and hypocrisies. Satire may employ fantasy; irony deals in realism.

Both forms typically parody the themes and patterns of romance to make their points. Protagonists are not larger-than-life; they are all-too-human, subject to all the ills of the world: physical weakness, other people's inhumanity, their own neuroses. Time passes and they must grow old and die. There is no feeling, as there is in tragedy and romance, of mysterious powers that link these people to something that transcends the world. Since they are merely human in a world that is far from ideal, their quests frequently remain unfulfilled as they pursue unrealistic goals or proceed wrong-headed and misdirected.

The heroic qualities of the main characters of romance are absent in the anti-heroes of irony or are employed by the hero-as-rogue who outwits the unscrupulous by becoming unscrupulous himself. The good and innocent are more likely to be victims than champions, and love is more often thwarted than conquering. The green world of romance is replaced by the harsh concrete of the city slum.

Characteristics of Satire

The satirist chips away at the huge ills of humanity: hypocrisy, self-deceit, smugness, pettiness, injustice. In some satires, people are shown accepting what they believe cannot be changed or retreating into rationalizations in an effort to escape. There are stories granting that the world is full of crime and folly, but counseling readers to laugh at the follies around them. Through humor and exaggeration, the satirist's audience has its consciousness raised and its perceptions sharpened.

Most satire is beyond the imaginative reach of young children, and few authors write in this form for them. The satiric aspects of *Gulliver's Travels* (Swift, 1726/1985) and *Alice's Adventures in Wonderland* (Carroll, 1865/1988) are for the most part absorbed without notice as the stories are enjoyed for their own sake. "The Emperor's New Clothes" (Andersen, 1974) is a notable exception, where children encounter satire in a form more manageable by them. Elements of satire occur, however, in contemporary children's fiction like *The Wish Giver* (Brittain, 1984), *The Whipping Boy* (Fleischman, 1987), *The Shrinking of Treehorn* (Heide, 1971), *Konrad* (Nostlinger, 1977), and *The Pushcart War* (Merrill, 1964).

Satire, in literature for children, is usually softened through fantasy and humor. Both *Konrad* and *The Pushcart War* are excellent examples. *Konrad is* a thoroughly delightful spoof on the wonders of a technological society that can produce anything, even children made to order in factories. The highly original classic, *The Pushcart War,* features a brave army of pushcart owners who outwit big business in New York City.

Characteristics of Irony

Ironic stories, like satiric ones, take place in the world of experience rather than in the world of innocence, and with them, too, heroism is impossible. They differ from satire in that no moral ideal seems possible.

Since the 1960s, much children's literature has been written in the ironic mode of most contemporary adult literature. An early story in this mode is *The Pigman* (Zindel, 1968), a story written for young adolescents which looks at tragedy from below, from the moral and realistic perspective of the state of experience. It stresses the humanity of its heroes, minimizes the sense of ritual inevitability found in tragedy, and supplies social and psychological explanations for catastrophe.

In *The Pigman*, two precocious, perceptive, lonely teenagers make friends with an equally lonely, strange old man, Mr. Pignati, who lives only through dreams of his dead wife and daily visits to his closest friend, a baboon at the zoo. The story is narrated alternately by the hero and heroine in a series of flashbacks, their attempt to make sense of all the crazy things they did. It is often funny in its digressions, wit, and candor, but the humor only serves to point up the irony that underlies it.

Alienated from their parents, John and Lorraine find in the Pigman someone who accepts them as they are, spoils them a little, and genuinely enjoys their company, luxuries not to be found in their homes. Their zany relationship flourishes in love and laughter; they have the run of his cluttered old house, sharing with him food and trips to the zoo. He buys them gifts of roller skates, and all three joyously skate down the hallway of his home. Human weakness and poor judgment are their undoing. Mr. Pignati suffers a heart attack after a hilarious skating session. While he is hospitalized, John and Lorraine invite friends to a party that turns his house into a shambles. His wife's collection of prized china pigs is smashed, her clothes ripped by the girls who dress up in them, and his belongings looted. In the midst of the chaos Mr. Pignati returns from the hospital. Although he forgives the stricken young people, who are not sure how things got so far out of their control, his gay spirit is broken. When they persuade him the next day to take a trip to the zoo to see Bobo, his baboon friend, he agrees half-heartedly to go. Once there he discovers that Bobo died while he was in the hospital. Mr. Pignati, weak from the heart attack, dies in front of the baboon cage.

John tries to sum up his feelings at the end, deploring life "in a world where you can grow old and be alone and have to get down on your hands and knees and beg for friends" (p. 144). He muses that, for that matter, maybe he and Lorraine are baboons, only of a different kind, and that his parents and everyone else are "baffled baboons concentrating on all the wrong things" (p. 145). The young people have faced reality and themselves, and found both confrontations unpleasant.

It is interesting to note that in a sequel to *The Pigman, The Pigman's Legacy* (Zindel, 1980), the unrelieved irony of the first book is tempered with humor. However, problematic aspects of living—as diverse as health care, communication gaps between the generations, and paying taxes—are examined through satire. In the circle of stories, the second story—though still in the ironic-satiric mode—is closer to comedy, ending as it does with hope and a promise of love, which John and Lorraine have come to realize is the Pigman's legacy.

Simple though it is, the familiar tale of The Gingerbread Boy is a good primer introduction to the ironic form. The Gingerbread Boy, about to be eaten, escapes and rolls down the hill on a quest for freedom and safety, narrowly escaping all who would eat him, and that is everyone he meets, including the family from whom he first escaped. Freedom seems certain until the Gingerbread Boy makes a friend of Piggy Wiggy—in some versions, Fox—who proves false. In the process of what seems a helpful act of carrying the Gingerbread Boy on his snout in order to cross a brook, the pig swallows him in one gulp. The Gingerbread Boy's quest is cut short unfulfilled.

Another example of a story in the ironic mode is *The Bomb* (Taylor, 1995), in which there are also elements of tragedy, as is common with this form. *The Bomb* fictionalizes a shameful chain of events in American history. Around the time of World War II, nuclear-bomb testing was conducted on Bikini Atoll with utter disregard or compassion for the people who inhabit the area. In this story, a young boy who tries to protest the ruination of his community loses his life in the attempt.

Other notable works in this genre include *We Are All in the Dumps with Jack and Guy* (Sendak, 1993), Marilyn Sachs's *The Bears' House* (1971), Louise Fitzhugh's *Nobody's Family Is Going to Change* (1974), and *Mrs. Fish, Ape, and Me, the Dump Queen* (Mazer, 1982). The novels by Fitzhugh and Mazer illustrate how humor is often used to ease the pain of "telling it like it is" in stories for young people.

The ironic mode is further accommodated in children's stories that use toys, animals, and diminutive people as protagonists. In this mode the protagonist is inferior in power even to ordinary people, a victim of others and the powers of nature and inferior in power and intelligence to the reader, who has the sense of looking down on a scene of entrapment, frustration, and absurdity.

However, the animals, toys, or diminutive characters do not necessarily see themselves as ironic victims (Fleming, 1981). Rather, like William Steig's *Dominic* (1972), they may perceive themselves as protagonists in the adventurous world of romance, in which danger is great but honorable motives, courage, and determination are rewarded. Excellent examples of such protagonists are found in *The Borrowers* (1953) and its several sequels, written by Mary Norton, and in *The Mouse and His Child* (Hoban, 1967/2001).

By using animals, toys, or diminutive characters as protagonists, authors are able to present, through the fantasy, an ironic view of life, while at the same time preserving the optimism and positive values of the comic and romantic modes, traditionally considered the most appropriate for children's literature. "If inferior in power or intelligence to ourselves, so that we have a sense of looking down on a scene of bondage, frustration, or absurdity, the hero belongs to the ironic mode" (Frye, 1957, p. 34). In the reader's eyes, the Mouse and his Child have ironic status because they are powerless, unable to move unless someone winds them up. However, they—like other toy and animal characters or diminutive people in stories—do not have an ironic view of themselves. Their positive viewpoint enables them to behave like heroes and heroines. Indeed, the Child undertakes a heroic quest and is successful in it.

Ironic stories typically reveal a bitter picture of existence: the contrast between ideals and reality. Some believe that children's literature must reflect life "as it is" and not see it through the rose-colored glasses of romance and comedy. There is merit in this view, of course, but irony and satire do not present the whole story of the human experience any more than romance and comedy do. Irony, in fact, proves to be romance turned upside down, the nightmare instead of the dream. Implicit in the ironic story is the dream of how things "ought to be."

COMEDY

When we speak of comedy, we are likely to think of laughter, but many forms of the comic plot in literature are not necessarily comical or humorous. They do, however, present a positive view of the human experience. Comedy is a form that celebrates the power of nature, human or otherwise, to renew itself, the power of life to overthrow the threat of death. It has to do with transformation, with the power of the imagination to raise experience above the limits of time and space, and to change the undesirable into the desirable.

Characteristics

The central idea of comedy is rebirth or renewal after obstacles have been overcome. The simplest pattern of comedy is expressed in the old cliché: boy meets girl, boy loses girl, boy and girl are reunited. Protagonists are kept from the object of their desires by a series of blocks or obstacles, often in the form of intransigent antagonists. The comic form usually involves a movement from one kind of society to another: from the rule of impossible, unreasonable people to the establishment of a new order where everyone is happy.

This ending is achieved by almost any means: miraculous transformations, coincidences, magical interventions. But the audience is delighted even when the solution is improbable, because they know that this is the only possible ending, the way things "ought to be." Even the intransigent characters are reformed and redeemed and become part of the new social order in the end, like Scrooge in *A Christmas Carol* (Dickens, 1843/1952).

The typical hero of comedy resembles Wilbur in E. B. White's *Charlotte's Web* (1952): well-meaning, likeable enough, but rather ordinary. Wilbur is aided by a cunning cohort, Charlotte, a character type common to comedy and related to the "tricky slave" of ancient Roman comedies, whose wit and daring frequently saved his charming but none-too-bright master. The chief blocking character is often a father figure or an outright villain, or is represented by an unfair or impossible situation that must be overcome, like the threat to Wilbur's life. Other comic characters include detractors of the hero, like Templeton the rat, and buffoons who contribute to the comic action with singing, clowning, and miscellaneous humor, like the gossipy goose in *Charlotte's Web*.

Like tragedies, comic plots may stretch from the limits of the ironic to the romantic. Julia Cunningham's *Dorp Dead* (1965) is an ironic comedy where the will to live triumphs over odds that must surely have left scars. Books like *Charlotte's Web, The Trumpet of the Swan* (White, 1970), and *Sarah, Plain and Tall* (MacLachlan, 1986) are romantic comedies at the other end of the scale; from beginning to end their mood is one of hope.

In this time of war and terrorism around the globe, many writers for children have written novels and biographies that show children struggling against all odds to survive in the imperfect world in which they find themselves. Such stories of hope and perseverance against staggering odds are exemplified in Deborah Ellis's (2000, 2002) two stories of Parvana, a child of war-torn Afghanistan, and in Cathryn Clinton's (2002) *A Stone in My Hand*, the harrowing tale of a young girl's existence in a Palestine filled with hate and terror.

Examples of the Comic Form

An excellent example of the comic structure in children's literature is one of the first books by Dr. Seuss, *The 500 Hats of Bartholomew Cubbins* (1938), a venerable favorite that is a comedy in the phase closest to romance. In this story there is a magical element that is never explained: the 500 hats that appear successively on Bartholomew's head are a phenomenon that "just 'happened to happen' and was not very likely to happen again" (unpaged).

Bartholomew, much like the heroes of Dickensian comedy, is a likeable chap, unpretentious and brave enough when he must be. Through no fault of his own, he is confronted with a wrathful and unreasonable king who demands that Bartholomew remove his hat in the king's presence. The hero tries to comply but cannot; whenever he removes his hat, another appears in its place. Like the hero of a picaresque tale, a juvenile Tom Jones, he is whirled off into a series of adventures, more or less an innocent victim of circumstances and situations largely beyond his control.

The characters are typical figures of comedy. The king is a blustering and unreasonable figure, foolish in his repeated attempts to divest Bartholomew of his offending hats. His retinue includes buffoon types reminiscent of the cooks and clowns of Shakespeare: the pompous prime minister, the ineffective and comical wise men and magicians.

Bartholomew faces death bravely and calmly enough in his stolid way, until he is saved—in the nick of time—by the magical powers that brought him into danger in the first place. The final hats grow more and more magnificent until the vain and greedy king, behaving true to character, covets one for his own. He pays Bartholomew a substantial sum for the splendid five hundredth, places it over his crown, and is appeased at last. Arm in arm, he and Bartholomew gaze out over the royal domain from the same vantage point, as equals. How such a reversal is accomplished is inherent in the comic structure itself. Everything moves toward the "happy ending," with the blocking characters converted at last to the hero's side.

The old tale of Cinderella is a prime example of the comic structure, its pattern enduring in displacements old and new and yet to come. It exemplifies comedy in the phase closest to romance, for it involves magical manifestations and metamorphoses. The worthy Cinderella endures against impossible odds, powerless against the cruel and unreasonable treatment of her stepmother and stepsisters who thwart her every wish and desire, including preventing her attendance at the prince's ball. Then her goodness is rewarded; her fairy godmother transforms her utterly. She must do as she is told (and she is used to that) and all will be well.

Cinderella at last is received into the society in which we all knew from the beginning she belonged; it is in effect a movement from illusion to reality. The illusion is always negative forces that must be dispelled, caused as they are by hypocrisy, injustice, and the like. Cinderella, of course, was really a princess in disguise. In the end, the prince recognizes this, and the king and queen receive her as if she were a long-lost daughter; even her stepmother and wicked stepsisters share in her triumph in most versions. The character of Cinderella is the embodiment of the wish fulfillment: Virtue and goodness are rewarded; things turn out "as they should."

The comic form is a favorite of writers for children, found in countless traditional tales like *Beauty and the Beast* (Osborne, 1987) and *Snow White and the Seven Dwarfs* (Grimm, 1886/1972) and in tales of survival—a popular theme for children's fiction— like Gary Paulsen's *Hatchet* (1988) and Elizabeth Speare's *Sign of the Beaver* (1983).

The main emphasis in comic literature, then, is on the creation of a new or better order or set of circumstances. This is often achieved by equating the new and better world with the season of spring, a time of beginnings and renewal. The world at the end of a typical comedy is renewed, better and more ordered, freer and more merciful than the old order it replaces. The marriage and the happy ending typical of comedies are symbolic of the establishment of a new, more just society.

The biblical Book of Revelation uses the marriage metaphor to symbolize an eventual happy ending to the human story. A bride from earth, known variously as the new Jerusalem, the church, or the community of saints, is united with the redeemer and with him enters paradise. The central form of the comic story is symbolic of hope, of possibilities for new and renewed life, of triumph over trials and difficulties, and of the power of love.

SUMMARY OF THE FOUR PLOTS

The main idea of romance, the first story, is adventure or action. An innocent, idealized person moves in a world beyond the ordinary and realistic world of experience and undergoes a quest involving a test of his or her human powers. The central idea of tragedy, the second story, is catastrophe or death befalling a hero who maintains those qualities humans consider heroic no matter what the hero's fate. Tragedies may be romantic or ironic depending on whether they feature idealized characters or more realistic ones. The controlling idea of satire and irony is the absence of heroism and the presence of chaos, confusion, misery, and injustice—the world of experience. Satire attempts to change the unsatisfactory condition by revealing through ridicule such things as hypocrisy. Ironists simply show things as they see them, and their point of view is a negative one. Comedy, the fourth story, moves out of ironic confusion; its central idea is the human spirit's potential for renewal. It ends with a transformation of ironic chaos. The comic spirit is one of hope for the future and faith in human endurance over time.

The stories that people tell are parts of a single story. That one story is people's search for human identity, a search that continues and will continue as long as there are people. It begins with an ideal world, moves through the less perfect world of human experience, and toward a vision of the return of the perfect harmony of Eden. There are moments when we catch a glimpse of that perfect world. For it exists in the minds of imaginative writers and in imaginations awakened by their words.

IMPLICATIONS FOR TEACHING AND LEARNING

Figure 5.2 is at once a review of the characteristics of the plot of each of the four narrative types and an example of an exercise in criticism undertaken by middle school students. These questions were developed by Cathy Swan's sixth-grade reading class in New Canaan, Connecticut, to be used as the basis for small-group discussion of stories and novels. John Willinsky (1991), after observing a class at work putting a story to the "test," noted that the exercise brought the class to the brink of literary knowing, in this case to a sense of symbolic meaning.

> A number of the students also took that extra step beyond naming the right archetype for the story. They were practicing literary criticism, with their insights slipping out off-handedly. . . . Such is the elusive nature of teaching and learning. But there is the added point here that within this theory of literature is buried the idea that these insights aren't directly about anything so much as the pattern of literature. (p. 167)

The unifying principles of literature provide an organizational scheme that enables students to see literature as a whole rather than as a collection of unrelated entities. It provides a way of relating together all the verbal constructs of our experience—both literary and subliterary—thereby providing a sense of the scope and extent of the human imagination as it works in creating verbal structures.

Identification of patterns and relationships is one of the major ways in which we learn. In discovering the patterns and interrelationships of literary works, students have a more-than-usual sense of the importance of literature as a study. For the whole—like a jigsaw puzzle—makes sense only when the right context is found for each of its parts.

An understanding of the unifying principles of literature liberates criticism because it provides a view that comes from stepping back from the works to better see their organizing structure and how they fit with respect to other works. It is not meant as a system to justify pigeonholing—paring and prodding each poem, play, and story until it fits into a slot. It releases students from the stultifying, myopic study of literature that centers in recall of bits and pieces of a work's content. It provides a way to broaden the perspective of discussions about literature.

FIGURE 5.2. Determining Characteristics of the Four Narrative Types

Romance Test

1. Was there a quest?
2. Does the main character have supernatural powers or special abilities?
3. Is the setting a fantasy (a dream or nightmare) world?
4. Does good triumph over evil?
5. Does the main character "live happily ever after"?
6. Do wishes come true?
7. Did the story make you feel that you can slay dragons?

Tragedy Test

1. Does the story show the main character's limits?
2. Does the main character have a fault?
3. Does the main character make a disastrous choice or mistake?
4. Does the choice or mistake affect the natural order?
5. Does the main character seem to be caught in a trap?
6. Does the main character die in the end?
7. Does the main character exhibit dignity and honor?
8. Does the story remind you that people have limitations?

Irony-Satire Test

1. Is the story set in the world of experience?
2. Does it discuss human limitations?
3. Is the main character all-too-human?
4. Is the main character a hero or a champion?
5. Does the quest remain unfulfilled?
6. Is the setting cold?
7. What is being attacked satirically?
8. Does the story attempt to change people's behavior?
9. Is there hope in the end?
10. Did the story teach you that we must fight the ills of humanity? How?

Comedy Test

1. Does the story show a positive view of life?
2. Is the main character likeable but ordinary?
3. Is there a clever, daring side-kick who saves the main character?
4. Does the story have a blocking character or situation?
5. Are there detractors who keep the main character from his/her goal?
6. Is there a major transformation?
7. Does this transformation seem magical or miraculous?
8. Do blocking characters convert to the main character's side?
9. Is there a happy ending with a move toward a better life?
10. Does the story teach you that with love and hope you can make a better life?

These principles are not to be learned by rote. What they can do is provide the teacher with a deductive framework to keep in mind during discussions with students. For the students, learning proceeds inductively; from broad experience with literature and nonliterary forms of daily experience, they begin—with guidance—to see for themselves patterns and relationships in what they read, see, and hear and to make generalizations. Students know a great deal more than they realize; their verbal experience has been built up by reading, listening to stories and conversation, watching movies and television, and listening to the lyrics of pop songs. The teacher—informed by a knowledge of literature's unifying principles—helps students to discover and express their knowledge. With the realization that literature is a coherent order of words comes a greater sense of its significance as a study and of its importance in our lives.

This realization grows out of experience. Experiencing imaginative literature is therefore the first step in the development of the child as critic. The focus in this book is on imaginative literature for several reasons.

The first reason is obvious: poetry and story appeal to children. Furthermore, the best poems and stories are illustrative of the wonders and marvels that may be created with words. Since they are born of the imagination, they have the potential for educating that faculty in readers and listeners. In addition, the unifying principles of literature are revealed through experience with poetry and story. Accordingly, the next two chapters (in Part III) are about the first aspect of criticism, experiencing literature. In Chapter 6, poetry is considered; Chapter 7 focuses on story.

PART III

Theory Into Practice

6

Poetry and Literacy

Poetry, the main body of which is verse, is always the central powerhouse of a literary education. It contributes, first, the sense of rhythmical energy. . . . It contributes too, as the obverse of this, the sense of leisure, of expert timing of the swing and fall of cadences. Then there is the sense of wit and heightened intelligence, resulting from seeing disciplined words marching along in metrical patterns and in their inevitable right order. And there is the sense of concreteness that we can get only from the poet's use of metaphor and visualized imagery. Literary education of this kind . . . can do something to develop a speaking and prose style that comes out of the depths of personality and is a genuine expression of it.

—Northrop Frye (1963b, p. 26)

In most classrooms, poetry, far from being a central powerhouse in literacy education, seldom plays even a small part in efforts to promote reading and writing ability. Few studies have been undertaken on its motivational potential for encouraging reading and writing or on its role in developing facility in language. This is not surprising, since poetry is typically consigned to a peripheral role in classrooms and is generally not considered to be a major factor in elementary programs to develop literacy. Of all the forms of literature, poetry is farthest removed from the practical and prosaic and therefore easily shunted aside in a shortsighted curriculum that sees it as a decorative distraction from the pursuit of utilitarian language arts and communication skills.

For more than 20 years, elementary and middle school teachers enrolled in my graduate class, "Poetry for Children," at Queens College have conducted informal research on using poetry in the classroom (Sloan, 2003). The results *in every case* indicate that more formal research studies designed to test the hypothesis "Poetry improves oral and written expression" would have significant positive results.

For the poetry class, I require a study. Each teacher, with a simple survey, assesses her class to determine what they know of poetry and their attitudes toward it. Usually, the children know very little about poetry. Unfortunately, many—especially older students—have developed a negative attitude toward it. Here are some comments from third and fifth graders: "It's babyish," "It's for girls," "Some of it doesn't even rhyme," "You have to figure out what it means."

Based on the findings from the informal survey, the teacher designs a "treatment" for that specific group of children that is intended to change attitudes for the better and to wipe out ignorance about poetry. *Delight, immersion, enjoyment, inundation* are the buzz words guiding teachers as they plan these treatments. We have discovered that, *without exception*, a concerted effort to use poetry in the elementary and middle school classroom, without abusing it in any way, even over a short time, has significant positive results in regard to the following: knowledge about poets and poetry, changed attitudes toward poetry in general, word awareness and interest in language, and developing skill in the creation of original verse. By abuse I mean, among other horrors, forced memorization, verse vivisection, assignments to write poetry with few prior examples of the form or no group efforts as examples, attempts to translate the "true" meaning of a poem into prose, and learning by rote the names of poetic devices and techniques and rummaging around in poems to find and list them.

While a few weeks is not sufficient time to see marked literacy development in children, this brief time is enough to see the *potential* for development. If nothing else, a systematic poetry program, properly presented not as stiff lessons but as occasions for delight in language, creates keen interest in words and all the marvelous and astonishing things they can be made to do. Without this interest in words, children have little motivation to make the considerable effort it takes to read and write.

THE PRIMACY OF POETRY

Formal literacy education typically begins with the inauthentic prose of the basal reader. In misguided efforts to teach the basics from a utilitarian base, we overlook what is truly basic—the child's natural propensity for the poetic: metaphoric expression, rhythm, rhyme, pun, riddling, wordplay in all its forms (Geller, 1985).

Generally, our notions about language are prose-based. Early in our education we become familiar with the distinction between poetry and prose. Along with the recognition of this distinction usually comes the conviction that prose is the language of everyday speech and is therefore the more natural means of expression. Poetry, as misguided in-school attempts to uncover and explain its "true" or "hidden" meaning seem to indicate, is widely considered to be an almost perverse—albeit often witty and ingenious—way of distorting prose statements. However, the truth is that prose, like poetry, is far from being the language of everyday speech.

> Prose is not ordinary speech, but ordinary speech on its best behavior, in its Sunday clothes, aware of an audience and with its relation to that audience prepared beforehand. It is the habitual language only of articulate people who have mastered its difficult idiom. (Frye, 1963b, p. 18)

Ordinary speech is characterized by short phrases, sketchy syntax, and repetitiveness, with many of the repetitions, like nonsense words in verse, serving as rhythmical filler. This teenager's speech is an example: "Like, I mean, the new guy is cute. Know what I mean?"

Verse and prose are both used to regulate and control the babble of speech. Prose, however, is the more difficult way to conventionalize it. Historically, verse precedes prose in a society's literature, often by centuries. Primitive poetry delights in catalogues: long lists of strange names, names that are potent in magic, that are keys to history, that summon up the deeds of heroes and gods. In this poetry everyday language is conventionalized, ordered to form, shaped, and controlled. Children, on their own, recapitulate the experience of primitive literature, turning easily toward the conventionalized, to riddles, chants, conundrums, and jingles (Opie, 1959). If their natural speech is any indication, young children understand that verse is a more direct way of conventionalizing speech than is prose.

Poetic Devices in Children's Speech

In poetry and in children's talk, abstractions are visualized and personalized; logic and sequence are subordinated to the insights of metaphor and simile. Figures of speech are seen for what they are, direct means of expression, rather than ornaments of language.

The poet, like the child, works with sensory experience rather than abstractions, using images rather than ideas and concepts. The poet typically employs the most primitive of categories, similarity and identity. Something is like something else or something is something else. "Like a small grey/coffee-pot,/sits the squirrel," says Humbert Wolfe (1962, p. 303); Vachel Lindsay tells us that "The Moon's the North Wind's cooky" (1983, p. 30). A child with a stomachache complains that his stomach is "broken."

That children love riddles is one indication of their poetic turn of mind. The riddle's use of pun and identification reflects the mental processes of young children. In a riddle what is being described is not the thing itself but its properties and effects, as in this riddle about a well: "As round as an apple, as deep as a cup, / And all the king's horses can't pull it up." Children's naturally metaphoric way of looking at things makes the riddle an appealing form for them. The riddle, where something is described in terms of something else, embodies the very essence of poetic thought.

If younger children's metaphoric sense is capitalized upon and preserved through riddles and other poetic forms, instead of finding the advanced study of poetry difficult, as those raised on textbook prose often do, they will recognize its associations and identities as the simple, natural, and direct forms of expression with which they are familiar.

Other poetic devices—rhythm, alliteration, onomatopoeia— are also natural elements of the child's own expression, which is repetitive, heavily accented, given to sing-song, whine, and croon. The following examples are from studies by graduate students in my classes at Queens College:

- Several students described how young children take a phrase or word, heard but not necessarily understood, and make a chant of it. One 2-year-old stamped around the backyard to "Zilch, zilch, zilch-zilch-zilch."

- An example of wordplay comes from a 7-year-old helping to carve a pumpkin: "The stuff inside is like orange gunk; it's like orange gook; it's like orange gluk; it's like orange glunk."
- Onomatopoeia is in a 5-year-old's account of how Tommy fell in a puddle: "Yeah! Tommy was riding SWISH! down past Roz and hit a rock SMASH! (smacks hands together) The bike fell over into that big muddy puddle—KSHHH!"
- There is rhyme in a 4-year-old's conversation with a bug: "Hello, bug wug. Buggy, wuggy, bug, wug. Glug!"
- Examples of rhythm, rhyme, alliteration, and assonance abound in playtime chants and jingles such as:

> Baby, baby, stick your head in gravy;
> Wrap it up in bubble gum,
> And send it to the navy.

As these examples from their speech and oral lore indicate, children are explorers of language. They love to pun, to play with words, to ask riddles featuring words that sound the same but have different meanings: "Why did the house call the doctor?" "Because it had a window pane." Like poets, children are fascinated by all the marvelous things that words can do: how sounds mimic what is being described, how puns are possible, how language can be made to "natter, patter, chatter and prate" (Merriam, 1974, p. 4).

In simpler societies poetry emerges as a primary need because it is seen as a simple and direct means of expression. In Eskimo, for instance, the word *anerca* means "poetry"; it also means "to breathe." Children seem intuitively to understand that metaphor, far from being mere decorative language, is a powerful means of linking thoughts to experience. One child, during a ride in a car, commented that the "road is a big waist and we're riding on the belt."

Primitive poetry is linked to movement, to the basic bodily rhythms involved in singing, dancing, marching. Children are kinesthetic creatures who delight in moving to rhythmic chants of words that take their fancy. Polysyllabic mouthfuls become rhythmic background for table-beating and pan-pounding. Children know how language and movement relate. They bounce balls and skip rope in time to chanted words; they tease in taunting rhythmic rhymes. They call on the magical powers of incantation.

White horse, white horse,
Bring me good luck;
  Good luck to you,
  Good luck to me,
  Good luck to everyone I see.

In young children, movement and language are inextricably bound.

Implications for the Classroom

Ideally, our literary education should begin not with prose, but with such things as "This little pig went to market"—with verse rhythms reinforced by physical assault. The infant who gets bounced on somebody's knee to the rhythm of "Ride a cock horse" does not need a footnote telling him that Banbury Cross is twenty miles northeast of Oxford. . . . All he needs is to get bounced. If he is, he is beginning to develop a response to poetry in the place where it ought to start. For verse is closely related to dance and song; it is also closely related to the child's own speech. (Frye, 1963b, p. 25)

Poet Eve Merriam also emphasizes the importance of experiencing poetry physically: "There's a physical element in reading poetry aloud; it's like jumping rope or throwing a ball" (Sloan, 1981, p. 959). She advises young poets not to intellectualize, but to respond to words with movement: "Use your whole body as you write. It might even help sometimes to stand up and move with your words" (p. 963).

To fail to capitalize on children's poetic language sense is a serious mistake. Good writing is based on good speech; the good speech of each individual is a direct reflection of personality. If we write in a way we never speak, our writing is sure to lack conviction and individuality. Rhythmic poetry can give children a sense of their own inner rhythms. Far from being frills on the edge of a literacy program, these activities—hearing verse, repeating it, moving to it, letting the music of the language sink in until it becomes part of you—are the power sources that fuel it.

It is an educational truism that we must begin instruction when children are in their development. Imaginative literature is exactly where they are. It makes good sense to have children read and listen to poetry, because verse is closer to their natural mode of expression than more utilitarian forms of language. They grasp analogies that older, more experienced minds reject as absurd. In intellectual development they move from the imaginative and pre-logical toward discursive, reasoned forms of thought. If we impose alien structures too soon—expecting children to read and write expository forms foreign to them—we invite failure and disinterest.

Scholars like Ernst Cassirer, Edward Sapir, and Otto Jesperson have confirmed that the essence of language is not communication. The egocentric speech of children is one indication that the purely communicative aspect of language has been exaggerated. Language in the young, who as they begin to learn language babble both to learn and for the sheer joy of the sound, is as likely to be expressive as utilitarian. Children delight in the repetition of words and phrases for their sound, even when their meaning eludes the youngsters. The affective aspect of language, sorely neglected in formal education, deserves primacy in the literary education of children.

Some years ago a film told the story of Victor, an adolescent captured in 1799 in southern France, where for years he had roamed like an animal, savage and mute. A young Doctor Itard undertook the boy's education. Acting on the assumption that language is produced primarily to serve practical ends, he struggled to teach Victor to communicate efficiently. The project was eventually abandoned and judged unsuccessful for a number of reasons. Among them was Dr. Itard's failure to realize how Victor used language. The child, for example, never used the word *lait* to obtain milk but only to express his pleasure after the enjoyment of it. Indeed, the few words Victor did master were spoken only when he contemplated their objects with joy or sorrow, not when he lacked anything.

Our advanced society places great value on the practical, prosaic, discursive mode of language and thought. We begin to believe that language began as a utility, that metaphoric expression is mere decoration or distortion of fact. Children are not so easily misled. With their natural affinity for the poetic, they thrive on poetic language. The prose route to literacy is a rough one, as teachers will testify who have to listen to pedestrian basal-reader prose haltingly read and peruse prose offerings that are like essays in a foreign language imperfectly learned.

Language is absorbed from top to toe, not by the head alone. Sylvia Ashton-Warner, in her celebrated efforts to help Maori chil-

dren toward literacy, discovered the significance to children of
the affective aspects of language. In her classic "textbook," *Teacher*
(1964), she writes:

> First words must have intense meaning for a child. . . . They
> must be part of his being. How much hangs on the love of read-
> ing, the instinctive inclination to hold a book. INSTINCTIVE. That's
> what it must be. . . . Words must be organically born from the
> dynamic life itself. (p. 30)

For Sylvia Ashton-Warner's pupils, written expression in the
words of their personal "key" vocabularies was stimulated by
dancing, because their teacher understood the basic relationship
of the two rhythms. In children, language is as basic and rhythmic as their body language and as inextricably bound to it, but—
perversely—in school we chain them to seats and insist that they
use only their minds in growing literate.

Far from being an unnecessary frill, poetry is essential to
the development of genuine literacy. For the elementary school
child, and the middle school student, as well, it is important to
note, this means the aesthetic experience of poetry, not prema-
ture analysis and explication of it. Poems chosen for presentation to children should be at the children's level of interest and
understanding.

Experiencing poetry by listening to it, reading it aloud, chanting it, and moving to its rhythms are prerequisite activities for
later, formal studies. Children who experience an early, pleasurable exposure to quantities of fine poetry and verse are less likely,
as students in high school and college, to experience difficulties
with poetic conventions: its compactness; its use of simile, metaphor, and personification; its employment of assonance, ambiguity, and pun.

To begin where children are, then, is to begin with verse, to
capitalize on their nature and their natural proclivities. Phyllis
Rogovin (1985), a teacher-researcher who collected examples of
poetic devices in children's speech, comments:

> Knowing that children enjoy using poetic devices when they
> relax and play, it is safe to assume that if they were carefully
> exposed to poetry, they could appreciate it as much as, if not
> more than any other form of literature. Daily doses of rhyth-
> mic and rhyming poems, similar to the patterns already famil-
> iar to them in the street, would be the starting point to capture

their interest and imagination. I have found that poems like David McCord's "Pickety Fence" [1974, p. 7] do just that. (p. 3)

BRINGING CHILDREN AND POETRY TOGETHER

Choice of Poems

There is one rule of thumb for the choice of poetry to be used with children: It should be the best available. It is essential that it be "poetic" in the sense of being imagistic and rhythmic. Good poems employ metaphor and image effectively and delightfully; they have strong sensory appeal; many illustrate patterns of repetition and rhyme. Poems chosen for use with children should speak to them at their level of understanding, but they ought also to stretch minds and imaginations with fresh insights, novel ways of seeing the world, and unusual but apt ways with words.

Riddles, good examples of metaphoric imagery, belong in a central place at every grade level in the elementary school. In riddles and conundrums, rhymed or unrhymed, the poet's way of looking at the world is clearly evident; analogy and association are used with telling effect. Early experience with epigrammatic sayings, concise and compact like proverbs, helps the child to understand the economy inherent in poetic expression. Many proverbs and epigrams are highly imagistic or metaphoric, illustrating at once two primary qualities of poetry.

Although it is the teachers' responsibility to bring the best of poetry to children, they are choosing for children and therefore need to read and listen to poems as a child would read and listen. What delights a child may seem simplistic to an adult, but delight is an important ingredient in poetry programs for children. The wise teacher is one who learns from the pupils, encouraging them to share their own favorites, whether from an anthology or from the oral lore of childhood: jingles, chants, game-songs, taunt-songs, word games, even the lively singing commercials learned from television and radio or lyrics of pop songs. Choosing poetry to use with children can never become an academic exercise.

Poems may be rhymed or unrhymed; they may be stories or lyrics; they may be old or new; they may be on any subject that might interest the children. Surveys by teacher–researchers in my classes at Queens College have found that children of all ages prefer humor and nonsense in poetry, poems that tell stories, and poems that rhyme.

For foolproof introductions to poetry, choose works suitable for children by such poets as these:

William Blake   Federico Garcia Lorca
Robert Browning   Marianne Moore
Emily Dickinson   Mary Oliver
Robert Frost   Christina Rossetti
Gerard Manley Hopkins   Carl Sandburg
Langston Hughes   Wallace Stevens
D. H. Lawrence   Walt Whitman

Also recommended are classic and contemporary writers of verse for children such as:

Arnold Adoff   Nikki Grimes
*Dorothy Aldis   David Harrison
Brod Bagert   *Mary Ann Hoberman
Byrd Baylor   Leland Jacobs
Harry Behn   *X. J. Kennedy
Rosemary and Stephen   *Karla Kuskin
   Vincent Benét   Dennis Lee
N. M. Bodecker   Edward Lear
Ashley Bryan   J. Patrick Lewis
Deborah Chandra   *Myra Cohn Livingston
*John Ciardi   *Eve Merriam
Kalli Dakos   A. A. Milne
Walter de la Mare   *David McCord
*Barbara Esbensen   *Lilian Moore
Norma Farber   Lillian Morrison
Eleanor Farjeon   Ogden Nash
*Aileen Fisher   Naomi Nye
Paul Fleischman   Robert Louis Stevenson
Douglas Florian   Nancy Willard
Nikki Giovanni   Janet Wong
*Eloise Greenfield   Valerie Worth

The asterisk indicates that the poet received the National Council of Teachers of English Award for Excellence in Poetry for Children. No list of poets is complete; every year new names are added. Consult reviews in *Horn Book Magazine* at the library to find reviews of new books of poetry.

Poetry as a Part of Daily Experience

Poetry cannot be relegated to an occasional lesson in its appreciation. As Leland Jacobs, educator and writer of children's verse, emphasized in his lectures to teachers, it must become an integral part of daily living, embedded in the ritual of the classroom. Effective teachers will have poems on the tips of their tongues for all occasions: If someone has new shoes, a new baby brother, or a case of the sniffles; if an early robin appears, or the first flake of snow, they will be ready at a moment's notice with an appropriate poem or know where to find one to read aloud. Teachers are advised to develop personal collections of poems to read from and for their students to browse in. A personal anthology is a ready resource when poems are needed at a moment's notice. Besides, children love to read their teacher's favorite poems. When I visited a former student's kindergarten classroom, I found that her personal poetry anthology, in a large photo album, was the children's favorite book in their classroom library. Its once white covers showed smudges made with hands eager to see the poems within.

Ways must be found to bring poetry naturally and regularly into the classroom. It helps to encourage the children to develop personal anthologies of their own, as well as classroom anthologies containing class favorites. Anthologies may be written or tape-recorded or both. Festivals of poetry reading may be organized, with readers taking their favorites "on the road" to share with other classes. Children in one class I know have a "gift of words" for every visitor to their classroom: Favorite poems—the children's own or those of published poets—are copied carefully by the students, the papers rolled and tied with colored yarn, and arranged in a basket for visitors to select from. One first-grade classroom I visited had poems displayed on large poetry posters, lettered and illustrated by the children.

Many teachers find the unit an effective way to bring substance and coherence to poetry presentations. Units may be developed by focusing on the works of one poet; by comparing or contrasting the works of two or more; by concentrating for a time on a type of poetry like the ballad, limerick, sonnet, and the like;

by reading and listening to poems on one topic or subject; by searching for poems that relate to material being studied in mathematics, social studies, or science (Cullinan, Scala, & Schroder, 1995). This last activity is especially useful in showing children that poetic insights are possible for all subjects, including those—like science and mathematics—typically talked about in discursive language.

The Importance of Oral Presentation

Poet Eve Merriam is a recipient of the National Council of Teachers of English Award for Excellence in Poetry for Children. *Out Loud* (Merriam, 1974) is both the title of a volume of her verse and also her poetry-presentation philosophy in two words. "If we can get teachers to read poetry, lots of it, out loud to children, we'll develop a generation of poetry lovers; we may even have some poetry writers. But the main thing, we'll have language appreciators" (Sloan, 1981, p. 960).

In the elementary school years, and even before formal education begins, children should experience poetry orally. Students develop an antipathy toward poetry only after they become independent readers, when there is a great possibility that poetry will become for them nothing more than static rows of print on a page, perhaps the subject of analysis and dissection, or something that they must memorize under pressure. The silent treatment of poetry can never result, at least for the young child, in an appreciation and enjoyment of poetry. Poetry should be read aloud, as effectively as possible, by the teacher, who in most cases will be the best oral interpreter the child will encounter. Recordings may be used for variety, but they are never a substitute for the live performance that involves direct sharing between a teacher and a class. Children should be encouraged but not coerced to read aloud to others, with preparation always preceding performance. All oral interpreters ought to prepare their presentations, selecting only those poems that they most enjoy, for these will be the best read.

Artistic responses to poetry (and other forms of imaginative literature) are particularly appropriate. Responding through art respects the aesthetic experience and extends it. Affective response is often intense and complicated, difficult if not impossible to put into words. Through nonlineal and multidimensional artistic responses students can come closer to an expression of their personal aesthetic experiences. The creation of visual art in response to poetry (and story) may take many forms. Janice Dressel (1988) describes how students created collages of words and pictures taken from magazines to express their response to and interpretation of literary works they had experienced. Using paint, clay models, or constructions of various kinds, students may visually render the personal meaning and significance to them of a literary work of art. In these renderings, children are encouraged to strive for a personal and interpretive creation rather than one that is simply literal or representational.

As often as possible, the oral experience with poetry ought to be accompanied with a physical response. Children should repeat lines and verses that have natural appeal, perhaps joining in on the refrain as they listen to a verse such as:

> A farmer went trotting upon his grey mare,
>   Bumpety, bumpety, bump!
> With his daughter behind him so rosy and fair,
>   Lumpety, lumpety, lump!
>
> A raven cried, Croak! and they all tumbled down,
>   Bumpety, bumpety, bump!
> The mare broke her kees and the farmer his crown,
>   Lumpety, lumpety, lump!
>
> The mischievous raven flew laughing away,
>   Bumpety, bumpety, bump!
> And vowed he would serve them the same the next day,
>   Lumpety, lumpety, lump!

Moving to the rhythms of the poem is to be encouraged. It is natural for little children to gallop to "Ride a cock horse," walk with "To market, to market," march smartly to "The Grand Old Duke of York," or hop in time with A. A. Milne's (1924) "Hoppity."

Poems may be acted out as well as moved to, their rhythmic qualities brought to life through physical response. For older children it is fun to act out the action words of a poem: "slink," "dance," "creep," "rush," and the like. The acting may be representational, with children taking turns miming each episode of, say, A. A. Milne's (1924) "The King's Breakfast" or "The Highwayman" by Alfred Noyes (1902), while others read the poem aloud.

Avoid Verse Vivisection

This is the advice of Leland Jacobs, a militant against the misuse of poetry in classrooms. Poems must be respected and enjoyed for what they are—imaginative constructs that are not translatable into utilitarian prose. No effort should be made to extract what is often erroneously called a poem's "real" meaning.

The question, "What does it mean?" has no place in the study of poetry at any level, because it fails to make a necessary distinction between imaginative and discursive writing. Trying to translate a poem into discursive commentary is a fruitless and wasteful procedure. The effort confuses children, giving them the erroneous impression that poetry exists only as a distortion of prose. Instead, the child should be helped to know, by means of the best examples and with enjoyment and experimentation, that poetry is a valid mode of thought.

Students in Leland Jacobs' children's literature classes at Teachers College, Columbia University, were treated to a telling example of how the experience of a poem may be twice ruined: by overteaching it and by treating it as discourse. Professor Jacobs recited "The Goblin" to classes of teachers and mimicked the absurdity of misguided teachers who would ask of a poem intended to be enjoyed solely for its sounds and rhythm such questions as "What does it mean?" "Where, children, does the goblin live?" "How many things does he do?" "Can you name each one in its proper order?"

THE GOBLIN

A goblin lives in *our* house, in *our* house, in *our* house,
A goblin lives in *our* house all the year round.
He bumps
And he jumps
And he thumps
And he stumps.
He knocks
And he rocks
And he rattles at the locks.
A goblin lives in *our* house, in *our* house, in *our* house,
A goblin lives in *our* house all the year round.

Rose Fyleman

If a poem requires considerable explication and commentary by the teacher before, during, or after the reading of it, it is probably the wrong choice for a particular group. Poems should stand by themselves, requiring few if any props, at eye level with children. Occasionally it may be necessary to clarify a concept or offer the meaning of a word before reading a poem to a class but, in general, even this practice should be avoided. A better plan is to encourage the children's own questions about points that bewilder or intrigue. In giving children freedom to experience poetry, teachers need to be listeners as students comment on how a poem affected them. In this early stage of criticism, experience of the poem is the best teacher.

The emphasis is always on delight rather than dissection. In Archibald MacLeish's words, "A poem should not mean but be." "It takes children a long time," say the Opies, "before they cease to be amazed that one word can have more than one meaning" (1959, p. 31). Certainly a literary education worthy of the name should see to it that this amazement with the delightful things that words can do is fostered and made to last a lifetime.

This can never be accomplished through unpalatable practices such as vivisection. Children's initial experiences with poetry must center in delight. Only if this is so are more analytical procedures possible and palatable as the child grows older. And even these must be planned to enhance and not destroy the essence of the poetic experience.

Experience of poetry, as with story, is the first step in criticism at the elementary and middle school level. A personal response—verbal, physical, artistic—to the aesthetic experience is the preferred first critical act for young students.

> In poetry
> Ideas explode in words on the page
> Raging, rejoicing,
> Voicing
> Hopes or joy or pain
> For now and again.
>
> *Glenna Sloan*

A SHORT COURSE IN POETRY

Teaching a course in children's poetry to teachers in the graduate children's literature program at Queens College over many years has led me to an important discovery. Many teachers do not include reading and writing of poetry in the curriculum for two main reasons: Experiences in high school and college classes have left them intimidated by poetry, and, although they know they are short-changing their students by not including poetry on a regular basis, they don't know how to begin. Poetry is not to be feared (Sloan, 1981); in fact, it is much to be desired as a valuable aid in literacy development (Sloan, 2003). Here follows a short course for teachers on bringing poetry and children together. (Also see the website (*www.ncte.org*) of the National Council of Teachers of English to read the cyberbrief, "Teachers to Teachers on Bringing Poetry and Children Together" [Sloan, 2001c].)

Getting to Know Poets and Poetry

My students ask: How can I learn enough about children's poetry to teach it? The answer: Begin by reading quantities of poetry in both old and new anthologies. Then, look for collections of verse by poets you enjoyed reading in the anthologies. Use plenty of Post-Its® to mark the poems that appeal to you. Buy a large photo album, xerox your favorites, and create your own anthology. Look for poems by outstanding poets, such as those who have won the National Council of Teachers of English Award for Excellence in Poetry for Children. You will find this list on the NCTE website. For bibliographic information about poets, consult two NCTE publications, Jeffrey S. Copeland's *Speaking of Poets, Volumes I and II* (1993, 1994).

As you read and select your favorites, note the common characteristics of poems: how they are made and how they are made memorable. You will note, for instance, that describing something in terms of something else (metaphor) is common to poetry: varicose veins, as one child poet put it, are "thunder and lightning"; "a white balloon aloft" is the moon; the bare branches of trees against the sky are like black lace. As you read and read, you may notice that many poems for children are written in rhyming two- or four-line stanzas (couplets and quatrains) and that some poems are simply statements made interesting with memorable comparisons and appeals to the senses.

Learning Facts About Poetry

To learn about the genre itself, read the little book, *Poem-Making: Ways to Begin Writing Poetry* (Livingston, 1991). It answers such questions as: What makes a poem a poem? Also, read what Pulitzer-prize-winning poet Mary Oliver (1994) has to say in *A Poetry Handbook: A Prose Guide to Understanding and Writing Poetry*.

Bringing Children and Poetry Together

The teachers worry: How do I present poetry to children so I kindle and not quench their natural delight in all the wonderful things words are made to do in poetry? Eve Merriam told me (Sloan, 1981) that teachers were likely to put poetry on a pedestal as something far above their reach. She suggested that they take poetry down from the pedestal and have fun with it.

Setting Goals. Begin by setting goals. Here are some of the common goals my students have articulated:

- To kindle, not quench children's interest in language through fostering delight in poetry;
- To help them appreciate the possibilities of language, including its playfulness;
- To use poetry as reading material;
- To use poetry that is read and heard as motivation and as a model for creating original verse;
- To learn through experiencing quantities of poetry something about the nature and variety of poetic form;
- To incorporate poetry into all aspects of classroom life and curriculum;

- To dispel the mystique that surrounds poetry; it is simply language at its best, to be enjoyed by all.

Begin with Inquiry.   Often, poetry study in school is limited to reading a poem or two. My students found that a planned sequence of study over time was needed for a meaningful engagement with poetry. In your class, begin with inquiry. You want to find out what your students know about poetry and poets; how they feel toward the genre. Create a simple survey to discover your students' knowledge and attitudes. Use questions such as:

What is poetry?
What do you think of when you hear the word *poetry*?
Do you enjoy listening to poetry?
Do you read poetry on your own?
Do you check out books of poetry from the library?
What poets can you name?
Have you tried writing poetry?
Do you own any poetry books?

Plan Ahead.   Using the information from the survey, plan a sequence of study to address your children's needs and interests. Some sequences will last for days, others for months. Methods and materials are geared to the children's ability level and stage of linguistic development. The possible approaches to such a sequence of study are limitless. Here are some examples:

- Work with one or more forms such as couplets, quatrains, limericks (older children), terse verse (two-word rhymes), and cinquain.
- Study the work of one poet or compare the works of two.
- Concentrate on one type of poem, such as the ballad.

If you are unsure about poetic forms, consult such books as Livingston's *Poem-Making: Ways to Begin Writing Poetry* (1991), David McCord's *Take Sky* (1962) and *For Me to Say* (1970), or Avis Harley's *Fly with Poetry: An ABC of Poetry* (2000).

What Works.   Whatever you choose to do, begin by immersing the children in poetry.

- Read to them, no strings of questions attached. *Out loud* is the best way to experience poetry.
- Encourage the children to bring in poems they enjoy to read to partners or to the class. (Always insist that they practice before they perform.)
- Display poems on charts.
- Flood the room with collections of poems.
- Record and play tapes of people reading poetry.
- Invite the principal or another teacher and class for a poetry read-in.
- Stage whole-group choral readings of poems.
- Publish the children's work on bulletin boards, in simply-bound books, and on tape.
- Have the children carefully copy a poem they love, roll it up, and fasten it with a ribbon. Keep a basket of these "gifts of words" for visitors to take away with them.
- Arrange for older students to read aloud to younger children.
- Form a band of traveling minstrels to read in other classrooms.
- Create a classroom anthology of the children's favorite poems.

Ease into Writing.   Gradually move students into the writing mode. Begin with simple, fail-safe forms like terse verse, couplets, or triplets. Work up to more complicated forms: A quatrain stanza is composed of two rhymed couplets. Encourage the children to write ballads, a series of 4-line stanzas in which they tell a story, a book review, a biographical paper on George Washington, or an account of a school trip *in verse.*

Don't be afraid of forms. Writing within the limits of a form has a game-like, puzzle-like challenge that children enjoy.

When the children try writing free verse, don't accept as finished work mere dull statements that contain no interesting images or comparisons. Do not assign poetry writing for homework. Try whole-class collaborative creations before asking the children to write independently. Never ask the children to write in a form they haven't experienced in quantity. Do not accept obviously poor efforts (couplets that rhyme but don't make sense, for instance.) For tips on coaching, read poet and teacher Georgia Heard (1989, 1999).

Remember: Poetry is the ultimate language art. For children learning the wonders of language, let poetry do most of the teaching.

7

Developing a Sense of Story

> The young child can be introduced to the myths, fairy-tales, leg-
> ends, Bible stories, which are central to our imaginative heritage,
> because all he needs to do to comprehend them is to listen to
> the story. This is not a passive response, but a kind of imagina-
> tive basic training. . . . As he grows older and his literary experi-
> ence increases, he begins to realize that there are a limited num-
> ber of possible ways of telling a story, and that he is already in
> possession of all of them. Hence he has, not only a sense of the
> structure of storytelling implanted in his mind, but a potential
> critical standard as well. . . .
>
> —Northrop Frye (1988, p. 54)

The importance of story in human lives goes well beyond literacy. Experience and intuition tell us this, and the knowledge is
confirmed in the work of narratologists, students of narrative and
of its significance in our lives (Culler, 1978). "Given the least
prompting, we are disposed to arrange around people and things
a meaningful sequence of events" (Rosen, 1985, p. 7; 1986). We
recognize the truth in Barbara Hardy's (1977) famous discussion
of narrative.

> My argument is that narrative, like lyric and dance, is not to
> be regarded as an aesthetic invention used by artists to control,
> manipulate, and order experience, but as a primary act of mind
> transferred to art from life. . . . What concerns me are the quali-
> ties which fictional narrative shares with that inner and outer
> storytelling that plays a major role in our sleeping and waking
> lives. For we dream in narrative, remember, anticipate, hope,
> despair, believe, doubt, plan, revise, criticize, construct, gos-

sip, learn, hate, and love by narrative. In order really to live, we make up stories about ourselves and others, about the personal as well as the social past and future. (p. 12)

THE HUMAN NEED FOR STORY

In *The Uses of Enchantment,* Bruno Bettelheim (1976) discusses the importance of story to our psychological development. Through story, especially the fantasy of fairytales, Bettelheim argues, we are offered a way to articulate and explore our view of the world—a safe, objective means of making "some coherent sense out of the turmoil of . . . feelings" (p. 24).

A child's "sense of story"—a gradually evolving awareness of story form—is both a literary understanding and a facet of general development. The objective spectator stance that story allows us to bring to experience provides us with the means "to articulate and explore our view of the world, presenting alternatives, clarifying dark corners, posing contradictions, reconciling conflicts within the realm of our subjective, personal experience" (Applebee, 1978, p. 134). Stories are read more with the imagination and the emotions than with the reason. They are not judged against external standards of truth and logic, as are informational pieces. People who know the ways of stories do not ask: Is there a Yellow Brick Road? Although it may not be found on a road map, they understand that it exists as an imaginative reality. Those who have had plenty of experience with story are ready and willing to suspend disbelief and accept a story's postulates. The realization—which comes through the experience of imaginative literature—that many unusual premises are imaginatively conceivable widens personal perspectives and opens one to a greater range of possibilities in thought and action.

In terms of literacy, as a child's sense of story form and convention develops, it becomes an internalized representation, a schema, which aids comprehension. Listening to quantities of stories is the best preparation for reading them independently (Lehr, 1991, p. 16ff). "Literary experience depends on the mastery of the underlying conventions which govern the exchange between author and audience; without the conventions no exchange can take place" (Applebee, 1978, p. 134). Immersion in stories is essential to the growth of a child's sense of what stories are and how they are made—their patterns, components, and conventions. This sense improves the readers' ability in predicting syntax and meaning, and in reading comprehension, in general (Meek, 1982; Smith, 1983; Wells, 1986). Not surprisingly, a gradually evolving awareness of story form manifests itself in stylistic richness and complexity in children's speaking and writing (Eckhoff, 1983; Fox, 1983; Hickman, 1986).

Stories exert a strong motivational pull on readers and listeners. Moved by a story that excites or delights, children are likely to want to read on their own. Simply experiencing stories as works of art, savoring reactions and responses to them—reveling in the aesthetic experience—is of first importance in the development of literacy.

For both psychological and linguistic reasons, listening to and reading stories are essentials in the child's development. Stories teach children to read and write. Stories help children to make sense of their inner and outer worlds. *Engrossing* stories convince them that reading is worth doing.

EXPERIENCING LITERATURE:
A CRITIC'S FIRST STEP

Experiencing literature is the first step in the study of it. Children can't talk about what they haven't experienced, nor can they make connections among works of literature unless they are well-read. Through television, comics, series books, and movies, most children are well-educated in the literary subculture. What they are likely to lack, and therefore what school must provide, is the experience of the best from among a wide variety of children's literature, old and new.

The experience of literature and certainly the study of it are often reserved for superior readers and reasoners. If children are slow learners or if English is a second language for them, common belief has it that they have time in school only to pursue utilitarian communication skills. This elitist approach to literary studies is nonsense, not to mention antihumanistic. Like all other children, the less intellectually gifted child or the child who has minimal English deserves literature (Heath, 1985; Rigg & Allen, 1989; Spack, 1985). To develop as critics, children must experience quantities of stories—and poems, of course, as discussed separately in Chapter 6. For some children, this experience may come at first only through listening.

Hearing Stories Read

Children understand with the ear what may be beyond them as independent readers. Reading aloud to all children, whether they can read for themselves or not, is a must for every classroom. There are numerous compelling reasons why.

First, there is the mutual pleasure that comes with reading to someone. At storytime, there are moments of true communion between children and an adult. Reading for no other purpose than shared enjoyment places much-needed emphasis on the aesthetics of reading, emphasis that is neglected in the relentless pursuit of main ideas and significant details in directed reading lessons.

I cherish memories of laughter and tears shared with children I've taught. At a reunion in the school where I taught in the 1950s, a man who had been in one of my third-grade classes said, "I remember how you always read to us; you made a reader of me."

Second, as my former third grader suggests, there is a motivational aspect in hearing books read. The very enjoyment they experience as listeners convinces children that reading is worth doing. Hearing a story interpreted by a competent, enthusiastic reader not only gives children pleasure, but the experience also brings a sense of what proficient reading can be like. For learners whose own reading may falter, this is essential modeling. Reading aloud assigns a special role to reading, signalling to the child that adults find reading worthwhile and enjoyable. Further, an oral presentation allows listeners to hear the storyteller's voice. Carefully crafted prose, like poetry, is meant to be heard; in imaginative literature especially, words are chosen for their rhythm and sound as well as their sense.

Third, regularly hearing quantities of fine stories read aloud significantly improves children's vocabulary and reading comprehension, and results in greater complexity and sophistication of syntax in both oral and written language (Meek, 1982). For learners of English, hearing the cadences of the language is of inestimable value in developing reading facility (Rigg & Allen, 1989).

A teacher need not be the only oral reader in a classroom. Children can read to partners, with benefits accruing on both sides. Older children can prepare picture books to read to children in lower grades. Some schools encourage adult volunteers to serve as reading partners in classrooms. A word of caution:

oral readers should prepare in advance. A peerless performer, poet Ashley Bryan told his audience in Atlanta, November 2002, at the annual conference of the National Council of Teachers of English that oral readers must prepare for three weeks before going public.

Selecting Stories to Read Aloud

Children ought to experience the widest possible variety of stories: myths, Bible tales told as stories, folktales and fairytales, tales of the heroes of epic and romance, fables, stories of contemporary life, modern fantasy, and all the rest. Most stories for children are in either the comic or romantic modes, but stories in the tragic and ironic-satiric modes or stories with elements of these modes are now written for children and need to be included with the other two types to ensure exposure to the full circle of story types. To know only romantic and comic structures is not to advance beyond childlike tastes, with subsequent problems in appreciating "heavier" stories like the Shakespearean tragedies encountered in high school.

Myths, Bible stories, fairytales, and legends are central to the critical process, because this traditional literature is to later literary works what still life is to painting: studies in form. Through experience with traditional forms of story, children not only internalize a sense of the structure of all storytelling, but also develop a potential critical standard, essential in a world of subliterary entertainment.

A knowledge of myth and legend, Bible stories, and ancient epics is essential to one's full appreciation of later literature with its countless allusions to the traditional stories. Deprived of the sources of allusion, the reader is like someone limited in mathematics through lack of knowledge of the multiplication tables.

The traditional stories of a culture put children in contact with many of the social myths that have figured in the development of their society. Every society has a central group of stories that inform not only its literature but other aspects of its social life as well. Literary works that express informing social myths are not invariably works of great literary distinction, but they are of interest nonetheless. In America, these stories often present a nostalgic vision of the country's early history and feature cowboys, pioneers, hunters, and self-made tycoons, together with biographical tales of mythologized heroes like Washington and Franklin.

The interests and developmental level of a particular group of children are the first considerations in selecting material to read to children. However, as professionals aware of the needs of a particular class, teachers will select some reading materials that match the children's interests and other materials that will spark new interests and broaden literary experience. For older children who have not encountered much of it, the wonders of modern fantasy—works by Lloyd Alexander, Ursula K. Le Guin, Brian Jacques, Madeleine L'Engle, Anne McCaffrey, Robin McKinley, Diana Wynne Jones, to name a few outstanding authors in the genre—can be an exciting revelation. Stories that children might not attempt on their own or comprehend if they did—the classics like *Tom Sawyer*, for example, with their many pages and often unfamiliar vocabulary—are among the best choices for oral reading to groups. Biographies and historical fiction are sometimes dismissed by children as difficult or dull. The reading aloud of one or two of the best of these—by writers like Sid Fleischman, Jean Fritz, Russell Freedman, Kathryn Lasky, Jean Little, and Milton Meltzer—will go far in correcting this misconception.

Literary excellence is another primary consideration in selection: Important themes, memorable language, well-drawn characters, plots with streamlined structures, complementary text and illustrations, and fresh, innovative treatment of a subject are among the criteria to be considered. The stories need to be well beyond mediocre, far past the trivial tales that merely mirror experience without examining its paradox, intricacy, and ambiguity. The less challenging literature is more accessible—because of its ubiquity and simplicity—and children are likely to come to it on their own. Most books we read aloud, whether humorous or serious, ought to give listeners a thing or two to wonder about, marvel at, and talk about. Among the contemporary authors who write fine books of substance for older children are:

Avi	Michael Dorris
An Na	Anne Fine
Natalie Babbitt	Paul Fleischman
Byrd Baylor	Paula Fox
Sandra Cisneros	Virginia Hamilton
Lucille Clifton	Florence Heide
Sharon Creech	Karen Hesse
Karen Cushman	Lois Lowry

Patricia MacLachlan
Walter Dean Myers
Donna Jo Napoli
Katherine Paterson
Gary Paulsen
Richard Peck
Ann Rinaldi
Cynthia Rylant
Ouida Sebestyen
Gary Soto

Elizabeth Speare
Jerry Spinelli
Suzanne Fisher Staples
Mildred Taylor
Cynthia Voight
Gloria Whelan
E. B. White
Diana Wynne Jones
Tim Wynne-Jones
Laurence Yep

Children of preschool and primary grade age are particularly responsive to stories featuring repetitive patterns and refrains, as in the enduring *Millions of Cats* (Gág, 1928) and *Caps for Sale* (Slobodkina, 1947), or in inspired retellings of favorite folktales such as *Anansi and the Talking Melon* by Eric Kimmel (1994) and Aaron Shepard's *The Gifts of Wali Dad: A Tale of India and Pakistan* (1995). Not only do the children enjoy predictable books, but research also shows that their predictability facilitates learning to read and comprehending what is read (Baghban, 1984).

Some authors who write for young children and use memorable language to tell engaging stories—with and without repetitive patterns—are:

Margaret Wise Brown
Anthony Browne
Pat Cummings
Tomie dePaola
Roger Duvoisin
Pat Hutchins
Arnold Lobel
Bruce McMillan
Patricia Polacco

Amy Schwartz
Maurice Sendak
Marjorie Sharmat
William Steig
Chris Van Allsberg
Bernard Waber
Rosemary Wells
Charlotte Zolotow

In studies of children's preferences in upper elementary grades and middle school, teacher-researchers found that fast-paced stories featuring strong characters in humorous or perilous situations had the strongest appeal (Sloan, 1988). They discovered also that, with practice, listeners can appreciate more leisurely, reflective writing. In one study lasting 15 weeks, a class of fifth graders began by listening to simpler books of less than 100 pages and ended able to listen attentively to the complex fantasies of Susan Cooper, Ursula K. Le Guin, and Lloyd Alexander.

Although teachers on occasion may, for various reasons, judiciously cut bits from the texts they read aloud, abridged or simplified versions of works generally ought to be avoided. An author's style is in the language the author used. When the language is altered, the integrity of the piece is lost. Edited versions or insipid retellings, where language is simplified, are little more than summaries. The best translations, the finest versions of old tales, or the most masterly contemporary retellings of them must be sought. (Excellent bibliographies of recommended versions may be found in *Children and Books* [Sutherland, 1997] and similar anthologies. See also Resources for Teachers at the back of this book.) The unique style of storytellers like Rudyard Kipling needs to be heard in the original. In Kipling's *Just-so Stories* (1902/1987), for example, the outrageous flights of fancy are related in this storyteller's singular voice and they must be read "just so":

> In the beginning of years, when the world was new and all, and the Animals were just beginning to work for Man, there was a Camel, and he lived in the middle of a howling Desert because he did not want to work; and besides, he was a Howler himself. So he ate sticks and thorns and tamarisks and milkweed and prickles, most 'scruciating idle; and when anybody spoke to him he said "Humph!" Just "Humph!" and no more. (p. 139)

THE MAGIC OF STORYTELLING

Teaching a graduate course in storytelling for more than two decades has taught me that anyone, whether shy or outgoing, gifted with a mellifluous voice or not, can develop storytelling skills for classroom use. We all tell stories all the time. To heighten and hone our natural storytelling abilities, we require only three things: motivation, a little instruction, and a lot of practice. It is unlikely that most of us teachers and librarians will reach the level of skill of the many professional storytellers performing today, Jackie Torrence, Diane Wolkstein, Heather Forest, and Donald Davis among them. Their polished performances shouldn't intimidate us, says Margaret Read MacDonald, folklorist and storyteller, because more than polish, we need "caring tellers in every home and community who will share story with the personal warmth and concern that only the intimacy of small-group storytelling can provide" (1993, p. 9).

Why tell stories rather than read them? It's not a matter of one to the exclusion of the other, but of using both means of presentation, for both have value. Here are some comments of teachers in my classes who discovered, as tellers, the unique merits of storytelling:

"I never knew how powerful storytelling could be."

"Maintaining eye contact with the children helped them to focus and concentrate on the story."

"The children listen so intently, their eyes on my face; I know they are visualizing the action."

"I love how I can directly affect the children; telling a story seems to make response and conversation easy and natural."

"There is nothing between you and the children, no book; I love how they hang on my every word."

"Storytelling is an exciting way to communicate; there is no book to detract from the closeness you feel."

"The children were amazed that I could 'talk' a story and wanted to know where the story came from; discovering that a told story is also in a book motivates reading."

Becoming a Storyteller

How to Begin.   The following advice is for adult readers of this book, but most of it can be offered as well to storytellers in elementary and middle school classes.

There are many fine books on how to become a storyteller. Begin by reading one like *Storytelling: Art and Technique* (Greene, 1996). Reading about storytelling will not make you a storyteller, however. You should start by selecting a story that you truly enjoy, because you will be working with it for some time. A folk tale is probably your best choice, although *short* short stories are also good, especially if your audience is middle school age. (For a selection of short story sources, see the Literary References section at the end of this book.)

Selecting a Story.   To find your story, read collections of the best versions, those that are well-written as well as authentic. The language should be rich, colorful, and descriptive; the tale should not be abridged. As an example of what to look for, note the difference between the fine, authentic version and the poorly-written, "basalized" rendition of "Two of Everything" in Chapter 1 of this book. An excellent place to find memorable retellings of classic folk tales is in a book published many years ago, but well worth searching for in libraries: Walter de la Mare's (1959) *Tales Told Again*. You will hear his poet's voice in every line. Be guided in your selections by the sources cited in *Storytelling: Art and Technique* (Greene, 1996) or another reliable text.

Choose a story that contains dialogue. Repetition of names, phrases, or bits of verse also adds interest, as in the delightful tale of "Tikki Tikki Tembo" (Mosel, 1968) with its many repetitions of the boy's full name: Tikki Tikki Tembo No Sa Rembo Chari Bari Ruchi Pip Peri Pembo.

Select a story that is not too long or too short; a rambling, slow-moving tale will lose your listeners. "The Fisherman and His Wife" (Hunt, 1983), for instance, is a story for an experienced teller who can add variety to the narration of a long sequence of similar events.

Learning the Story. It is never wise to memorize your story word for word, as you may forget a word and suddenly dry up. Besides, recreating the story with each telling brings vitality and a sense of immediacy to the performance. You will, however, want to memorize bits of verse that occur in the story or turns of phrase that can't be improved upon and should be delivered just as they were written. Learn or *overlearn* the story by reading it many times, silently and aloud. Then, tape record the story and listen over and over again as you drive in the car, dust the furniture, or clean out the dishwasher. If it helps you, write the key scenes on cards or make a flow chart, a story map, or story board of the action.

When you think you know the story, try telling it aloud to your full-length mirror. Record your "performance." Be sure to go all the way through, no matter how much you forget or how often you falter. Note the parts that need more work. Listen again to your original taping and, as soon as you can, tell the story to a live audience, even if it's only one long-suffering relative.

Imagine the events of the story as you tell it. See it happening in your mind's eye. Be sure to use enough descriptive language to allow your audience to visualize from your words; paint pictures in the listeners' minds.

Vary your pitch, volume, and tempo as required. Be animated and fully absorbed in your telling. Never draw attention to omissions you may make. If you omit a vital part, don't apologize; find a way to improvise and insert the missing piece of information. Keep going. Remember, your audience doesn't know the story. They will be unaware that your version is not as perfect as you would like it to be. Don't point out your flaws and the audience won't notice them.

If you're telling to a group, include all, in turn, in your gaze. Maintain eye contact. Be conversational, but intense. Use pauses for effect; practice making the audience occasionally wait in suspense. Move and use gestures, if you wish, but keep them under control. Avoid aimless movements like patting your hair or twisting a button on your shirt. Don't pace back and forth. In other words, don't distract the audience from the words they are hearing.

To review, then, here are nine habits of highly successful storytellers:

1. Choose stories you love.
2. Overlearn, but don't memorize.
3. Record practice tellings either on videotape or on an audio-cassette.
4. Practice before a mirror.
5. Visualize while telling.
6. Control gestures.
7. Maintain eye contact.
8. Vary pitch, volume, and tempo.
9. Do not draw attention to flaws in your performance.

Developing a Repertoire. Your story kit should contain a variety of material. Examples of good materials are carefully crafted personal or family history and lore, folk tales, short stories, book excerpts, participatory stories, finger plays, call-and-response activities, accounts of historical events, and biographies of famous people and national heroes. For help in building a repertoire of short-story hour "stretchers," see the classics *Juba This and Juba That* and *With a Deep Sea Smile* (Tashjian, 1969, 1974). For innovative approaches to storytelling, there is Bob Barton's (1986) *Tell Me Another*. The Weston Woods company (see Teachers' Resources at the end of this book) publishes an excellent collection of audiotaped tellings by professional storytellers.

Storytelling and Literacy

The benefits of storytelling are numerous, some of them similar to those of reading aloud, some of them unique to storytelling. An important benefit is the sense of community that sharing a told story imparts. There are no distractions in this shared experience, no book to peer at. Listeners are part of a performance; their awareness is heightened as they enter into the telling. Relaxed, enjoyable, happy experiences with books and the words found in them can only have a positive effect on a child's interest in learning to read.

In storytelling, the child is offered a gift of words. At the end of the story there should be no prying questions by the teacher; a moment of silence is far more appropriate. Let the children comment and question, if they wish. Although hearing stories develops listening skills and familiarizes listeners with the conventions found in stories—the latter is a prerequisite for the full comprehension of them—it is surely not productive to test comprehension with a series of questions following a telling. Far better is an art activity (not always the drawing of a picture, either) that "tests" comprehension as effectively as a teacher's questions.

Storytelling is uniquely conducive to motivation. Children are known to want to read for themselves the sources of stories they have heard. One teacher commented, "The children wanted to know where I got the story. I can see how storytelling is a great way to get children more involved with reading." Another reported, "At the end of the story, *Too Much Noise* (McGovern, 1967/ 1992), I showed them the book the story came from. They were excited and wanted to borrow it."

Book-talking by the children or the teacher stimulates interest in reading. A teacher writes that her third graders "enjoy diving into the books that I have book-talked." A book talk, the perfect alternative to the written book report that no one reads, is not the labored relating of a plot, but rather the enticing telling *as a story* of an exciting, dramatic, or humorous excerpt from a book, with a few words of introduction to set the scene. Book talks are shared personal responses to books. Unlike the book report, they are vital language-arts activities involving reading, writing, speaking, and listening. I have seen children of all ages writing and revising in order to perfect a book talk that says just enough to capture interest but not enough to give away the secrets of a good book.

Storytelling deserves a prime place in the curriculum. As a teacher new to junior high school, I was required to "teach" a selection of Greek myths to ninth-grade students. "Have the students read the myths and give them questions to answer," was the department chair's advice. This led straight to boredom and rebellion. The students had difficulty with the Greek names and lost interest in the stories. Only when I prepared the stories for telling and gave them my best dramatic delivery did the students appreciate the tales of Demeter, Persephone, Prometheus, and the rest, and we were able to move on to further related reading and writing. For fourth graders, reading the tales of famous explorers in their texts was lonely work. Yet Henry Hudson, Cortez, and Balboa all came to life in our shared experience of their stories when I learned them well enough to tell them.

Highly recommended is a comprehensive book, *Teaching Through Stories: Yours, Mine, and Theirs* (Roe, Alfred, & Smith, 1998), that illustrates how storytelling can enhance every corner of the curriculum. In their Preface, the authors say:

> Storytelling is a powerful tool for teachers who integrate instruction across the curriculum and for teachers in many separate content areas. . . . Stories can be a vehicle for working on many literacy and content skills and understandings. (p. xv)

THE CLASSROOM INDEPENDENT READING PROGRAM: WHY AND HOW

Listening to stories—and poems, as discussed in Chapter 6—is essential in a literary education. So is the independent reading of genuine texts, most of them stories. My reasons for emphasizing stories in the individualized or independent reading program are discussed earlier in this chapter. The conventional, predictable structures of stories, when readers are familiar with them, help to make these printed texts comprehensible. Stories are read primarily for enjoyment, for affect, for an aesthetic experiencing. Certainly on a first reading, readers needn't struggle to remember facts and details to take beyond the initial experience, as they often must do when they study informational material. Stories have a mysterious hold on most of us; few people of any age can resist the pull of a good story. Independent reading is not part of a directed reading lesson. It is time for the application of the skills learned in directed reading lessons, for individual exploration and experimentation, and most of all for enjoyment.

Many reading programs in elementary and middle schools deal almost entirely with how to read, even though we are far from being certain exactly how reading is accomplished. We do know that reading is a skill that is developed by actually practicing it with genuine reading materials and not by filling workbooks with exercises that relate peripherally to it. That is why an independent reading component is absolutely essential in all literacy programs.

Every effective reading program has three components: directed reading lessons, skill-building exercises, and a regular in-school program of independent reading. (Such a program is often called "balanced reading.") Directed reading lessons may use a variety of materials: stories, passages from science or social studies texts, newspaper articles, novels, and poetry. In many literature-based literacy programs, literature—stories and poems—is used for directed reading lessons. This is entirely acceptable, providing that the literary works are treated as works of art and not as informational pieces. However, directed reading lessons, whatever their content, cannot be considered the whole reading program.

At least half the time allotted for reading in school should be spent in individualized or independent reading, defined as reading for enjoyment or enlightenment, material—with emphasis on imaginative literature—that children choose for themselves. This, it should be noted, is a straightforward, simple procedure that requires no kits, manuals, or complex doctrine for its implementation. There is no guru of independent reading, unless Jeanette Veatch, Professor Emerita of Arizona State University, might be called one. Her little book, as applicable today as when it was written, *How to Teach Reading with Children's Books* (Veatch, 1968), is a study in simplicity and sound advice that takes the mystery out of teaching with children's literature. Many of its ideas are incorporated into the following suggestions for the implementation of an independent or individualized component of the reading program—which I have personally and through my students tested in classrooms, grades 1 through 9.

Acquiring the Books

An independent reading program centers on books and time in school to read them. Since it is advisable to keep a classroom book collection from becoming static, a good plan is to borrow books from the school or public library for several weeks at a time. Librarians offer invaluable help in selecting books tailored to the needs and interests of a group of children.

Library books may be supplemented with donations from the children themselves, dividend books from class membership in book clubs, or gleanings from garage and library sales.

Two to three books per child is generally considered the optimum size for the classroom library, with books ranging in difficulty from easy to challenging. The classroom collection, chosen with the children's interests and ability levels in mind, should consist mainly of stories at the elementary and middle school levels, including biographies and historical fiction. Volumes of poetry and plays also belong in the collection. A suitable classroom library reflects the developmental needs and the interests of a particular class and is not viable unless these are taken into consideration.

For a class of older, resistant readers, in which several spoke English as a second language and many had never read a book in its entirety, the teacher prepared a selection of "mini-books," manila folders holding short pieces chosen to interest her group of aliterates: magazine articles, editorials, the occasional poem, works of short fiction. Another teacher of a similar group included in the classroom library picture books whose content made them acceptable to older students, among them *The Last Free Bird* (Stone, 1967), *Crow Boy* (Yashima, 1976), *An Extraordinary Life: The Story of a Monarch Butterfly* (Pringle, 1997), *Jumanji* (Van Allsburg, 1981), *Starry Messenger*, a biography of Galileo (Sis, 1996), *Pink and Say* (Polacco, 1994), *She's Wearing a Dead Bird on Her Head!* (Lasky, 1995), and *Call Me Ahnighito* (Conrad, 1995).

Thousands of books are published each year; thousands go out of print. Through a close association with children's librarians, teachers have access to lists of recent publications, reissues in paperback, award-winning books, and titles of the books children actually check out of the library.

Most teachers enjoy the research necessary for selecting books for their classes. Ours is a golden age of children's literature. The finest contemporary artists have illustrated distinguished picture books. A selective list of these artists follows:

Verna Aardema	Leo Lionni
Aliki	Arnold Lobel
Molly Bang	David Macaulay
Marcia Brown	Mercer Mayer
Eric Carle	Robert McCloskey
Barbara Cooney	Gerald McDermott
Pat Cunningham	Barry Moser
Diane and Leo Dillon	Helen Oxenbury
Roger Duvoisin	Peter Parnall
Tom Feelings	Jerry Pinkney
Ann Grifalconi	Alice Provensen
Gail E. Haley	Martin Provensen
Syd Hoff	Robert Quackenbush
Nonny Hogrogian	Maurice Sendak
Pat Hutchins	Nancy Tafuri
Trina Schart Hyman	Chris Van Allsburg
Ezra Jack Keats	Rosemary Wells
Steven Kellogg	Ed Young
Jack Kent	Margot Zemach
Karla Kuskin	

Dozens of writers whose books are catalogued as youth literature are admired by adults who get to know their work. In addition to those authors cited earlier in the chapter, the following are notable writers for older readers:

Joan Aiken	Madeleine L'Engle
Bruce Brooks	Jean Little
Hester Burton	Anne McCaffrey
Leon Garfield	Scott O'Dell
Mollie Hunter	Philippa Pearce
Diana Wynne Jones	Zilpha Snyder
M. E. Kerr	Ivan Southall
E. L. Konigsburg	Susan Fisher Staples
Jane Langton	Jill Paton Walsh

A Place for Nonfiction

In choosing books for children, I have given the highest priority to works of the imagination: poems and stories. These genres, through the use of imagery, symbol, and extended metaphor, lend themselves to interpretation because of their ambiguities and complex evocations. Through wide reading in children's literature, however, it becomes obvious that the line between fiction and nonfiction is often blurred (Carr, 1982, 1987; Crook & Lehman, 1991). This is particularly evident in biographies. It is also true of books that, although they do not tell a story in the traditional format of characters coping through a definite sequence of beginning, middle, and end, do make a vivid appeal to the child's imagination and sense of wonder. The nonfiction works of skilled, sensitive creative artists may indeed be considered within the categories of poems and stories as part of children's total literary experience. Such works ought to be included in classroom libraries and in units of study.

In the nonfiction works of Aliki, Tomie DePaola, Lois Ehlert, Russell Freedman, Gail Gibbons, Joe Lasker, Kathryn Lasky, David Macaulay, Bruce McMillan, Milton Meltzer, Gary Paulsen, Glen Rounds, Cynthia Rylant, Diane Stanley, and Peter Sis—to name a few outstanding artists in the genre—are embodied the characteristics of fine fiction and poetry: rhythmic pacing, suspense, memorable metaphorical language, and a sense of wonder in the mysteries and ambiguities inherent in all aspects of life on the planet.

The melding of the factual and the poetic is often experienced to the greatest extent through the medium of the picture book. One striking example is *Starry Messenger* (Sis, 1996), where words and pictures combine to present an intriguing and insightful portrait of Galileo. Others include *Chicka Chicka Boom Boom* (Martin & Archambault, 1989), a highly imaginative alphabet book in lively rhyme that tells a "story" of alphabet letters clambering to the top of a coconut tree, and *Voices of the Heart* (Young, 1997), a totally original rendering of Chinese characters that all carry the symbol of the heart.

The Great Fire (Murphy, 1995), winner of the National Council of Teachers of English Orbis Pictus Award for Outstanding Nonfiction for Children, is one example of the superb work of this non-fiction writer. His account of the horrendous Chicago fire of 1871 is a page-turner, as full of suspense as any novel.

Heartland (Siebert, 1989) movingly combines poetic text and magnificent paintings by Wendell Minor to spellbind as well as impart information about farming in the Midwest. The list of fine examples of such books is virtually limitless, as researchers will discover in their quest for the best books in all genres that will capture children's interests and ignite their imaginations.

Finding the Best Books

For those who need guidance in choosing the finest books available for children, a good place to begin is with the Caldecott and Newberry award-winning and honor books (runners-up). The Randolph Caldecott medal, named for a nineteenth-century British illustrator of books for children, is awarded each year for the most distinguished picture book for children published in the United States. The John Newbery Medal, named for an eighteenth-century British publisher who was the first to publish books especially for children, is given annually for the most distinguished contribution to literature for children published in the United States. Selection of both awards is made by a committee of the American Library Association and lists of winners may be found on their website: www.ala.org.

Guided Reading of a Picture Book or Novel

A guided or directed reading of a picture book or novel is an effective way to launch an independent reading program. The oral presentation of a book (preferred in this case) or the silent reading by all students of the same book provides a common experience, which becomes the basis for discussion by the entire class or small groups within it. Some teachers find it good practice to start by modeling discussion techniques with the whole class. Prepared by a guided reading experience, independent readers proceed with greater confidence toward richer experiences with books they read on their own.

Study Stories as Entities. Some procedures for directed reading—and other teacher-guided approaches to study—are recommended; others need to be avoided. For one thing, the story must be experienced as an aesthetic whole before it is "studied." This doesn't preclude the occasional stopping at a climactic point to ask students to predict what will happen next. Actually, prediction—asking about what students will read or hear—is a highly desirable strategy; it leads to more critical thinking than does questioning to recall bits and pieces of a story already read or heard. However, the story as an artistic whole always must be preserved.

Stories Are Fiction, Not Fact. Another point must be kept in mind: Stories are imaginative constructs, not informational treatises or assemblages of facts. Stories go more for affect than fact. Therefore, the personal experience of a story is an important part of literary criticism. Interpretations of the text in the form of examples and illustrations from the student's own life represent a higher order of thinking than do factual answers drawn verbatim from the text. Students should approach an imaginative work more with the imagination than with reason.

Divergent and Convergent Thinking. Consideration of a work centers on certain key words: imagining, theorizing, hypothesizing, evaluating, synthesizing. Divergent thinking, where a number of possibilities—about a character's motivation, say—are posed and tested, is valued. (Examples: What is going to happen now? What's another possibility?) So is convergent thinking, in which students must listen to each other, reflect on the story, and decide on the validity of interpretations resulting from divergent thinking. (Examples: Which prediction do you think is most accurate? Which of our predictions are still valid? No longer valid?) In talking about books, the aim is not to have a quiz in which there are right and wrong answers but to have a shared discussion of possible interpretations of a text. Ferreting out facts about the story is, of course, the opposite of this.

Common Elements in Story. Each story is unique, yet the same elements are found in every story: characters; setting; point of view; language, including dialogue; plot, which contains a conflict or problem, suspense, foreshadowing, climax, denouement; tone; and theme. The focus of a book discussion should be less on facts about a story's content and more on how these elements are combined to make meaning in the story. For this reason, specific questions on each book are often unnecessary; indeed, reams of questions after each chapter are a sure indication of overkill. It is usually better to base discussion on questions that apply to stories in general. In this approach a work is not dissected under a microscope. Instead, students step back from the work the better to see its shape and form; stepping even further back allows students to see works in relation to each other. The analogies and resemblances students find in all their literary experiences should be stressed in discussion.

Content in Terms of Form and Structure. In developing questions to help children—directed or undirected—in the exploration of literary works, teachers need to think of the works in terms of their structure and form, not merely in terms of their content. Of course, in the discussion of literature, content cannot be ignored. However, it always can be considered in relation to the form and structure of a work. Characters often behave the way they do in order for a story to develop along certain lines; characters may, in fact, be examined structurally. For example, in *Charlotte's Web* (White, 1952), Templeton, an undesirable character, is probably not one children would choose to emulate or to have as a friend, but he serves the purpose of the plot precisely because he is undesirable. (These two rather pointless questions about characters encountered in a story are often asked of children: Would you do as X did? Would you like to have X as a friend?)

Each reader and listener brings to literature personal likes and dislikes that color and enrich each response. The content of literary works may challenge values and offer new and provocative possibilities for thinking about experience. While literature relates to each one's life experiences, these relations cannot be the basis for systematic criticism. Nor can a view of literature as purely content provide such a basis. Children need to be discouraged, as they undertake the stage of criticism beyond personal response, from considering works solely for messages, morals, key ideas, and miscellaneous general knowledge.

The Tale of Peter Rabbit (Potter, 1902), for example, may be seen as a moral tale. Read one way it teaches that if you disobey your mother you may be endangered, lose your clothes, feel ill, and be sent to bed with medication. Another valid interpretation of the content is that disobedience can lead to excitement. In either case, the literary point of the story is lost. Without Peter's character and behavior there would be no story, for his tale is in the form of the romance, the adventurous quest, which requires a courageous hero to go forth, successfully complete a quest, and return home triumphant.

ENCOURAGING WIDE READING

Getting children to read widely can be difficult. Youngsters are wary when it comes to both food and books, insisting that they don't like what they haven't even sampled. Children tend to prefer the familiar. Studies by teachers in my graduate classes showed that, in general, students left entirely to themselves to select their reading material were likely to always choose the same type of books. Moreover, most readers regularly chose books that offered little or no challenge in terms of readability.

One boy concentrated solely on sports fiction; other children in the 9–12 group read exclusively works of fiction depicting everyday life, like those of Judy Blume, Beverly Cleary, Carolyn Haywood, Johanna Hurwitz, and Ellen Conford. Some children never read fiction at all; they simply leafed their way through informational books, looking at pictures. In every case, after a planned effort to introduce these children to challenging books that reflected their interests, all of them responded by reading more widely.

Interest Inventories

As part of their systematic efforts to encourage wider reading, teachers report success with interest inventories. Open-ended questions like the following were found to elicit the best response:

When I grow up, I want to _____
During my free time, I enjoy _____
Outside of school, my main interest is _____
The kind of story I like best is _____
If I wrote a book, it would be about _____

One teacher, discovering that a fifth-grade girl enjoyed riding, drew up for her a personalized list of fine horse stories that included classics such as *King of the Wind* (Henry, 1948), *The Black Stallion* (Farley, 1941), and *The Winged Colt of Casa Mia* (Byars, 1981).

For a boy, an able reader in sixth grade, who revealed in his interest inventory that he liked stories from the twilight zone, another teacher prepared a list that included *The White Mountains* (Christopher, 1967), *The Eyes of the Amaryllis* (Babbitt, 1977), *The Ghost of Thomas Kempe* (Lively, 1973), works by William Sleator, including *Rewind* (Sleator, 1999), and Philip Pullman's (1995) *The Golden Compass*.

Responding to negative comments about reading in her batch of inventories ("I'd rather do anything than read" was the response of several students), one of my graduate students promised the resistant fourth graders books that were both funny and short. Her list, which helped to convert some nonreaders, included *Chocolate Fever* (Smith, 1972), *The Twenty-one Balloons* (DuBois, 1947), *Mr. Popper's Penguins* (Atwater, 1938), *Lizard Music* (Pinkwater, 1976), *Help! I'm a Prisoner in the Library* (Clifford, 1981), and *The Dreadful Future of Blossom Culp* (Peck, 1983).

A teacher-librarian, realizing that too much time is wasted by children gazing at the spines of books on library shelves, provided them with lists based on the information gleaned from the interest inventories she administered. Among her lists were "Ten Top Authors of Mysteries," "Ten Golden Oldies," and "Ten to Make You Laugh Out Loud."

Oral Introductions to Books

Word-of-mouth is always the best advertising. When I taught in Toronto in the 1950s, we had no library in our old downtown school. Once a month, my third graders and I trekked along College Street to Boys and Girls House, the children's room of the Central Public Library. At the end of the journey, we were rewarded with book talks, the librarians introducing, by reading aloud enticing snippets of stories, a wide variety of books spanning a broad range of content and readability. Invariably, the books the librarians introduced—whether classic or contemporary, easy to read or not—were always those the children chose to carry back to school with them.

The power of advertising, in particular the personal testimonial, is awesome. One teacher initiated a campaign in her classroom to open the eyes of her sixth-grade realists to the glories of modern fantasy. She read widely herself, determined to advertise the genre with the best possible books. She selected to advertise such books as *The Owl Service* (Garner, 1968), *The Keeper of the Isis Light* (Hughes, 1981), *The Fledgling* (Langton, 1980), *A Wizard of Earthsea* (Le Guin, 1968), *Space Race* (Waugh, 2000), and *Christmas in Camelot* (Osborne, 2001).

This teacher featured displays of these books in her classroom, but the main part of her advertising campaign was oral. As she read the books, she noted passages in them that were particularly tantalizing; these she read aloud when she gave book talks. She took time to create one-page scripts for Readers Theater, featuring passages of dialogue directly from the books, chosen to interest children in reading the entire book. Groups of students gave prepared readings of the scripts to the rest of the class. The teacher reported that, although her display included many more books than were presented through book talks and Readers Theater performances, the books that she personally introduced were the ones the children clamored to read for themselves. Eventually, most of these sixth graders were reading fantasy, giving their own book talks, and preparing new scripts for Readers Theater.

Another teacher initiated The Sixty-Second Salestalk, in which her students had to "sell" to the class a book that they enjoyed. This lively method of reporting, the teacher found, was more effective by far than lists of books in persuading others to read. Students wanted to read what their classmates had read with enjoyment. In addition, the timed talks gradually, with practice, became better organized, more detailed, and more innovative.

RESPONSES TO INDEPENDENT READING

The Student–Teacher Conference

The conference is an essential part of the independent reading program. While it is usually a student-teacher conference, it need not be so exclusively. Parent volunteers, students from higher grades, and even classmates may conference with readers. Students need not conference after every book they read, although that option should be open to them. Holding a conference ought to be treated as a special time, an opportunity for students to share orally the experience of their book. Oral sharing of what one reads is a natural, pleasurable response to reading. During the conference—most last about 10 minutes—students should be encouraged to read aloud from their books a portion that had significance for them.

To hold a conference, teachers need not read the book. The child is the talker, the teacher the listener. Teachers soon discover, by careful listening, whether or not the child has read and comprehended the book. Quizzing children on the details they recall is to be avoided. Long drawn-out retellings of the plot are discouraged. Students need to understand that there are no "right" or "wrong" responses to a book. The teacher is interested in the students' opinions. Asking "Why?" after the following questions, where applicable, is a strategy that has been used with success by many teachers during conference time:

Did you finish the book?

What do you remember about the book?

What caught your interest most?

What pleased (or frightened, surprised, impressed, annoyed) you?

Was this story like any other you've read or heard or seen?

Was there anything in the story that relates in some way to you or your life?

What type of story was your book? (adventure? myth? legend? folk- or fairytale? mystery? science fiction? fantasy? everyday experience? biography? historical fiction?)

Who tells this story?

Where and when does the story take place?

What problem or situation gets the story started?

Is the problem or situation solved by the end of the story?

Was it the ending you expected?

Was the working out of the story believable?

Is this story like any other you know?

Probe, using what the child has said: "You said that Joel's friend drowns [in *On My Honor* (Bauer, 1986)] and Joel goes home without telling anyone. Why do you think he did that?"

The Child's Record Keeping

While there is no one formula or set procedure for a successful independent reading program, there is one emphatic negative: Do not assign formal, written book reports. These are the kiss of death to motivation for reading.

In an independent reading program, reading is all-important. What happens after the reading needs to be a natural, real-world activity, not a school-type, reading-related activity. There are no strings of questions to answer after a book is read. Record keeping for the children is kept simple. For example, titles and brief evaluative statements may be written on index cards and filed so other readers can consult them when choosing books.

Response Journals

To emphasize the personal experience of a book, especially the aesthetics of the experience, children are encouraged to keep response journals. There is no one way to keep a response journal. However, to prime responses, teachers can suggest that readers note parts that interested, frightened, surprised, troubled, or pleased them, or answer questions like these:

> What feelings did you experience during reading?
> Did the story leave you feeling satisfied? Why or why not?
> If you could speak to the author of the book, what would you say or ask?
> Were events in the story similar to occurrences in your own life?
> Have you read, heard, or seen a story like this one?
> Would you read another book by this author?

Some students will want to note in their journals words or phrases that caught their attention. Young children may respond with pictures and dictated statements before they have facility with writing. They should also be encouraged to write as much as they can on their own; this is a place where invented spelling is entirely acceptable. The response journal is like a diary, to be shared with the owner's permission and never to be graded.

The Teacher's Record Keeping

The teacher keeps anecdotal records of conferences; these become the basis for small-group and individual directed reading and skill-building lessons. Such general things as enthusiasm, interest, and articulateness are noted. If the child reads aloud, the process provides valuable clues about reading strengths and weaknesses, as follows:

> Does the child show anxiety or discomfort during the reading?
> Does the child read with appropriate expression, making use of punctuation, thus indicating that what is being read is understood?
> Is the reading word-by-word or in meaningful word groupings?
> If the child makes miscues (substitutions, omissions, etc.), do they change the sense of what is being read?
> Does the child notice and attempt to correct miscues?

Some teachers find it useful to periodically tape record samples of children's oral reading so children (and parents) can chart progress throughout the year. Tape recordings are also useful in self-evaluation.

Creative and Literary Responses

Although reading a book for pleasure can be its own reward, children also enjoy responding to art with art: writing, drawing, dramatizing, sculpting, creating (or at least planning through storyboards) videotapes or films, and making games. The following is a sampling of the dozens of possible responses:

- Writing reviews like those found in magazines and newspapers (a real-life activity unlike the book report, which is found only in classrooms)
- Writing a sequel to a story or developing an incident that might have occurred in the book
- Creating a Readers Theater script by extracting dialogue from a particularly funny or interesting scene, xeroxing it, cutting it in strips, and arranging it on a sheet in the form of a playlet, with narration where necessary
- Making oaktag mobiles with pictures illustrating key scenes from the story
- Writing and illustrating an advertisement for the book
- Writing a fan letter to the author
- Planning a TV mini-series based on a book: choosing the scenes, casting the characters, designing the set
- Creating a family tree for the characters in the book
- Drawing and lettering a pictorial map that shows the story's setting
- Making paper cutouts and clothing for the main characters in the book
- Creating a sequence game for others to play by sketching key scenes on file cards for players to lay out in order
- Writing a poem about the story or a character in the story

CONCLUSION

In this chapter we have considered the experience of literature and initial responses to it. Criticism is centered in knowledge. One's sense of story grows with experience of story. Developing a sense of story through listening, reading independently, and responding through talk and art is central to criticism. But wide reading without study leaves readers in the same position as that of pianists who play by ear. They know when it sounds right, but they don't have the knowledge to explain why it does. Critical ability grows through experience and reflective study. What this constitutes is the subject of the next chapter.

GUIDING THE READING EXPERIENCE

To assist teachers in facilitating discussions on reading, examples of questions are included here. Note that these questions are not tied to one particular story but may be applied to stories in general. (Refer to Chapter 8 for further examples of questions to elicit discussion.) In leading book discussions, it is always wise to begin by listening closely to the initial free responses of the children and building upon them. For instance, if at the conclusion of a story a child says, "That's not a good ending" (a comment on plot), beginning discussion will center on plot, in this case probably with a question prefaced by "Why?"

Type of Story

- *Every storyteller constructs a make-believe world that may be very like our own or entirely different from it. What signs and signals indicate whether a story will be more fanciful than realistic?*
  Good examples are talking animals; exaggeration; strange, improbable situations, characters, or settings; stories that begin: "Once upon a time. . . ."
- *If the world created by the author is far different from the one we know, how does the author make the story seem possible and believable?*
  The author creates the world down to the last detail. For example, C. S. Lewis gives his magical land of Narnia a complete geography, with land forms, plants, and weather.

Setting and Plot

- *Where and when does the story take place? How do you know? If the story took place somewhere else or in a different time, how would it be changed?*
  Readers will recognize that specific time and place are less important to some stories than to others. In historical fiction like *One Is One* (Picard, 1966), the medieval setting is central to the story; *The Pushcart War*

(Merrill, 1964) could take place in no city other than New York; exactly where *Konrad* (Nostlinger, 1977) takes place is less important than character and plot.

- *What incident, problem, conflict, or situation gets the story started?*

  Here readers and listeners focus on form, recognizing that a story begins at a particular point, usually with a conflict or an unresolved situation.

- *What is the basic shape of the story?*

  Successful quest: romance form; overcoming obstacles to some desired end: comic form; unfulfilled or partially fulfilled quest: irony-satire form; prevented in some way from reaching a desired end: tragic form. Younger students will readily understand these concepts through less technical terms: The quest pattern may be described as home-adventure-home, a circular story shape.

- *What does the author do to create suspense, to make you want to read on to find out what happens? Is what happens made credible and plausible? How? Did the author prepare you for what happens? How?*

  Suspense occurs because there is set up a situation that must be resolved; this resolution is delayed and detoured through dramatic scenes that deliberately delay and detour as they lead inevitably toward it. The author prepares you for what happens through foreshadowing but keeps you guessing as to the nature of the resolution. If the characters are made interesting and appealing enough, the reader wants to know their fate. Actions and events are made credible and plausible because they develop organically from the interplay of character and plot. There are no characters introduced only to serve the plot, no coincidences that make the plot seem contrived.

- *How is the story ordered for telling?*

  For example, chronological order, a series of episodes or incidents, flashbacks, or told through letters or diary entries.

- *Trace the main events of the story. Is it possible to change their order? Leave any of them out? Why or why not?*

A well-constructed story develops organically, action developing out of previous action with a sense of inevitability.

- *Suppose you thought of a different ending for the story. How would the rest of the story have to be changed to fit the new ending?*

  Consideration of this question helps readers to recognize unity in structure; a story is an organic whole, the ending inevitable, given its beginning and middle. Also considered here is character development in relation to incident.

- *Did the story end as you expected it to? What clues did the author offer to prepare you to expect this ending? Did you recognize these clues as important to the story as you first read it or listened to it? Why are these clues important to your overall reaction to the story?*

  Clues, foreshadowings of what is to come, are often not apparent to inexperienced readers until the ending is reached. How subtly they are used is a mark of the author's skill and a structural aspect of story interesting to study. The plausibility of a story often hinges on the use of foreshadowing.

Characters

- *Who is the main character in the story? What kind of person is this character? How do you know? Do you sympathize with the character? Are you interested in the character's fate? Why? Can you figure out from the story why the characters behave as they do? Do you recognize here any character types that you know from other stories?*

  We learn about character through description, through the character's behavior, through what the character says and what others say about the character. Good writers reveal characters by showing dramatically what they are like rather than telling about them. Readers are meant to sympathize and identify with the main character of a story; when they do, because the character is like them or has a problem that interests them, they want to read on to find out how the character will fare. Writers need to let us know what motivates a character's actions. Motivation may be complex, but it should be believable.

- *Do any characters change in the course of the story? If so, how are they different in the end? What changed them? Does the change seem believable?*

    Readers see how, through incident and experience, characters change and develop; good storytellers make the change believable and inevitable. Some signs of a possible change are in the character from the beginning.

- *Some characters play small but important roles in a story. Pick out a bit player from a story. Why is this character necessary to the story? Do you recognize this character as similar to minor characters in other stories?*

    Minor characters act as foils, helping the reader to more clearly see a main character through contrast. Minor characters may be used to move a plot forward.

Point of View

- *Who tells the story? Is it told in first person—I? Is it the omniscient viewpoint of the all-knowing author, who uses third person—he, she, they? Is it limited omniscient point of view, where, although the story is told in third person, it concentrates on the thoughts and feelings of a central character? Is it the dramatic or objective point of view, which, like the camera, records action without comment? How does point of view affect tone, characterization, and credibility?*

    Young readers can begin to discuss the complex and fascinating question of point of view in stories. Some first-person novels feature young protagonists so precocious it is difficult to believe in them. First-person and limited omniscient viewpoints lend a sense of immediacy to the action; readers are one with the viewpoint character. However, the viewpoint is also limited to this one character.

Mood or Tone

- *Does the story as a whole create a definite mood or feeling?
  How is it created? Does the mood or tone change during the
  course of the story? How does the author signal this change?*
  Descriptions, particularly of settings, create mood; a
  lighthearted tone may be established through dialogue or when a character embarks on a trivial quest;
  a serious tone is set when a quest is serious. An author's
  language conveys tone and mood. The point of view
  used in a story influences tone and mood throughout.
  The imagery and symbolism used in a story establish
  tone and mood; certain patterns of imagery are associated with positive and negative experiences. For
  example, the harsh concrete world of the city sets the
  tone and mood for Walter Dean Myers' explorations
  of ghetto life.
- *Did you have strong feelings toward the story?*
  Anger, hopelessness, fear, loathing, delight, joy, fear,
  sorrow, sympathy.
- *What did the author do to make you feel strongly?*
  Created sympathetic characters believably and set
  them in dramatic situations, making readers experience along with them and therefore care about what
  happens to them.

Style

- *Does the style of writing fit the subject? Do the characters
  speak naturally and in keeping with their setting? Is the
  language rich in imagery and in memorable ways of expressing ideas? Does it flow rhythmically when it is read
  aloud?*
  A casual contemporary style may not suit the substance of an ancient tale. Good writers have an ear
  for dialogue, letting us hear each character's distinc-
  tive voice. A good, imaginative writer helps readers
  and listeners to visualize the action in clear detail. In
  a good book, language is used with flair to express
  unusual or telling insights.

Theme

- *What is the idea behind the story that gives point to the whole?*

    If a book leaves one thinking, "So what?" the theme is probably trivial or lacking altogether. Truly memorable literature examines the issues that concern people most: matters of love, loyalty, purpose in life, survival, courage, friendship, and the like. In a well-written story, thematic lessons are presented indirectly through the dramatic action, never preached or taught. Exploration of the informing ideas of a story is an important aspect of criticism and critical thinking; to do this exercise, children must analyze, synthesize, interpret, theorize, and hypothesize—all higher-order thinking skills.

Symbol and Metaphor

- *What examples of this technique did you discover in the story?*

    Talking about the "meaning" of a literary work is a highly complex process. For one thing, a work may be so richly layered that two or three readings might be required to tease out the text's significance. Furthermore, what is significant and meaningful for one reader may not be so for another. What one makes of a text is not necessarily what another sees in it; each response is personal and unique. An author may use symbol and metaphor to express meaning indirectly. The underlying theme of a book is not directly stated and often is expressed through symbol and metaphor.

    Here is an example of a symbol from *Wringer* (Spinelli, 1997): The pigeon who comes to Palmer's window is a character in the book, but he may have even more significance symbolically. Taking a non-literal look at the pigeon, readers might consider him to be an embodiment of Palmer's fate and ultimately of his freedom to fly in the face of public opinion.

Making Connections

• *Is the story you read, though different in content, like any other story you have read or watched in its form and structure?*

A journey or quest; a struggle or predicament that is solved by magical intervention; a series of episodes of equal importance; the occurrence of magical change (metamorphosis); a theme like good triumphing over evil; a motif like disguise; mistaken identity; a pattern of three: trials, journeys, or wishes; a magical talisman; spells; or curses.

• *Think of all the characters in the story. Are any of them the same or similar to characters in other stories, cartoons, comics, movies?*

Brave hero or heroine, crafty villain, trickster, clown or comic character, wise advisor, helpful friend, foolish one, underdog who wins against all odds, charming rogue, anti-hero or "loser," etc.

Reading Critically

• *Books are written by individuals with specific viewpoints, beliefs, and philosophy. It is easy to take for granted ideas presented in a story or poem. Are your responses truly the product of your own thinking or do you simply parrot ideas that most people in the culture seem to believe? Do you confront a text and its premises, always questioning, always looking for discrepancies and contradictions within it? Do you read reflectively and critically, watching out for manipulative texts that perpetuate stereotypes or racist and sexist beliefs? Do you read as a critical activist?*

It is a teacher's responsibility to help students of all ages to become critical, questioning readers. Readers need to be alert for generally accepted but erroneous beliefs about the role of women and girls in society, for instance, or of ageist biases, or unfair, stereotypical portrayals of ethnic groups or individuals.

Noting Illustrations

Literary elements—plot, character, mood, tone, setting, and theme—are all present in picture books, and they may be studied through both text and pictures. The size of characters, their place on the page and relation to setting and other characters, the choice and juxtaposition of images, the use of certain colors and lighting, all have literary significance.

While the cumulative rhyming text of *Drummer Hoff* (Emberley, 1967) tells the tale of the firing of a cannon, the right question will help children to discover how the final pictures reveal that the book as a whole carries a message of peace.

During an examination of *Mufaro's Beautiful Daughters* (Steptoe, 1987), children might consider why the artist chose always to picture Manyara in a harsh light. Young children will readily see how *Rosie's Walk* (Hutchins, 1968) is a study in suspense. They will recognize that David Catrow's gloriously exaggerated illustrations for *She's Wearing a Dead Bird on Her Head!* (Lasky, 1995) emphasize the foolishness of this silly fashion in dress.

8

Growing as Critics

The critic's function is to interpret every work of literature in the light of all the literature he knows, to keep constantly struggling to understand what literature as a whole is about.
—Northrop Frye (1963a, p. 44)

To understand what literature as a whole is about students need to engage in a process of discovering for themselves how literature is unified. In Chapters 6 and 7 we explored what I consider to be the first phase of criticism: broad experience of imaginative literary works. Experience elicits response, which is also an aspect of criticism. First experiences and responses are or ought to be centered on the aesthetics of the works of art and their affect. The next phase of criticism involves an exploration of the unifying principles of literature, as delineated in Part II of the book. This chapter suggests how—with no diminution of the aesthetic experience—this exploration may be accomplished.

LEARNING THROUGH DISCUSSION

Talking is a major way in which students express their responses to literature and—through the process—amplify, clarify, and extend those responses, while at the same time working their way into a deeper understanding both of a particular work and of general literary principles. Time for purposeful talk after the experience of literature is analogous to the lab after a presentation in science. It is a time for experimenting with ideas, exploring concepts, making observations, and drawing conclusions (Hill, Johnson, & Noe, 1995; Short & Pierce, 1990).

Generally, an oral rather than a written response to the literature read or listened to is preferable for elementary and middle school students. Young children for whom extensive writing can be physically taxing are likely to regard lengthy written answers to reams of questions, character studies, and plot summaries as punishment.

Literary study involves *exploration* of ideas, *sharing* of responses, and *growth through reflection.* Through purposeful group discussions, these characteristics of literary study—literary criticism—are better realized and developed. One important aspect of literary study is expressing ideas—orally and in writing—about stories, poems, and other literary works. A major goal of the study is to develop the ability to articulate the ideas and feelings literature elicits.

The process of discussion must be taught; children cannot be expected to come to class with mastery of this difficult but profitable technique. Many of the teacher-researchers in my classes advocate modeling as a mean of building skills in discussion. A small group volunteers to discuss a text before the whole class; afterwards, the process is critiqued by the observers who have developed in advance a list of criteria for successful discussions. Volunteer groups may be videotaped for later viewing and evaluating by themselves and by the entire class. One teacher reports that in her class small discussion groups audiotaped their sessions throughout the term, eventually using copies of these audiotapes as part of their portfolios.

Discussion has two major emphases: courtesy and participation. Children need to practice the ritual give-and-take that discussion requires. They need to learn to listen, wait their turns, assimilate and weigh what they have heard, and build upon this when they speak. From their first encounter with a new class, teachers need to work to establish a climate of mutual respect where ideas and opinions are heard and valued. This is particularly important in literary studies where, if the discussion is in response to questions that require genuine reflection and critical thinking (as they ought to be), there are no "right" and "wrong" answers.

Talking in Small Groups

A distinction needs to be made between small- and large-group discussion. Whole-class discussion, unless it follows discussion in small groups, is unlikely to be more than exchange among a few. Only a limited number of students in a class of average size can participate at once, comments are likely to be addressed to the teacher rather than to other pupils, and un-engaged minds are apt to wander. Children of all ages can be taught to work together in small groups.

The group process is an invaluable one where children have the opportunity to express their ideas, to test their notions in relation to those of others, and to engage in divergent and convergent thinking. In the group process, ideas are amended, elaborated upon, defended, and supported. Children, with guidance, learn to summarize, to synthesize, to qualify. They also benefit from exposure to others' vocabulary and usage (Cohen, 1986).

Work groups for literary or any study are best if they are heterogeneous, with their composition frequently changed. Slower learners should have the opportunity to work with faster learners in an atmosphere of mutual help and support; the least articulate and the verbally facile will mutually benefit from working together. Common interests, personal preferences, and individual needs will also determine the composition of groups. Research has determined that five is the optimal group size (Cohen, 1986).

Learning to work cooperatively in groups is a developmental process, with first experiences planned for success. With the teacher's help, the children themselves can develop the ground rules that will govern their small-group work. The first small-group activity might well be a session in which groups work on these rules, subsequently pooling their ideas in a large-group sharing session.

"Literature circles" is another term for literature discussion in small groups. Kathy Short (Hill, Johnson, & Noe, 1995) comments on the discussion process:

> In literature circles, readers must think collaboratively with each other, not simply work together cooperatively. . . . Children do not simply contribute their part of completing a task; they listen carefully and think deeply with other group members to create understandings that go beyond those of individual members. The dialogue in these groups leads children to new perspectives on literature and their lives. (pp. x–xi)

The Teacher's Role

Effective teachers help to create the structure of a subject in students' minds. The unifying principles of literature are the teacher's deductive framework. Aware of the principles, the teacher devises learning sequences that allow students to inductively discover them.

As an example, suppose a group of fourth graders have all read the same novel, *Stone Fox* (Gardiner, 1980). Provided with a set of questions that, ideally, they have developed and that apply to novels in general—a selection similar to the discussion questions listed in Chapter 7—they meet in small groups to discuss the novel.

Teachers do need to work with the children to set specific purposes and establish time limits. In the beginning, short sessions are advisable. To be avoided is the ruin of the process when bored participants, talked out, turn to paper planes, spitballs, or harassment of others.

Once a clear purpose has been established for a group-talk session, teachers function as facilitators of discussion. Circulating from group to group, they sit in for a time to facilitate the group process and provide information as requested by the children. Offering quantities of unsolicited information is to be avoided.

In facilitating the group process the teacher may

- Encourage participation: "Has everyone given an opinion on that point?" "Mary, do you agree with what's been said so far?"
- Ask for qualification: "Your idea about the character is interesting, Mario. What was your reason for thinking that?"
- Help the children to get at the thinking behind comments, by asking "Why?" and encouraging group members to do the same of each other.
- Handle the monopolizer with a tactful but firm comment: "Wait a minute, Kyle; Sheena isn't finished."
- Encourage group members or the designated leader to summarize ideas.

More structured discussion may be an outgrowth of children's free responses. Teachers need to listen closely to questions and comments children make after they hear a story or poem. These will be fruitful starting points for small-group discussion conducted independently or led by the teacher. Sometimes these comments lead to purely literary discussions: "That ending just doesn't follow from what went before." At other times, comments may signal the need for research and further talk: "How long do elephants usually live?"

Assigning Roles to Discussants

To facilitate discussion, teachers in my classes and I have found it effective to assign roles to at least some of the children in the small group (Daniels, 1994). We found that words often did not flow without encouragement, especially with inexperienced small-group participants. With fifth graders, I used the following roles with considerable success:

- *Scribe*—designated note taker.
- *Word Detective*—in charge of looking up unknown words in the dictionary.
- *Kickoff*—starts discussion with a quote or question.
- *Riddlers 1 and 2*—prepare searching questions, preferably beginning with *Why?*
- *Participation Police*—verbally prod non-participants.
- *Data*—a resource for background information or items that needed researching.

Assessing Growth

A reader responds to a text in a variety of ways (Beach, 1993). Teacher-researchers discovered that a child's typical, *unguided* response was to a work's effect on emotions. Some comments from researchers' reports were: "I liked it." "It was okay." "It was exciting." "I wanted to read on to see what would happen." The second most-common response was to the narrative: what a story was "about." Only with experience and guidance did students get beyond basic responses to substantive discussion about connections between the story and personal experience or between the story under consideration and other stories they had read or viewed.

Teachers' questions and comments may be designed to elicit different types of response. The goal is to help children progress from literal or factual understanding through more complex levels of thinking: interpretation, analysis, synthesis, application, and critical evaluation.

Both in posing questions and in assessing growth, the following description of progressive levels of thinking, based upon Benjamin Bloom's venerable but useful *Taxonomy of Educational Objectives, Handbook I: Cognitive Domain* (1956), is helpful to keep in mind:

- Basic response is the literal recall of facts and order of events. (Asks or answers questions beginning What? How? Who? Where? When?)
- Interpretative response involves reading between the lines to make inferences and reading thoughtfully to draw conclusions, to analyze (see how the parts relate), and to synthesize (bring disparate ideas together in new ways.) (Asks or answers questions that begin Why?)
- Application of ideas and facts is another higher-level thinking skill. This involves applying discoveries from the text to other texts and to one's own experience. It includes the application of general literary knowledge to a particular text in discussions of imagery, style, symbol, plot, motifs, and the like.
- Comments and questions that signal critical evaluation also involve literary knowledge and are likely to center on comparisons or discussion of similarities and differences among works, including, in addition to other printed texts, non-print presentations such as television and movies. As with all response beyond the literal level, there are no "right" or "wrong" answers, but the best answers are fully supported.

With elementary and middle school age students, probably the most favored means of response is oral, through small-group discussion or individual conferences. In assessing development in response, observation is crucial. As the teacher circulates from group to group, she notes—perhaps with a chart to facilitate recording—how participants respond. She looks for growth in the number of responses a child makes, the amount of detail in the response, and the gradual development of higher-level thinking abilities and articulateness. Besides charts and anecdotal records, teachers report excellent results with audio- and videotaping of group discussion, the participants reviewing the tapes against *their own formulations* of what constitutes good discussion in small groups.

LEARNING SEQUENCES IN
LITERARY CRITICISM: DISCUSSION

A learning sequence may be a single session or series of sessions, depending on its purpose. It may be a discussion or another type of activity, such as those suggested later in the chapter. Sometimes teachers will serve as facilitators in group discussions or as resources to groups led by student leaders. To help students toward an understanding of literary principles, teachers may select poems and stories for presentation that exemplify the principle that students will discover inductively. The following are examples of such sessions.

Conventional Patterns in Story

The aim of the session is to lead young children toward an understanding that stories come in conventional "shapes."

Teacher: We have read *Where the Wild Things Are* (Sendak, 1963) and *The Tale of Peter Rabbit* (Potter, 1902). It's true that they are stories about very different things, but let's think about ways in which they are alike.
Children:
- Max and Peter have adventures.
- They get into danger.
- Lots of things happen to them.
- They get home okay in the end.
- Everything ends happy, except Peter is sent to bed.
- But he did okay; he got away from Mr. McGregor.
- Max didn't really go away; he had a dream.
- But he went away in his dream; it's the same thing.
Teacher: If you were to draw the shape of the two stories, what shape would it be?
Children:
- They both end up where they started.
- Max leaves his room but he comes back to it.
- So does Peter.
- They both leave home, have adventures, and come back.
- Then it's a circle; the stories are shaped like a circle.
Teacher: Do you know any other stories with that shape?
Children:
- In "Jack and the Beanstalk," Jack goes to the giant's castle and comes back home.
- In *Sylvester and the Magic Pebble* [Steig, 1969], Sylvester in the end gets to be himself again, home with his parents.
- Even E.T. gets to go home at the end of the movie!

The Quest as a Shaper of Stories

The aim in the following discussion is to help older students discover how the hero story relates to the dialectical aspect of literary structure. The quest of heroes and heroines involves efforts to restore harmony, right a wrong, or find their own sense of identity.

Teacher: The old tale we just read, about Gilgamesh, the Sumerian king who searched for everlasting life, is a typical hero story. Think of other hero stories you know. How are they alike?

Students:
- The hero goes searching for something important to him, like Sir Lancelot looking for the Holy Grail.
- Or Jason searching for the Golden Fleece.
- Sometimes he tries to get rid of a monster.
- The way Perseus does when he goes after Medusa.
- Or St. George when he kills the dragon.
- Sometimes the hero isn't happy with the way things are, so he sets out to change them.
- Moses did that.
- So did Robin Hood.
- The heroes in fairytales go to seek their fortune.
- In *Arrow to the Sun* [McDermott, 1978], the boy has to find his father to prove his identity.
- Heroes and heroines are always looking to change things.
- To make things better.
- A hero story has some kind of search in it.
- Or a test. The hero has to prove his courage.
- Sometimes there's a search *and* a test; Hercules has to survive 12 tests if he wants to keep on living.

Teacher: Your examples are all from ancient hero tales. Is it the same for modern stories?

Students:
- Superman sets out to right wrongs.
- So does Luke Skywalker.
- In *Dicey's Song* [Voight, 1982], Dicey takes her family on a long journey to their grandmother's when her mother disappears.
- In *Call It Courage* [Sperry, 1940], Mafatu thinks he's a failure, so he leaves home, maybe to die, but he finds out that he has courage.

- In *Dogsong* [Paulsen, 1985], Russel and his dog team escape modern life to find their own true song.

Conventional Characters

Through examination of the hero story, the concept of recurrent character types may be developed. As discussed in Chapter 4, the evil goddess of the myth is related to the witch of the romance, to the evil stepmother of fairytales, and to the impossible female parent of modern realistic stories in the ironic mode. The helpful goddess of myth, the kindly sorceress of romance, the fairy godmother of the fairytale, and the kindly mother figure in the modern realistic story are also related.

Children will discover that certain types of characters are associated positively with the hero or heroine's quest, while some are aligned against it. Some characters exist to make main characters look more heroic, to give them help, even to give them someone to talk to. Children will note that there may be neutral, flat, or static characters in many stories who play a small role in moving the story forward.

The aim in the following discussion is to help younger students discover that certain character types are important to the structure of stories.

Teacher: What gets most stories going?
Students:
- You have to have some kind of problem to get it started.
- Sometimes there's a war, kind of, between two kinds of people: good guys and bad guys.
- A story usually has good guys and bad guys.
- Or good girls and bad girls.
- A lot of stories are just struggles between people on one side and people on the other.

Teacher: We just read one of Dr. Seuss' first books, *The 500 Hats of Bartholomew Cubbins* [Seuss, 1938]. Is there a "bad guy" in that story?
Student: The Grand Duke Wilfred.
Teacher: Why is he in the story?
Students:
- He makes it interesting because he's so cruel and nasty.
- Mean characters are usually interesting, even though you don't like them much.

- Like Templeton the rat in *Charlotte's Web* [White, 1952].
- Wilfred in this story is the opposite to Bartholomew; he's a bully and Bartholomew is basically just an innocent nice guy.
- He's the opposite too because he's rich and royal and Bartholomew is poor and ordinary.
- That makes you wonder how things will turn out. Wilfred has all the power.
- He puts suspense into the story because he threatens Bartholomew's life.
- You need somebody like him in a story because it's someone for the main character to fight against.
- You need that for a good story.

Patterns of Imagery

As discussed in Chapter 4, two structures underlie literary imagery. The cyclical pattern is exemplified in the association of certain seasons and times of year with particular stories or parts of stories. Beginnings and quests, for instance, are likely to take place in the "merry months" of May and June, as in the old ballads. Endings and failures are often associated with the "death" of the year: fall and winter. Triumph, the full powers of the hero, and the like are most often associated with "high summer," when nature is also at her peak of growth and beauty.

A dialectical structure is also present in literary imagery. People's dreams and desires are associated with gardens and visions of paradise; their nightmares with deserts, threatening forests, and wastelands. Settings reflect atmosphere and mood.

Some colors are associated with dreams; others with nightmares. Dark colors may have sinister associations because the darkness of night can cause fear; the golden light of the sun is reassuring. Peaceful animals and birds like the lamb and the dove are on the side of good in stories; serpents and ravens typically belong with the evil side.

Three examples of learning sequences dealing with imagery follow.

Sequence for Primary Grades. The aim of the first sequence is to help young children develop some awareness of patterns of imagery in stories.

Teacher: Let's try a game, something like "Twenty Questions," on the stories we know. The categories are animal, vegetable, and mineral. Which animals are "good" characters in stories? Which aren't?

Students:
- Animals that are used to being with people, like the horse in "The Goose Girl."
- Or the cat in "Puss in Boots."
- Pigs are good! There's Padre Porko.
- And Charlotte the spider.
- Foxes are pretty bad. One ate the Gingerbread Boy.
- Wolves are bad, in stories anyway. One eats Red Riding Hood's grandmother.
- Dogs are always good.

Teacher: Think about the natural surroundings in stories you know, the trees and plants and the ground around them. What are they like in the stories you know?

Students:
- When Dominic [Steig, 1972] was in danger, he was deep in a forest.
- So was Red Riding Hood.
- Rapunzel was sent away to a forest and then to a kind of desert where nothing grew.
- No sun ever shone on the place where Medusa lived.
- Sylvester turned into a rock, the opposite of being alive.
- And he felt loneliest in the winter when the ground was cold and covered with snow.
- But snow can be part of a happy story, like *The Snowy Day* [Keats, 1962]. It depends.
- And forests are okay if your home is in the forest.
- A lot of stories end up with people in castles.
- Or at home where they're comfortable.

Sequences for Upper Elementary and Middle School Grades.
The aim of the next sequence is to help students toward an understanding of the dialectic structure underlying literary works.

Teacher: Stories show the difference between our dreams—what we want most—and our nightmares—what we fear and dread. In your experience, is that a true statement? Let me hear your thoughts on it.

Students:
- Stories usually begin with a problem or a situation where things aren't all they should be.
- People want to change that.
- Take slavery. Books about Harriet Tubman, like *Freedom Train* [Sterling, 1954], show how she leads people out of a nightmare to safety.
- *The Girl in the Box* [Sebestyen, 1988] leaves you feeling depressed because what happens to her is a nightmare that doesn't have an end.
- The same thing with *The Year Without Michael* [Pfeffer, 1987]. He's still missing at the end of the book.
- But most stories move from bad to good, from what isn't wanted by the main characters to what is wanted.
- A lot of times it's all too easy. Things work out well as if by magic. That's not true to life.
- And some stories show only the nightmare side and that leaves you feeling down. *The Bumblebee Flies Anyway* [Cormier, 1983] is like that.
- Even in that story there's a dream of what could be and the boy tries to make the dream happen.

The aim of the following sequence is to help middle school age students discover in literary works patterns of imagery that reflect natural cycles.

Teacher: In nature, what happens in spring and summer?
Students:
- Plants grow. Leaves come out.
- Everything is alive.
- Things are green and growing.

Teacher: What happens in fall and winter to natural things like plants?
Students:
- Leaves die and fall.
- Nothing grows.
- The sky is often grey.
- The wind is cold.

Teacher: Think about this: Even though they may not mention the seasons directly, stories might be described as being spring/summer or fall/winter stories. Or, to put it another way, dur-

ing the course of a story, the action may move from spring/
summer to fall/winter and perhaps back again to spring.
Students:
- "The Ugly Duckling" is a good example of the way a story
  moves from winter to spring. It's springtime when the
  happy ending comes.
- *Beauty and the Beast* is the same.
- At the beginning of "The Sleeping Beauty," everyone is
  asleep, almost as though they were dead. When the Prince
  comes and kisses the Princess, everyone wakes up and the
  thorn hedge around the castle starts to bloom.
- A lot of stories move in circles like the seasons. For awhile
  everything looks dead, the way it does in fall and winter,
  but at the end, things are brighter.
- Some stories never get brighter, like *Slake's Limbo* [Holman,
  1974]. At the end the boy is still a homeless person.
- But there's some hope, because at least he has moved out
  of the depths of the subway.
- In some stories, the main character dies or almost dies, but
  reappears at the end.
- In the myth about the god, Osiris [McDermott, 1977], he
  dies, but he is actually brought back to life again.
- In *Call It Courage* [Sperry, 1940], life is pretty cold and
  harsh for Mafatu in the beginning. He even wants to die.
  But at the end, he comes home a new person.
- You could say he was reborn.

Associative Language

The literary imagination seeks to associate and identify
the human mind with what goes on outside it. The language of
literature is associative, using simile and metaphor to express
this identity. In the imaginative logic of literary thought and
language, therefore, two unlike things may be said to be like
each other or to be each other. (My love is like a rose; my love is
a rose.)

The logic of metaphor, which insists that "this is that," is not
the logic of reason; it is an *imaginative* logic that illustrates how
the imaginative writer goes beyond nature to show a world absorbed and possessed by the human mind. In poetry, for instance,
it is not only legitimate but highly desirable to tell the "truth" by
means of analogy and association—truth that cannot be defended

or refuted in discursive terms. Poetic expression, which uses associative language to make its own sense, should be regarded by children as a valid mode of expression, and not as a distortion of prose. If children are able to grasp this basic understanding of poetic expression in elementary and middle school, problems of understanding or accepting the "difficult" images of the poets in high school and beyond may be minimized.

Children ought to become aware of the logic of metaphorical language in literature, not by collecting similes and metaphors as if they were so many colorful pebbles, but by seeing for themselves, as they read and write, the worth and value of using concrete and sensory imagery to express ideas.

Sequence for Primary Grades.   In the following discussion, the teacher leads young children toward an awareness that the literary imagination seeks to suggest an identity between the human mind and the world outside it by using metaphor, the language of identification: this is that.

Teacher: Just before class I saw Peter galloping across the school-
     yard. You looked happy.
Student: I was pretending to be a horse, a really fast one like I saw
     on Saturday at the race track. Running makes me feel good.
Teacher: Yes. Now I want everyone to act out for us what feeling
     happy is like for you. Let's push back the chairs and tables
     to have room to move. Now, show us with your whole body
     what feeling happy is like. (The teacher might provide music
     as the children proceed with movement mimes, some in
     place, others moving about the room.)
Teacher: I saw lots of happy, freed-up people just now. Mary, were
     you flying?
Students:
   • I was. I was a bird.
   • I was floating like a cloud.
   • I was a fish swimming.
   • I was a rabbit running.
   • I was sunshine.
   • I was a tree getting blown by the wind.
   • I was swinging in a swing.
   • I was singing a song.
Teacher: Everybody acted out feeling free and happy by being
     something else. I wonder why.

Students:
- That's the way you have to do it.
- If I just stand here feeling happy you couldn't tell. I had to pretend I was a leaf twirling around in the air.

Teacher: In order to show what it's like to be happy, you have to use a comparison. That is, you say that feeling happy is like other things or is other things. Let's put into words what you acted out. (Teacher prints "Happiness is . . ." on an experience chart or the board and records the children's responses under these words.)

Students:
- Happiness is flying like a bird.
- Happiness is a leaf twirling in the wind.
- Feeling happy is the warm sun.
- A balloon!
- The sound of the bell on the ice-cream truck.
- A ride on a swing.
- Happy is the smell of roast turkey cooking.
- Happy is eating ice cream.

Teacher: Do you know what? We've made a poem by saying what happy is like. You did just what poets do. Who can explain what I mean?

Students:
- We said that feeling happy was like something.
- We said feeling happy was something else.
- We said feeling happy was smelling or tasting something.
- Or something you can hear.
- Or even taste.

Teacher: Let's read our poem.

Sequence for Upper Elementary and Middle School Grades.
The aim of the discussion is to lead the students to an understanding that certain patterns of imagery are associated with the expression of positive and negative feelings. The students have experienced a number of poems of their own and of the teacher's choosing, including the following:

HERE WE COME A-PIPING

Here we come a-piping,
In Springtime and in May;
Green fruit a-ripening,

And Winter fled away.
The Queen she sits upon the strand,
Fair as a lily, white as a wand;
Seven billows on the sea,
Horses riding fast and free,
And bells beyond the sand.

Traditional

CITY AUTUMN

The air breathes frost. A thin wind beats
Old dust and papers down gray streets
And blows brown leaves with curled-up edges
At frightened sparrows on window ledges.
A snow-flake falls like an errant feather:
A vagabond draws his cloak together,
And an old man totters past with a cane
Wondering if he'll see Spring again.

Joseph Moncure March

DARK GIRL

Easy on your drums,
Easy wind and rain,
And softer on your horns,
She will not dance again.

Come easy little leaves
Without a ghost of sound
From the China trees
To the fallow ground.

Easy, easy drums
And sweet leaves overhead,
Easy wind and rain;
Your dancing girl is dead.

Arna Bontemps

IN TIME OF SILVER RAIN

In time of silver rain
The earth
Puts forth new life again,

Green grasses grow
And flowers lift their heads,
And over all the plain
The wonder spreads
        Of life,
        Of life,
        Of Life!

In time of silver rain
The butterflies
Lift silken wings
To catch a rainbow cry,
And trees put forth
New leaves to sing
In joy beneath the sky
As down the roadway
Passing boys and girls
Go singing, too,
In time of silver rain
        When spring
        And life
        Are new.

                            Langston Hughes

Teacher: Think of the poems we have shared lately. What were
    some of the subjects they dealt with?
Students:
    • They talked about people.
    • And animals.
    • A lot of them were nature poems.
    • I think most of them expressed feelings.
Teacher: What feelings do they express?
Students:
    • Sadness, sometimes, like in the poem "Dark Girl." It's
      gloomy, because, after all, she's dead.
    • So is "City Autumn" sad. It makes you think of dark, rainy
      days. There's not much hope in it.
    • Some of the poems we heard were happy, though.
    • Yeah. Like the one by Langston Hughes, "In Time of Silver
      Rain."
    • Most of the poems we read by e. e. cummings were happy,
      like the one that starts, "In just-spring."

Teacher: In the poems we read and others you know, what season is associated with positive feelings? negative feelings?
Students:
- The happier poems, like "Here We Come A-Piping," are set in spring.
- The sadder poems usually mention fall when the leaves are falling and things are dying. Like "City Autumn."
- Or it's the coldest time of the year the way it is in "The Ballad of the Harp-Weaver" [Millay, 1924].

Teacher: Why would this be so?
Students:
- In spring and summer grass and trees are alive and growing. In a poem about death, you'd probably not want to describe a season like that.
- You'd want images from fall and winter when nature sleeps or dies.
- Images of cold wind and frozen ground go better with sorrow than images of sunshine and spring rain.
- Unless you want a contrast.

Teacher: Can you say more about that idea?
Students:
- Let's say you were writing a poem about a baby's death. If you said it took place on a beautiful, sunny day, it seems to me it would make the death even harder to take.
- I agree. There's a contrast like that in "The Ballad of the Harp-Weaver." The boy's mother dies on Christmas Eve, which is supposed to be a happy time.
- It's also the coldest time in many parts of the world: midwinter.
- Right. The poem makes the point that it's the worst winter for cold in history.

Teacher: I like your ideas.

Intertextuality: Reading for Connections

Likenesses unify both literature and less-than-literary imaginative verbal constructs. A growing understanding of how literary and non-literary structures interrelate leads us to understand more fully the significance of imaginative literature in our daily lives. Learning theorists have established that one of the major ways we learn is through identification of significant patterns and relationships in what we study. Moving toward an understanding of the unifying principles of literature offers students insights that are unique to this approach. Here is an opportunity to step back from individual works and discover how literary entities fit with respect to each other.

This way of looking at literature does not preclude the use of other approaches to literary study. What it does do is offer a broader perspective on what imaginative verbal constructs are. I worked with a group of fifth graders in a middle school in Queens, New York using a holistic approach to literary study that included personal response and critical analysis of the conventional aspects of texts. We then moved into a systematic examination of inter-relationships among texts.

Responding to the statement, "In folktales we have the blue-prints for all stories that come after them," students proceeded through inquiry. What were the elements or motifs common to folktales? These are some of the recurrent patterns they discovered:

- Plots that feature quests or journeys. These often include trials the quester must face, temptings, twists of fortune, moments of profound insight (epiphany), transformations, loss and recovery, rescue from evil, goodness rewarded, good winning over evil, the righting of wrongs, and the triumph of the underdog.
- Characters who are either for the quest or against it and who either help or hinder the quester. Typical characters are a good, well-meaning protagonist; evil villains; characters—often friendly birds or animals—that exist simply to assist the protagonist; wise men and women; tricksters; and simpletons.
- Settings such as highways, forests, riverbanks, oceans, islands, towers, castles, deserts, rocky wastelands, and pleasant meadows and dells.

The students commented on the liberal use of certain numbers in countless tales. For example, 3 and 7 are often used as the number of trials or tests to be endured or the number of years someone served in bondage or spent on a quest. They found in the tales such motifs as the talisman, prophecies, oracles, wishes, and spells. They noted that weather and time of year were significant in the stories: Quests often began in the spring; success also coincided with spring, the time of rebirth, while the greatest trials and crises took place in winter, a time of death and dormancy.

Once the "blueprints" were established, the children examined modern stories to see if these elements were present. They found them more easily in fantasy than in realistic fiction. A selection of their discussion, which was based on common experiences with books they first enjoyed when they were younger, follows.

Students:
- *Sylvester and the Magic Pebble* [Steig, 1969] is a story about loss and recovery. Sylvester is lost when he turns into a rock, but his family gets him back at the end.
- There's a good example of transformation. Sylvester turns into a rock and back again into a donkey.
- And the transformation is because of a talisman, a magic pebble.
- And a wish, don't forget. Sylvester's mother wishes he was with them again and he changes from a rock back into a donkey. The wish comes true because of the pebble.
- Sylvester gets rescued in the spring, when leaves and flowers are starting to bloom.

A reading of *Higglety Pigglety Pop!* (Sendak, 1967) elicited these remarks:

Students:
- Jennie leaves home on a quest because she's discontented. She says there must be more to life than having everything.
- This whole story is like a dream or a vision or something. It doesn't make much sense to me.
- Well, that makes it like folktales. Lots of times the stuff in them couldn't really happen. Things change shape, just like they do here. In *Cinderella* the pumpkin turns into a coach and mice into horses. Here Baby turns into Mother Goose.
- There was a shape-changer in the TV show, *Deepspace Nine*.
- Right. And in an ad, a motor oil bottle turns into a tiger.
- There's no villain in this story.
- What about the lion? The lion seems to be a villain.
- Jennie's black leather bag is a talisman.

  • Anyhow, Jennie's quest turns out okay. She gets what she
    wanted.

A reading of *Brave Irene* (Steig, 1986) produced these
comments:

Students:
  • Irene keeps trying to deliver that dress even when it's really
    hard for her. Bad things keep happening.
  • She's being tested. And she doesn't give up trying. A real
    hero.
  • You mean *heroine*. There's loss and recovery when she loses
    the dress and finds it again.
  • At the end, when she finally does what she set out to do,
    there's food and a ball, just like in lots of fairytales.
  • A happy ending.

It was more difficult for the students to make connections
between the old tales of fantasy and a modern, realistic story.
However, connections were possible. This is what the group said
about *The Great Gilly Hopkins* (Paterson, 1978).

Students:
  • Gilly doesn't go on a journey, but she has a quest. She wants
    to find her mother and live with her.
  • In a way, you could say Trotter is like the wise woman or
    fairy godmother in fairytales. Don't you think so? She's on
    Gilly's side and she gives her good advice.
  • There's a transformation; at least I think so. Inside, Gilly
    changes. At the end she accepts what happens without
    making trouble. Once she would have made trouble.
  • Gilly doesn't get tested or have trials.
  • I think she does get tested, but it's through what happens
    and how she feels, not by what she has to do.
  • She makes things happen. She takes chances.
Teacher: Could you say she tempts fate, something like Molly
    Whuppie (De la Mare, 1983) in the old tale?
Students:
  • I think she's a trickster character.
  • Or maybe just a brat.
  • Same thing.

LEARNING SEQUENCES IN LITERARY CRITICISM: ACTIVITIES

The following are activities designed to develop an understanding of the unifying principles of literature, as delineated in Part II. Although they may involve discussion, they go beyond it into other areas of response.

Classification and Categorization

It will help students to become aware of recurrent archetypal structures, patterns, and themes if they work to classify in various ways what they read and hear.

● Working in groups, students might classify characters according to their power of action: Is it greater than a human's, less, about the same? Comic and cartoon characters should be included: Superman is like a god, Charlie Brown is an ordinary chap.

● Another profitable critical activity involves collecting examples of literary archetypes from television, comics, advertising, and films. As examples: the detergent that fights dirt as the knight fought the dragon; images of paradise in soft-drink commercials; cars that are cougars and rabbits; hand cream that magically transforms chapped hands; the "Cinderella" story: a young man can't get a date until the "fairy godmother" in the form of the right mouthwash transforms him.

● Students can identify archetypal plots such as the "Cinderella" story or the "Jack-the-Giant-Killer" story in television serials or soap operas, movies, comic strips, and advertisements. Examples: The "Cinderella" plot is found in many advertisements for cosmetics, which show magical transformations that result in the conquest of a lover; the "Jack-the-Giant-Killer" plot is in the episodes of Batman and Superman.

● Stories may be classified in a number of ways, the sophistication of the classifications varying in accordance with the ability of grades and classes within grades. Here are some examples of categories.

Stories that end happily or sadly
Stories of successful and failed quests
Stories of dreams and of nightmares

● To make students aware of color and how it is used in
people's symbolic acts, students can be asked to show how colors may have positive and negative symbolic associations. Gold
(yellow) is positive as the imperial color in the Far East, wealth,
and light; negative as deceit, cowardice, and treason. Red is positive as courage, love, and fervor; negative as violence, revolt, and
sin (scarlet letter "A"). Positively, purple is associated with royal
dignity, wisdom, and religious leaders; negatively, with mourn-
ing. Green may stand positively for hope, growth, and life, but
negatively for jealousy.

The students might exchange their ideas on why brides,
graduates, and surrender flags use white; why sailors wear blue
and Brownies wear brown; what colors are used on flags to sig-
nify danger and why; why red is used on valentines; why mourn-
ers wear black (do they do so in every culture?); what colors are
associated with Halloween, Thanksgiving, Christmas, and so on,
and why.

● As exercises in the study of archetypal imagery, students
can create picture essays of comic or happy visions of life, or
tragic or sad visions of life. (Refer to Table 4.1 in Chapter 4.)
Happy visions are characterized by images of communion, friendship, love, and marriage; domesticated animals; gardens, parks,
roses, lotus, and groves; temples, precious stones, and castles. Sad
visions usually involve bullying villains, betrayed heroes and
heroines, and isolated people; preying animals and birds; sinister forests, desolate wastelands, and littered city streets; deserts,
rocks, and ruins.

Analysis

Criticism may focus on analysis of literary and nonliterary
experiences. These activities are intended as oral exercises.

● Students can analyze movies, television dramas, or serials,
using the following questions: Does the story show an upward or
downward movement? What is the condition of the characters as
the story begins? What is their state at the end? Is the imaginative

view of the human situation basically happy and triumphant, or tragic and futile?

Are any of the following archetypes found in the stories: the dream that tells something about reality; the perilous journey in quest of something; someone expelled from society for a crime; the messenger who speaks from the world of the dead; the death of a noble person; the slaying of a monster; the transforming power of faith and love; betrayal of an innocent; recognition of a truth that changes someone's life; the idea that good action is rewarded, and so on.

● To introduce the dialectical principle, students can explore the metaphorical significance of the prepositions *up* and *down* in language and literature. Moses goes down into the land of Egypt; Elijah's chariot goes up; when we're sad, we're down, and when we're happy, we're up; a book by Booker T. Washington is called *Up From Slavery*; the prisoner-singer sings from "Down in the Valley"; Jacob saw a ladder going up to heaven; Rapunzel let her hair down so her love could climb up to her in the tower; Moses received the Ten Commandments on top of Mt. Sinai.

● Students might compare contemporary fiction with folktales to see how ancient archetypes appear in modern stories: the magical talisman; the curse or spell; the pattern of three attempts or three trials; transformations; mistaken identity or disguise; character types like the trickster, the underdog, the noodlehead; the triumph of good over evil. Some examples are

> James Bond's elaborate technological devices are magical in effect, like the magic talisman of the ancient hero—a cloak or helmet that causes invisibility, a sword that never misses its mark.
>
> Luke Skywalker has with him the same "Force" that has sustained heroes of all times.
>
> Yoda, one of the wise old men of literature, is Luke's teacher and advisor.
>
> In police shows there are often three tries to catch a killer.
>
> Situation comedies are filled with stock characters like the henpecked husband, the buffoon, the heartless female.
>
> In countless stories, good triumphs over evil, if only in the last few seconds of a show.

Critical Response Through Art, Drama, and Speech

Working in groups, students may make the following kinds of response to the literature they experience.

● To explore patterns of imagery, students might develop picture essays (with drawings or magazine pictures) that show positive and negative images: straight roads or mazes; trees in bloom or rows of telephone poles; domesticated animals and beasts or birds of prey; homes and prisons; productive people and derelicts; gentle waterfalls and destructive floods; human compassion and human cruelty.

● In a debate on the issue, "There are no heroes or heroines in modern life," students can consider the following questions: What is the definition of a hero or heroine? Has this definition changed over time? If there are modern heroes or heroines in real life, who are they? Who are our fictional heroes and heroines? Can anyone be a hero or heroine? How?

● Students can create "Me" collages with drawings or magazine pictures. Students find images from the animal, vegetable, and mineral worlds with which they identify: dog, whale, elephant, mouse; artichoke, tomato, turnip, cabbage; jewel, rock, razor. Crests may be made to adorn the collages, showing pictorially the meaning of a student's name. (Sally Smith uses a picture of a blacksmith on her crest.) A variation of the exercise is to divide the collage into two parts: "Me" and "Not Me." The opposing images show what the person rejects or does not identify with.

● Groups might dramatize, through mime, interesting metaphors from their reading. As in charades, the team acts out the metaphor while the others guess.

● To a drumbeat, students can mime changes (transformations). The leader says, "You are holding something very hot; as the beat slows, it changes into a small, pointed object; as the beat quickens, it becomes a bird or butterfly that is set free."

● With movement and mime, students can transform themselves imaginatively in quick succession into three different objects: a baby, a rock, a swaying tree.

THE UNIT APPROACH TO LITERARY STUDY

The unit—a sustained learning sequence—is an effective way to integrate language arts activities and to help young critics grow in making connections among literary works. The unit is built around a set of books, say three to five, related by theme, plot, structure, topic, focus, style, or any other common element. Through the use of carefully planned units, students learn that "in literature you don't just read one poem or novel after another, but enter into a complete world of which every work of literature is a part" (Frye, 1963a, p. 27).

The ways of organizing units are unlimited. The study in social studies of colonial America is enhanced by a unit that features several of the fine books in historical fiction dealing with the period. Great literary themes like survival or basic literary archetypes like the quest provide significant focus for units of study. Such diverse topics as bedtime, giants, friendship, or peer relationships are only a few of the countless choices available. A study of literary types, such as the fable or the cautionary tale, is another way of setting up a unit. To focus on several works by the same author is still another organizing principle, as is organization around a type of discourse such as biography, drama, journals, memoirs, and correspondence.

The three to five core books or works are read aloud in part or, preferably, in their entirety to the whole group. These listening and discussing sessions are an important feature of the unit approach. The books chosen for this stage of the unit must offer ideas that are worth thinking, talking, and writing about. In style they should be worthy of emulation because student writing may be modeled on them.

The sequence for presentation is planned so that one discussion leads into the next. New stories are considered in terms of those that went before so that students may readily discover significant relationships and recurring patterns. Joy Moss (1984) suggests use of the following kinds of questions to guide discussion (for more on questioning see Chapter 7):

- *Questions that set the stage for reading.* These may involve examination of the title and illustrations. They may, for example, ask the students to predict on the basis of these. Background information is supplied and discussed.

- *Questions that focus on the basic story.* These questions ask for information that is directly stated in the text or supplied through illustrations. They also deal with who? what? where? why? and story elements such as character, plot, and setting.
- *Questions that involve interpretation.* Here students make inferences, comparisons, and generalizations. They might consider a character's motivation, for example, or the theme of a work.
- *Questions about the craft of story.* Here aspects of form and structure are considered, the genre or type of writing, the techniques of writer and illustrator.
- *Question about the interconnections in literature.* Stories are compared in terms of story elements: characters, plots, settings, themes, style. Characteristics of genres may be considered.
- *Questions that relate the story world to the student's world.* Here students give subjective responses to books, which may include putting themselves into a character's place, or they may evaluate a character's ideas in terms of their own. (Do you think Ruth made a good decision? What would you do if you had found the treasure?)

Twenty-five to 60 books on the topic or related to it are made available for independent reading. When possible, related reading should involve works in as many different types of discourse as applicable—fiction, nonfiction, poetry, songs, journals, sections of newspapers—for both the shared and independent reading. Units are planned around three main objectives, as follows: learning about literature, independent reading, and writing or other responses.

Extensions of the reading-listening experience need to have roots in the actual experience. Writing, for example, might continue the exploration of themes or ideas presented in the literature or be modeled after the selections themselves. (A unit on fables leads naturally to the creation of original fables.)

Some works—and poetry always—lend themselves to oral reading. Folktales are natural choices for dramatization. Biographies may be recast as ballads. Questions raised in a work of fiction can lead to research in informational works and result in discursive writing. Reports may involve a variety of creative responses, as in a mixed-media presentation (taped recording with homemade slides or transparencies for the overhead projector; videotaped documentary with voice-over commentary).

In teaching criticism, the holistic unit approach obviously has much to recommend it. Students move from experiencing to extending experience through writing and art. Talking together is the major means by which students examine literary works. The focus is on making connections and seeing relationships. Units provide a means of shaping and focusing literary experience in productive ways.

CONCLUSIONS

Criticism comes from the Greek *kritikos,* meaning a "judge." A judge's right to be on the bench is based on knowledge of the law. A literary critic's obligation is to know as much as possible about literature, how the parts work separately and where they fit together in the whole.

Literacy is not something that occurs as the result of reading a book or two. Nor will reading every book in the library guarantee the reader an educated imagination. The development of literacy and the education of the imagination through literature are cumulative processes resulting from a systematic and progressive study of literature. And the early study of literature must take its place in a continuum of study if the cumulative benefits of a literary education are to be realized.

Becoming a literate critic begins when we experience and respond to our first stories and poems. It continues in further response that involves exploration, reflection, and making connections. "Whatever value there is in studying literature, cultural or practical, comes from the total body of our reading, the castle of words we've built, and keep adding new wings to all the time" (Frye, 1963a, p. 39).

LITERARY CAPABILITIES

In conversations with children about their responses to the literature they read and hear, it helps teachers and caregivers to have a sense of the level of literary understanding that is typical of children at different stages of development. What follows are generalizations of literary capabilities by age group as developed by students in my graduate classes after observing and recording the reactions and responses of individuals and groups of children.

Preschool

- Learns through listening; will attend to the reader's voice even when material being read is beyond understanding.
- Learns what books are and how they are used.
- Helps to "read" stories by joining in on repeated words and phrases.
- Responds with body movements like pointing, clapping, and talking to the book and its characters.
- Follows the story sequence through pictures.
- Insists on accuracy in retelling and rereading.
- Begins to distinguish among different types of books: make-believe stories, stories about everyday life, books that invite participation.
- Becomes selective, preferring some stories, poems, and types of books over others.
- Repeats independently words and phrases from books.
- Engages in reading-like behavior: holds book, turns pages, "reads" by retelling from memory.
- If asked for comments about a book, is likely to tell what happened in it, often focusing on one incident.

Primary Grades

- Listens to longer, more complicated stories and books.
- Asks more "Why?" questions about characters, pictures, and plots.
- Watches cartoons and stories on TV and recognizes stock characters (hunter, hunted) and basic plots (the chase).

- Anticipates what will come next in a story.
- Shows need for resolution in stories.
- Categorizes stories more precisely.
- Recreates previously experienced stories and/or creates original ones through pictures, dramatic play, writing, or dictating.
- Repeats jingles and rhymes from books and TV and begins to enjoy puns, riddles, and jokes.
- Distinguishes between make-believe world of stories and reality.
- Begins to read independently, often choosing what has been read aloud.

Middle Grades

- Reads independently and selectively; enjoys stories with dramatic action and conflict or humor.
- Knows story genres: folktale, myth, fable, fantasy, realism.
- Understands and uses literary terms: character, plot, flashback, suspense, point of view.
- Predicts outcomes.
- Recognizes recurrent character types: hero, heroine, villain, minor supporting characters.
- Distinguishes tone and mood.
- Notes similarities among characters in different stories: "This stepmother is a witch!"
- Recognizes the style of particular authors and prefers one over another.
- Becomes interested in who makes stories and how and enjoys reading about and meeting authors. Favorite question of authors: "Where do you get your ideas?"

Upper Grades

- Is familiar with patterns of recurring images and their significance: Confusion and chaos contrast with peace and serenity; light and calm contrast with darkness and storm.
- Recognizes allusion and metaphor, although often is unable to articulate this knowledge without help; enjoys wordplay; appreciates jokes, puns, and riddles.

- Child's own original writing features characters and plots that reflect viewing and reading.
- Resolves own stories more satisfactorily, if only by expedient means: character in a tight spot wakes up—the adventure was only a dream; an extraneous character is introduced to "save the day."
- Associates literary experiences; stories read and heard are compared with those seen on TV or in movies.

9

The Process of Writing

The art [of writing] cannot be learned, in the strict sense of the word, but through wide reading one can at least absorb some of the essentials. I mean, incidentally, reading everything—not just fiction but poetry (especially poetry), drama, history, biography, philosophy. By paying close attention to the way words work in the hands of the masters, and by reading copiously, one may if one is lucky (and a little gifted) acquire a style of one's own. But trying to become a writer without having been a reader is like setting forth to sail across the ocean in a boat without sails.
—William Styron (Gallo, 1977, p. 10)

Forty prominent authors were asked what they would like to see the schools do to improve the writing of students (Gallo, 1977). From those who responded, among them five recipients of Pulitzer Prizes, came a clear message: Read to write.

"The urge to write is the child of the love of reading," wrote John Hersey (p. 1). From Mary Stolz: "I have never known or known of a writer who was not a reader from the first dazzling moment when the letters assembled themselves and became the WORD" (p. 8). William Styron said, "The only absolutely indispensable factor in the teaching of writing is, it seems to me, an insistence on the necessity of *reading*" (p. 10).

These are the words of Elizabeth George Speare, twice winner of the Newbery Award for her distinguished contribution to literature for young people.

How wonderful if we could present a young writer with an intriguing Lego set of words with which to fit together his

181

thoughts! On second thought, we do have such a treasure, an inexhaustible Lego set of words. We have books. (p. 24)

If physically we are what we eat, then linguistically we are what we read and hear. In one study, the researcher found, not surprisingly, that the writing of children mirrored the style used in their basal readers (Eckhoff, 1983). Since the language children listen to and read is reflected in their writing, models need to be chosen with care. They have to be the best and they must be experienced in profusion. Experiencing a single short story or even a half dozen simply is not enough for would-be story writers. They must first be caught by pleasure in language as it is used in this or any other form. Then, through extensive experience followed by reflection and discussion—criticism—they are taught by the form itself.

All this takes time, as it should. Writing—like reading—is not something one masters in a year or two or even twelve. It is, or ought to be, a process of growth and development over a lifetime.

Of necessity, writing grows out of reading. What writers write comes out of their experience with written words. Children who have never heard or read limericks can't write them because they are unfamiliar with the conventions of the form. The same is true for all literary forms, each of which shapes language in its customary ways. Criticism, which involves the study of these forms, includes writing in them.

WRITING IN THE CLASSROOM

Just as we learn to read by reading, we learn to write by writing. Therefore, opportunities to write must be plentiful. Ideally, these opportunities should grow out of the actual experience of children, especially their reading experience. In *Learning About Biographies*, Myra Zarnowski (1990) describes how extensive reading of biographies by fourth and fifth graders led directly into their writing of biography. First, they learned about the subject—in one instance, Eleanor Roosevelt—by listening to the teacher read aloud and by reading for themselves. After they had listened or read, the children wrote in their journals what impressed them most in the biographical material on Eleanor Roosevelt. In groups of four to six, they brainstormed to prepare a list of events remembered from what they had read or heard read. Then they were ready to write their own biographical "snapshots," which consisted of a picture of an event in the subject's life and a description of it. The snapshots were then arranged in chronological order for display.

The snapshot approach to writing biography is one of four approaches to writing biography described in *Learning About Biographies*. Each approach is illustrative of good practice for writers in any literary form. First, the children were immersed in their subject through an unhurried, pleasurable program of reading and listening. Then they were prepared for writing by plenty of pre-writing activities: discussing the content and form of biographies, making notes in their journals of their personal responses to the material, asking questions, reading to answer them, brainstorming for ideas and impressions, ordering and organizing. They worked in small groups, sharing first drafts and deciding how revision would improve them.

Writing, like reading, is an individual act. But research shows that small support groups help writers to flourish (Atwell, 1987; Calkins, 1986; Graves, 1983). In a classroom where there is a climate of encouragement and support, children grow by reading and listening to each other's work in a workshop setting. Oral reading of one's work makes the work come alive; rough spots are revealed through reading aloud. To know that you will have a sympathetic audience for your words is to have an added purpose for writing.

Teachers need to remember that writing is developmental. Whatever a child writes is a beginning. Like any new growth, it must be tended and encouraged. To keep it growing and developing is the important thing. Shaping and pruning can come later. Marking things right or wrong is likely to stunt growth or cut it off altogether, especially in the case of imaginative writing and journal entries. We'd do well if we brought to children's attempts at writing the same tolerance we show for their first attempts to speak.

COMPOSING POETRY AND VERSE

Literature grows out of other literature, and experience with poetry is the best way to foster its creation. One or two poems will not do this, Children in elementary and middle school need to hear poetry *in quantity*. They need themselves to say it aloud; to respond to it with movement, questions, and comment; to become so steeped in verse that they are able to discover how poems are made. Then they need guidance and freedom to experiment with their own poetic creations.

The poet Kenneth Koch (1970), acting on the assumption that children are natural poets, went into inner-city classrooms to help children express their "wishes, lies, and dreams." He found it important to take children seriously as poets.

> Children have a natural talent for writing poetry and anyone who teaches them should know that. Teaching is really not the right word for what takes place; it is more like permitting children to discover what they already have. (p. 25)

When education for literacy is begun by developing and releasing "something they already have," children are likely to respond with the energy, enthusiasm, and creativity that Koch describes in his book.

Freedom Through Form

Writing according to a form or convention is both a discipline and a freedom. Young poets' creativity is helped, not hindered, by introducing them to poetic patterns and structures (Schertle, 1996, p. 434).

A good way to become familiar with the wide range of excellent children's poetry available today is a series of browsing sessions in the library. Many teachers find it useful to have an anthology of personal favorites, and suggestions for compiling it are provided in Chapter 6.

Familiarity with poetry will reveal that there are many recurrent poetic forms. The following list is only a selection of them: rhythmic lists (rhymed and unrhymed), chants, cinquain, riddles, concrete poems that take on the shape of what they describe, couplets, elegies, epics, epigrams, epistles, epigraphs, found poems (children's notes, bits of newspaper copy, scraps of conversation), free verse (no regular beat and no rhyme), light verse, haiku, limerick, a statement or line arranged on a page as poetry, and exotic forms like the pantoum, rap poems, sonnets, and senryu (Harley, 2000; Heard, 1989; Livingston, 1991; Padgett, 2000).

Wide, non-threatening experience with poetic forms is likely to inspire attempts to write in them. Poems are first enjoyed—read aloud perhaps more than once for the sound and the sense—and then examined to see how they are made. Many poems, for example, are simply statements made special by their placement on the page and by the unusual imagery and keen insights they contain. Children need to learn how poems are made through a process of discovery. The teacher might lead the inquiry by asking children to take a close look at a printed poem. What do they notice about it? That the following verse is a series of questions is an easy discovery to make, just as its rhyme scheme is easily discoverable.

> Does the restless sea grow weary?
> Does it long to lie still and rest?
> Does it tire of cries of sea birds?
> Does it seek an end to its quest?
>
> *Glenna Sloan*

It is especially important that children discover that poem-making is challenging and fun; that it most resembles playing a game or solving a puzzle. Creating a not-serious septone may help them to understand this.

Examples of selected poetic forms follow, presented as suggested material for learning sequences, some of which will culminate in writing by students.

Septone. The septone is seven lines of free verse (unrhymed) based on your or someone else's phone number. The number of syllables in each line is dictated by the phone number. The following, based on the number 645–6663, is an example of a septone and also of the form called apostrophe, in which something that can't answer is addressed:

> Sand dollar, suddenly
> Here on the sand
> Wet from your journey,
> How far have you traveled?
> Where did your frail body
> First begin its tumbling
> Toward shore?
>
> *Glenna Sloan*

Terse Verse. Then there is the foolishness of terse verse, a two-word rhyming form favored by the picture book creator, photographer, and author, Bruce McMillan. Second graders made these: "Peg Leg," "Big Rig," "Duck Cluck," "Run! Gun."

Riddles.   Not only are the puns and wordplay of riddles aligned to the mental processes of children, but they are also helpful in showing children how the literary devices we call simile and metaphor work. The French poet Mallarmé's prescription for writing poetry was to describe not the thing but the effect it produces. This is what happens in riddling.

Experience with the form can lead naturally into the creation of original riddles. Groups may work together with a secret object like an apple seed, a paper clip, a birthday candle, an acorn, or a book mark. They may describe their object literally or imaginatively in terms of the effect it produces.

One group, working with an apple seed, cooperatively developed this riddle:

> From my growth came Eve's downfall;
> And from it will come health
> Without doctors.

Rhythmic Repetitions.   The child's natural propensity for rhythmic patterns should be indulged. In response to Byrd Baylor's *Everybody Needs a Rock* (1974), children found a personal rock and described it as in this example:

> My rock is rough
> As rough as sandpaper;
> My rock is silent
> Like a tree;
> My rock has lines,
> Black and white,
> Like a zebra;
> My rock is just right,
> Palm-size.

The sonorous repetitive rhythms of the Bible supply powerful patterns to examine and try to emulate.

PSALM 150

> Praise ye the Lord.
> Praise God in his sanctuary:

> Praise him in the firmament of his power.
> Praise him for his mighty acts:
> Praise him according to his excellent greatness.
> Praise him with the sound of the trumpet:
> Praise him with the psaltery and harp.
> Praise him with the timbrel and dance:
> Praise him with stringed instruments and organs.
> Praise him upon the loud cymbals:
> Praise him upon the high sounding cymbals.
> Let everything that has breath praise the Lord.
> Praise ye the Lord.

The biblical litany uses parallel arrangements of words, variation in line length supplying a rhythmic sweep when the whole is read aloud. A holiday or holy day can be the inspiration for such a poem, the teacher offering the starting phrase as a primer, "Let us be thankful for . . ."

Catalogues and Lists.   Catalogue verse is as old as Homer. Vivid imagery, the basic stuff of poetry, is the heart of it. An entire class may participate, the younger children dictating their ideas on a common subject while the teacher transcribes, arranging the lines in different lengths for maximum rhythmic appeal. Children brainstorm, trying to use as many sensory expressions as possible. The theme might be the classroom itself; the "poem" grows with items like "the whirr of the pencil sharpener," "the woolly smell of damp coats drying on a winter afternoon," "songs off-key," "the dusty taste of a chewed pencil."

In the title poem of *Honey, I Love*, Eloise Greenfield (1978) gives a list, in joyous rhyme, of things well-loved. Rupert Brooke's (1915) "The Great Lover" was a stimulus for these lines:

> These I have loved:
>> Sunlight on a cat's silken back,
>> Clear June days,
>> White sails like birds in flight across the bay,
>> Green trees flecked with bits of blossom,
>> And the icy touch of water as I dive.
>>> *Glenna Sloan*

Haiku.   The haiku, which originated in Japan long ago, is a miniature lyric, the essence of a moment expressed in words. It is generally believed that the haiku must have 17 syllables arranged 5, 7, 5 in 3 lines. However, traditional Japanese writers of haiku count sounds, not syllables. What is important is the vivid, precise expression of an idea, in which the reader has something to look at, hear, smell, taste, or touch. Most haiku do not use metaphor.

> Now who thought of that?
> Of giving a little bug
> His own bright night light.
>
> *Glenna Sloan*

Cinquain.   The word, from French, means "a grouping of five." The form has 5 unrhymed, smoothly flowing lines of 2, 4, 6, 8, and 2 syllables, respectively.

> First snow,
> Surprise in fall,
> Melts soon on my warm palm,
> A promise of winter-white days
> To come.
>
> *Glenna Sloan*

Limericks.   Nonsense verse is a particular delight for children and may be used to reintroduce the joys of verse to older children who are skeptical of poetry or disenchanted through negative experiences with it. Children enjoy the bounce and speed of a limerick, recognizing with smiles its suitability for humorous subjects, and easily following its rhythmic pattern by tapping it out. They enjoy trying to fit words into the pattern of the limerick. There are many excellent examples to guide them, none better than the playful works of Edward Lear.

> There was an old person of Ware,
> Who rode on the back of a bear:
> When they asked, "Does it trot?" he said
> "Certainly not!
> He's a Moppsikon, Floppsikon bear!"

Couplets, Tercets, and Quatrains.   Rhyme is an aspect of poetry that need not be stressed with children. The creation of telling, vivid, fresh images is a more poetic endeavor. But children are intrigued by rhyme, and many of the poems written for them rhyme. Reading and writing rhymed couplets is an enjoyable exercise. Children will enjoy supplying the rhyming word when couplets are read aloud.

> The world is so full of a number of things
> I'm sure we should all be as happy as————.

Tercets are 3-line units that may rhyme in 2 lines or all 3.

> Dogs are very persuasive pets:
> Mine begs and flatters;
> What he wants, he gets.

Quatrains are 4-line stanzas with a possibility of a variety of rhyme schemes: aabb, abab, abcb.

The class or a group within it may choose a common subject for their couplets, tercets, or quatrains, pooling their creations to make one long poem. Common topics may be descriptions of classmates, each person's impression of a common experience, or an individual expression of a dream or wish.

Ballads. This old form has been used by storytellers for centuries. Traditionally, ballads are written in 4-line stanzas: lines 1 and 3 have four beats; lines 2 and 4 have three beats and usually rhyme, although other rhyme schemes are possible. Old ballads, like those that tell tales of Robin Hood, often have refrains, as in "Robin Hood Rescuing the Widow's Three Sons."

> Now Robin Hood was to Nottingham gone,
> With a link and a down, and a day.
> And there he met a silly old woman,
> Was weeping on the way.

A Bible story, myth, folktale, or an incident from current events or history might serve as a topic for classroom balladeers, working alone or in groups. Jan Shapiro, a middle school student, composed a ballad to retell the story of "The Princess and the Pea." Here is an excerpt from her 17-stanza ballad.

> One night the rain came down in sheets
> The thunder crashed and roared;

When all at once a knock was heard,
On Daddy's castle door.

"Oh, please, kind sir," a young girl cried,
"The night is cold and wet,
My travelling friends have left me now,
Misfortune I have met."

The king, he let the young girl in,
A princess, she did claim;
She said she came from far away,
Princess Rose Ann was her name.

Epics.   In a middle school classroom, where students worked
in groups writing, critiquing, and revising their creations, many
weeks were devoted to reading aloud the *Iliad* in Richmond
Lattimore's translation (Lattimore, 1951). One 11-year-old, inspired by the historical novels of Rosemary Sutcliff, created an
original epic about Marius, a young galley slave. An excerpt from
"For Marius Was Free," a 75-line poem arranged in three "books,"
illustrates how the rhythm and poetic devices of the *Iliad* were
absorbed by the poet.

As he entered the hold, they sprang upon him,
As lions spring upon the unwary buck,
And they grappled with him and bound him.
When morning dawned the boy awoke
To feel sharp pain in his head
Where they had struck him with a wooden club;
Where bonds had been, there was now a shackle,
And he was chained to a bench with others, unlucky,
A slave in the galleys of
King Solomon's Navy.

As the days became weeks,
And the weeks months,
He learned the ways of the rowers
From the man Jason, who was his friend.
So also he learned to eat the black bread;
And, as the jackals fight for the scraps
On the bony carcass that is left to them
By the lions, so he fought

For the scraps left to them by his master.
But, above all, he learned to hate.
. . .

Laurence Woodruff

"Prose" into "Poetry"

An important aspect of verse is its arrangement on the page,
as this example of "prose" into "poetry" from a second-grade student illustrates. The original story looked like this:

my dog. my dog is black with white. One black paw, the
others white my dog is noisy He barks a lot and he wags a
lot. And he eats a lot. My dog is My Best Friend. We run.
We play and we have fun.

Rearranged it looked like this:

MY DOG

My dog is
Black with white
One black paw,
The others white.
My dog is
Noisy
He barks a lot
He wags a lot
And he eats a lot
My dog is
My Best Friend
We run
We play
We have fun!

An imaginative and sympathetic treatment transforms what
is in prose unnecessary repetition into an element of poetry,
respects the child's natural expression, and offers the encouragement to undertake more literary endeavors, poetic and otherwise.

Poetic patterns may also be created by the alert teacher from
the children's conversation. These poems, transcribed on expe-

rience charts or the board, are useful as reading material and as evidence that words may be ordered in different ways. In the example below, the teacher joins a group of first graders to talk about a trip to the zoo. Transcribed on an experience chart, the conversation might look like this:

Teacher: What did you see at the zoo?
Students:
    A lion, a lion, I saw a lion.
    Monkeys.
    I saw monkeys.
    I saw lots of monkeys.
    I saw a big baboon.
    A *big* baboon!
    At the zoo
    At the zoo I saw a hippo,
    A huge old hippo.
    At the zoo. . . .

Writing should take place in a fail-free situation, where any honest effort is welcomed. Imaginative writing ought not to be used for formal evaluations. It is an outlet for personal expression; some students will be more comfortable than others in producing these works, but all should have the opportunity to try.

Composing poetry ought to be fun, its gamelike qualities always emphasized. Working with words to form is like fitting together the parts of a puzzle. As teachers, we need to emphasize poetry as wordplay. We need to focus on the fun of writing verse. In a conversation, Eve Merriam (personal communication, 1980) complained that too many teachers put poetry on a pedestal and make of it a solemn, serious study. Poetry needs to be pulled off the pedestal so students can romp with it.

> Young people should certainly be encouraged to write, for everyone can learn to write poetry up to a point—the point of discovering how difficult it is to write it unusually well. To get past that point is no mean achievement, as it is well past the substandard level of naive or doggerel verse which is the usual mode of amateur expression. But the purpose of such encouragement is to breed a love of poetry, not to breed poets. (Frye, 1956, p. 290)

WRITING IN PROSE FORMS

The knowledge of a story form and structure, acquired inductively through experience with story, is applied by students in composing original stories. Compositions are most often in words, but they can also be in movement (drama), shapes and design (graphic art), or images recorded on film or videotape. Indeed, constructing compositions without words gives children a sense of how the imagination creates artistic wholes, and these processes complement their efforts in written composition.

Young students are likely to have a greater affinity for story than for discursive forms. It is through story that they order their experience and orient themselves to the world. In the process of studying the stories of others, they learn that these constructs involve aesthetic ordering of experience through language and form. Criticism that emphasizes literary form and structure helps young writers to see that they share with all storytellers the same problems of creative construction.

Literary Forms Stimulate Creativity

In the process of ordering experience through language, children benefit from a consideration of form. Poetic patterns have been shown to be necessary input in the process of freeing children to create their own poetry; story patterns have the same function. Providing children with patterns that give shape to their imaginings saves them hours of frustration; creativity is aided, not curtailed. All too often children are required to write stories without sufficient pre-writing activities, which include examination of models and brainstorming ideas.

From their study of story, children know how story is made (see Chapter 7). Some teachers find it useful to brainstorm a cooperative story with their students. An eighth-grade class of mine developed as a group project a contemporary realistic story. Calling upon their considerable experience with realistic fiction to develop their ideas, they decided that they needed to show a strong character using her own resources to overcome obstacles that prevented her from achieving a goal. Someone suggested a plot idea: our heroine—a talented actress—wants to attend an arts camp to study acting, but her mother, convinced that acting is an unsuitable career, refuses to pay the tuition. The young actress—the students agreed to call her Liz—was endowed with character traits, determination being foremost among them. She must try, and fail, the students decided, in several schemes to raise the tuition money. Many schemes were proposed, but it was eventually decided that these had to be limited in number (they settled on three) or the plot would lose momentum.

Liz should attend the camp, it was decided after long argument, but not in the expected way. To make the story interesting, there needed to be an unexpected—but plausible—twist in the plot. Liz had made every possible effort on her own, and now, the students decided, she could use some help. In the end, Liz's drama teacher—like the wise woman or fairy godmother of older tales intervenes—making it possible for her to attend the camp, and with her mother's blessing. In this learning sequence, which lasted several weeks, the students struggled with many artistic problems, finding the greatest difficulty in manipulating incidents to make their story plausible and believable. (The completed book, now out of print, was published as *Spotlight on Liz* by Macmillan of Canada in 1979.)

Impersonal forms provide structures into which children can project feeling un-self-consciously. Impressions and experiences may be unique, but they require a conventional form for their expression in words. Ideas of what originality is are often exaggerated; the best writers have always used the forms and conventions, and even the ideas, of those who came before them. Child writers may be encouraged to do the same. They may rewrite a story in a different form—a myth as a story poem, say, or an adventure story as a play. They might retell a traditional folk- or fairytale, sometimes with a contemporary setting. The triad form of the typical folktale might be used as a pattern for a story with a modern setting. The heroic quest is not limited to ancient tales of romance, but may feature heroes and heroines very like their youthful creators, struggling to attain some worthy goal. Tall tales, with their larger-than-life characters outdoing themselves in marvelously implausible endeavors, are ready-made templates for original tales. Young writers may create their own myths of origin (*pourquoi* tales) along the lines of the myths of the ancients or following the pattern they discover by reading or listening to Kipling's (1902/1987) *Just-so Stories*.

The archetypal patterns and motifs found in stories are the building blocks for creating new tales. There are

Repetitive patterns (three trials, three journeys)
Transformations (literal and psychological)

Clashes between good and evil, with the conventional triumph of the good

Contrasting characters such as the good sister-bad sister duo
of countless folktales

Conventional rewards for good or courageous behavior

Helpful characters like loyal sidekicks or wise men and women
who provide main characters with help and advice

Tricky characters who outwit

Underdogs who come out on top

Talismans and amulets that bring good luck

Prophecies, spells, and incantations

A story may be told from different points of view. Folktales,
for example, are usually third-person accounts. Rewriting the tales
in first person brings a new perspective to the tale and gives students firsthand knowledge of how a literary technique operates.

Stories may be recast in different forms. The journeys of the
explorers can become the subject of narrative poems. Excerpts
from novels may be written as plays or television scripts. Historical events may be described in letters or diaries created by students. A class newspaper, complete with editorials, feature stories, cartoons, and classified advertisements, can make another
historical period come alive.

Suggestions to Encourage Writing

Like other skills, writing improves only with practice, feedback, reflection, and more practice. Children should write every
day; not just "school exercises" but meaningful writing for an
actual audience.

Journals.   A journal is a private, diary-like, ongoing piece of
writing. In it writers record their thoughts, experiences, reactions
to incidents in their life or material they have read, hopes, dreams,
and plans. The writing is shared only if the author gives permission. *Journal articles are never corrected by a reader.* A written
response to the content of the journal is all that is permitted.

Short Takes.   Show a provocative picture from a newspaper
or magazine. Children work alone or with partners to describe
what is happening in the picture. As models for their writing, they
consult newspapers to note how captions are written.

Photo Essays. These may be on any subject, from a class trip to a celebration of autumn foliage. Children take pictures and write captions for them, arranging them on a bulletin board. Each person in a class might create his or her own photo essay, using pictures and captions to create a kind of autobiography. For example, a student shows herself eating her favorite food, wearing her favorite color, playing her favorite game, and so on.

Story Skeletons. For the writing center, create such story skeletons as these:

Last night in bed I was frightened
by_____

Interviews. Questions for interviews are prepared in advance. Notes are taken as the children interview parents, grandparents, a public figure in the community, the principal or school nurse, a classmate, etcetera; the list of possibilities is endless. The material is edited and a final version of questions and answers produced for the bulletin board or school newspaper.

New Year's Resolutions and Creative Alibis. Children enjoy writing about themselves and their actual experiences. Resolutions are self-explanatory. An example of a creative alibi is: "I didn't do my homework because my turtle died and I had to bury it."

Tall Tales and Hyperbole. Reading tall tales could provide the motivation for children to write an exaggerated account of an event. Featuring themselves in the account keeps interest high.

Recipes. Create recipes not only for food, but for anything the children can think of.

Mix together:
Gooey messes,
Toothless grins,
Wet kisses,
Big bear hugs.
You have
My little brother.

Glenna Sloan

99-Word Story. Professional writers are often held to a strict word count in their pieces. Challenge older children to write a story in 99 words. It must have a problem or conflict that is resolved in the course of the story. For example:

SURPRISED BY THE TRUTH

Elyse, 14, sometimes secretly wished that her little sister, Sarah, would vanish. "Why do I always have to babysit?" Elyse complained.

One day, on a trip to the department store to buy Sarah jeans, the toddler disappeared. Frantic, Elyse and the store's security staff searched the store. "Pest or not, I want her back," Elyse thought, a little surprised at her own feelings. When a security officer located Sarah asleep on a bed in the furniture department, Elyse wept with joy and relief, holding the toddler close. "How can I think one way and feel another?"

Create Food for Thought and Talk. Children write or dictate brief anecdotes that feature moral or ethical dilemmas. All the language arts are in action as individuals or groups of writers read their scenarios aloud and then discuss them with the audience.

Entering the coat room at school, Annie sees Sue going through the pockets of each of the jackets hanging there. As she watches, Annie sees Sue take money from a coat pocket. Folding the bill, Sue quickly slips it into the pocket of her jeans. Annie, unseen by Sue, leaves the coatroom. What should she do about what she has seen?

Create Games. On index cards, students write out questions and (on the reverse side) answers on any subject: science, social studies, mathematics, etcetera. In pairs or small groups they play the game they create, first writing out rules and a scoring system.

Encourage children to create their own lists of writing activities that interest them.

Case Studies in Composition

The following are illustrations and examples of learning sequences in which literary forms provided the patterns for original writing.

Patterns from Predictable Books. A group of first graders in St. Brigid's School, Brooklyn, New York, created a story of their own using the repetitive pattern of *Do You Want to See Something?* (Merriam, 1965). The picture book text begins, "Do you want to see a dancing flea? In the circus there's a tent. In the tent there's a ring. In the ring there's a pony . . ." and so on until ". . . there's a mouse. . . . And on that mouse there is a dancing flea."

The children and the teacher, Marie Woods, read the text together several times. Then the teacher asked if the children wanted to create a story of their own using the patterns of the one they had just read. They did.

"Do you want to see new shoes?" was their first line, because a boy in their group was wearing new shoes that day. "In the city there's a school. In the school there is a classroom. In the classroom there's a boy. And on that boy, on that boy are two new shoes." Each child chose a line to copy and illustrate on a sheet of construction paper. The teacher made a cover and stapled the pages together. Soon the first graders were reading their own story (Sloan, 1980).

In a third-grade class, the children read and listened to many books that used highly predictable language patterns (Sloan, 1988). As the culmination of the learning sequence, they created their own predictable books. Here is an example of a book on shapes and colors.

> This color is dark blue. (Letters printed in dark blue)
> And this is a triangle. (Drawing of a triangle)
> So this is a dark blue triangle. (Drawing of a triangle
>   colored dark blue)

The book continued through several shapes and colors.

> This color is red.
> And this is a circle.
> So this is a red circle.

Traditional Literature as Models. Folktales, myths, and fables have provided patterns of story form for writers of every age. Here is a fourth grader's version of a familiar tale:

> Once upon a time Tom Quick came to school to show off his new red sports car to his friends. He bragged about how fast it went. Tom told everyone that his new car could beat any other car in a race.

Just then, Bill Pokey drove up in his beat-up piece of junk car. Tom and his friends started teasing him about his car. Bill got out of his car and said to Tom, "I bet my old piece of junk car could beat your sports car in a race." So they agreed to have a race around town.

The race started. Tom took off very fast and Bill's car was very slow. Tom was so far down the road that he couldn't see Bill's car anymore. As he passed by McDonalds he saw some of his friends. He stopped and said to himself, "I'll win the race, so I have time for a hamburger."

Tom was having such a good time with his friends that he lost track of time and didn't see Bill drive by. At last Tom said, "I've been here too long. I'd better go." He got into his car and drove away fast.

When Tom got to the finish line, Bill was already there. Bill laughed at Tom. "I told you I could beat you!" (Curran, 1987)

Another fourth-grade class read many myths of origin, particularly those found in the mythology of native Americans: "Why the Robin Has a Red Breast," "How the Rabbit Got His Short Tail," and others. Then they wrote original myths that explained, among other things, why the grass is green, why eyes are different colors, why dogs bark, why birds sing and frogs croak.

Short Stories as Models.   One junior high school class read and studied short stories for weeks. The students and the teacher read aloud a wide selection of stories, old and new. In small groups, working inductively, the children described short story techniques: few characters, economy of expression, early establishment of setting and situation, and the like. They then discussed possible subjects for short stories.

Those who were unable to settle on a story idea were encouraged to retell myths and Bible stories with contemporary settings and characters. One boy, for example, wrote about a man called Noah, taunted by neighbors who thought him mad to be building a boat in his backyard when the nearest body of water was a meager creek on the other side of town.

STRANGE LITTLE OLD MAN

Noah Gransby was a slow, old man who could never complete anything he began. That is why his actions the past few months had puzzled the townspeople of Lamptonville. Their concern was stimulated as they watched him limp slowly, day after day, from his tiny brick house to the almost as tiny supply store across the street. They caught brief glimpses of him lugging heavy lumber daily into his barren, undernourished back yard. No one offered to help him, and most people participated freely in the loud, continuous laughing and ridiculing of Gransby.

A few reconnoitering individuals soon discovered what he was doing. But they were more puzzled by their findings. Others refused to believe it and went to see for themselves. Soon everyone in Lamptonville knew that old Noah was building a boat. A boat? It rarely rained even in the summer here, and a few inches of snow was all the precipitation in winter. And Gransby was building a deep water vessel! The nearest body of water was Craig's Creek: ten feet wide, several inches deep, and almost a mile away on the other side of town. Poor old Gransby. The townspeople had sensed his decline. Yet, why would a madman go to the extent Gransby was going to?

The sun left Lamptonville and dark clouds crawled overhead. And then one day . . . rain . . . and for forty days . . . rain. Finally, a sparkling gem of brilliance lit the sky and a rainbow hovered at the horizon. A small white dove flittered around, and beneath it, the hull of a boat sank slowly beneath the water's surface. Noah Gransby could never complete anything he began.

Peter Gross

Writing took place in class. The all-important first paragraphs were tested on others and revised again and again. Final dog-eared drafts were polished and read aloud. Proofreading was important because the stories were published for distribution to other classes and to parents. A copy of the publication, which included a short story from each student, was placed with the library's collection of short stories for circulation (Sloan, 1972).

Plays from Narratives. A sixth-grade class enjoyed preparing scripts for Readers Theater after examining play form. Scripts were performed for other classes in the school. What follows is an example of a Readers Theater script created from the book, *Anastasia Krupnik* (Lowry, 1979).

Anastasia Krupnik

Characters: Narrator, Anastasia, her Mother and Father.

Narrator: Anastasia Krupnik is a ten-year-old girl. Her mother is
a painter. Her father is a college professor and a poet. They are
together in their living room.
Anastasia: Why did you have to name me Anastasia? None of
the other kids can spell it, so when they have to vote by secret
ballot, nobody ever votes for me. Like when I was nominated
for class secretary, only 4 people voted for me. The other 22
voted for Mary Ellen Bailey.
Father: The reason they didn't vote for you is because the class
secretary has to have good handwriting. And your handwriting
looks like hieroglyphics. That time you tried to forge
an absence excuse, you got caught right away, remember?
Because no parent—no adult—would be caught dead with
handwriting like that.
Anastasia: No adult would be caught dead with a name like
Anastasia. Why did you guys name me that?
Father: Interesting question. Choosing names is a fascinating procedure. Have you chosen one for the baby yet, Anastasia? What
thought processes did you go through in choosing?
Anastasia: If I didn't have such a dumb name, Washburn Cum-
mings would have liked me better.
Mother: What's wrong with your name? I think it's a lovely name.
Anastasia: You have to pay extra, for pete's sake, to have it sten-
ciled on a tee shirt. There are too many letters. That's one thing
wrong with it.
Father: Well, I'd be willing to fork over the extra money that a
long name costs.
Anastasia: Look at me! I mean, look at my body.
Father: Not bad for ten years old. The legs are a little skinny, but
I've seen worse.
Anastasia: I mean, look at my chest and picture my name
across it.
Father: You know, Anastasia, my mind works verbally. Your
mother is the one with the visual imagination. Why don't you
have her look at your chest?
Narrator: Anastasia walks across the room to her mother, who is
knitting clothing for the baby she is expecting.
Anastasia: Picture my name across my chest.

Mother: Wait 'til I finish this row. Okay, let me look. Yes. I see
   what you mean.
Anastasia: Into the armpits. Right? The letters would go right into
   my armpits!

Handling the Skills

The problem of perfecting and polishing skills in spelling,
grammar, handwriting, and punctuation is minimized when children work cooperatively on something they want to do. Choice is
an important factor in writing as well as in reading. Children need
to know that there are many ways of responding in writing to the
literature they read and hear. Poems, play scripts, essays, advertisements, book reviews, short stories, and interviews are some of
the possibilities open to them. Production not perfection is the rule.
Invented spelling is encouraged.

Writers need an audience. When children write together, the
audience is ready-made. If they know that others are interested
in their ideas, they will work harder to perfect the skills necessary for effective communication. When composing comes first,
handwriting, punctuation, standard spellings, and the like are put
in their place—one of importance in facilitating communication,
but always as part of an editing process, coming after having
something to say and someone to say it to.

Authentic assessment (Hill & Ruptic, 1994) goes hand in hand
with authentic literacy activities. Lois Bridges (1995, p. 8) out-
lines six defining principles of authentic assessment:

- Authentic assessment is continuous.
- Authentic assessment is an integral part of the curriculum.
- Authentic assessment is developmentally and culturally
  appropriate.
- Authentic assessment focuses on students' strengths.
- Authentic assessment recognizes that the most important
  evaluation is self-evaluation.
- Authentic assessment invites active collaboration: teach-
  ers, students, and parents work together.

Working with small groups and individuals, teachers give
help with mechanical skills *where it is needed*. In every class
there is such a wide range of language ability that it is a fruitless endeavor to drill spelling, punctuation, and all the rest with

an entire class. The individual conference is more helpful; during it children can read aloud what they have written, a process that will reveal, among other things, how a piece should be punctuated.

Pre-writing sessions are all-important. In them necessary vocabulary is provided as required and ideas are brainstormed. Cooperative group efforts in composition assist the less able when they eventually write independently. Fully stimulated and prepared to write, children are ready to push their pencils, not chew them in frustration.

The practice of having children write a piece for the teacher to grade has no value as a learning experience. Confronted with a page of prose that seems to require major surgery, it is the rare teacher who can refrain from using the red pencil. As with reading, teachers need to note individual difficulties and work one on one or with small groups as required to help those who need special instruction and encouragement.

If a teacher does write a comment on a child's work, it should be in response to the ideas found there, to indicate that the writer has communicated something of an experience, interest, dream, or emotion. If, for example, a young writer tries to communicate, in halting prose, delight in a new pet, the teacher's comment responds to the effort: "Your cat sounds just like mine. I'd like to hear more about him."

Writing is a developmental process and a highly personal one. As a means of evaluation, examples of written work are filed in the children's portfolios. Self-evaluation is encouraged. In conferences, teachers and students note strengths and weaknesses in written work, and writers press on. What children need to know is that writing is a craft that continual effort may improve but never entirely perfect. The best professional writers struggle all their lives to express their thoughts precisely in contrary words that slip and slide out of their skilled control.

One's language is a part of oneself. To continually criticize children's language use is to make them feel inadequate as human beings. Writing especially is challenging and a little daunting for many students. More than training in technique, they require encouragement. Good teachers are like the poet Marie Ponsot, who for many years taught writing at Queens College. To her students she communicated her conviction that everyone can write. All they need to do is begin. Unintimidated, guided, and encouraged, countless students in her classes discovered that she was right. Expression through written words is not reserved only for professionals. The fulfillment that can come from writing is available to everyone at all levels of ability.

Nothing should be done to discourage children's efforts. Everything must be done to ensure that they experience some measure of the pleasure and satisfaction that can come through putting their feelings and ideas into written words.

Publication

Most children delight in seeing their work in print in classroom publications. An excellent form of publication that particularly appeals to children is the creation of their own simply bound books. These may be produced as class projects or as the work of individuals or small groups. They may be illustrated or decorated and include title pages, dedications, and tables of contents.

Young students enjoy creating shape books: a collection of tall tales in an appropriately shaped book, for example, or Thanksgiving poems in a book shaped like a pumpkin. Stories may be printed on charts or oak tag for room displays.

Class magazines or newspapers are excellent ways to publish compositions of all kinds. Another form of publication is a "talking" magazine or newspaper, with children recording on tape pieces they have composed. Use of the computer takes the drudgery out of revising, editing, and preparing class newspapers and books. Even young children can prepare texts for printing.

FILM AND VIDEOTAPE
IN THE LITERATURE CURRICULUM

Movies and television especially are criticized for leading children away from reading and writing. Perhaps our best defense against the overpowering presence of film in children's lives is to incorporate it into literary studies. References to stories on film belong in discussions of printed stories and need to be welcomed and encouraged.

All the aspects of archetypal criticism that apply to printed stories apply as well to stories on film. Children will be encouraged to draw upon their experiences with film, in and out of school, in their discussions of literary principles. Just as they can learn to read printed stories perceptively, noting point of view, mood, tone, how characters develop and interrelate, and the like, so they can be taught to "read" film with greater perception.

Literature on film and literature in print have aspects in common, although each medium makes use of techniques unique to it. The film, with unusual juxtaposition of images, variations of angle, and length of shot, can create a metaphorical language of association without using words.

Shooting characters from below can make them appear overpowering and menacing. A long shot of an individual alone in a desolate place evokes feelings of loneliness. Darkness and shadow often symbolize the evil, menacing, or threatening; light and color are associated with their opposites. Images of landscapes and natural surroundings, as well as weather, create mood and atmosphere.

Film makers, as well as writers, must find ways to begin, develop, and end a story. The elements of story—character, setting, plot, theme, mood, tone—are all present in filmed narratives. Especially interesting is point of view, generally the camera's, which is usually omniscient and relatively objective.

The composition of filmed stories by students encompasses several aspects of the process of literary criticism. It involves a creative response as well as an analysis of the elements of story. If a printed story is to be adapted for filming, students need to be aware of the story in terms of its structure, deciding, for instance, what key scenes are essential to the re-creation of the story in movie form. They must note details of the characters' appearance to suggest appropriate casting and costuming. In reading or listening to the story, students must have visualized settings in order to design them for the film.

When the project involves the creation of an original movie, the storytellers must consider story structure: how and where it should begin, how and by whom the plot will be developed, how suspense will be maintained, how it will reach a satisfying ending.

Usually, the first step in the making of a film is the creation of a storyboard, a sequence of sketches that plan the story shot by shot, with instructions for the length and angle of each included in a caption. The storyboard has some obvious possibilities for teaching students to trace a sequence of events and for helping them to see how a story is formed.

Besides the regular fare of television and the movies, many excellent films and videos of quality children's literature have been created. Seeing these dramatizations is often motivation for children to read the books on which they are based. Fine books are adapted for television and aired on Reading Rainbow and Wonder Works. The Weston Woods Company creates superior film adaptations of fine children's books.

The use of filmed and printed literature together makes possible cross-media comparisons. The children will draw many conclusions about the unique characteristics of each medium. Films, for example, do not require descriptions of either the characters' appearance or the setting, since the viewer sees these details. In printed literature we can read what a character feels and thinks; film is more suited to showing the physical rather than the mental state of characters. Films reveal the characters' thoughts through their actions to a far greater degree than does the printed story.

Students will find it interesting to discuss the relative merits of each medium. In a classroom where printed literature is a lively art, no one will accept film as a substitute for it.

Postscript

Mathematics, social studies, and science all have their places in the curriculum. They are established as subjects of study: their content and methods of instruction receive serious consideration. It is still not so with literature. Yet literature, of all people's creations, is one of the greatest sources of nourishment for developing minds and imaginations.

It has the capacity to delight; it is meant to be enjoyed, and children in a time of illiteracy and aliteracy need to be convinced of its value through encounters with the best it has to offer. Literature is a humanistic study, and studies in the humanities are essential to our survival in a technological world where things can easily become more important than people. Literature has a civilizing influence. Because it deals with all human experience—our dreams and our nightmares—literature can show us both sides of the coin: what it means to be human and what it means to be inhumane.

Preoccupation with "teaching reading" has led us away from serious consideration of what it means to be truly literate. To become literate, children must read genuine literature from the beginning. Learning to read is learning to read literature, and learning to write—the other side of the literacy coin—is learning to write through literature. Literature *is* the language art. All other language "arts" develop from and through it.

At the elementary level, the literature itself, carefully chosen, must do most of the teaching. A light touch is required as we engage in literary criticism with young students. Literature is an art, and art is first of all to be experienced and savored. Aesthetic and creative responses to it must be nurtured. But experience and response are not enough. The study of literature takes place in school, and educators concern themselves with fostering growth and development. The growth of young critics depends on going beyond experiencing to reflecting on what literature is and how it works.

As defined here, literary criticism is an all-inclusive concept that includes experiencing literature, responding to it, reflecting on it, and creating it. Its practice does not depend on commercially prepared programs, narrow doctrines, or prescribed courses of study. No textbooks are necessary. What is needed to teach literary criticism is literature itself, genuine literature of all kinds and in great quantities. In this wealth of material all children will find some things that will compel them to listen, to read for themselves, to talk about what they read, and to try to create literature of their own. An informed, enthusiastic teacher is there to bring children and literature together, to listen, to ask the right questions, to inspire, and to nurture creative effort.

The development of language ability, whether reading or writing, is a cumulative development. Unlike other studies, it develops from the inside out. When words engage our feelings and imaginations, we are motivated to read them. When our feelings and imaginations are stimulated, we have a need to use language to express them.

Children in large numbers have not thrived on instructional diets that serve up imaginative literature only as dessert. These children turn to television to satisfy their desire for fantasy, their need to hear language that jingles, rhymes, and sings. For many of them reading is an onerous activity confined to classrooms.

With children, feeling comes first. They want to read what makes them laugh or cry, shiver or gasp. They need stories that reflect what they have felt but had no words to express. They need the thrill of imagining, of being in some character's shoes for a spine-tingling adventure. They deserve the delight that comes with hearing language that puns and plays. For children, reading must be equated with imagining, wondering, reacting feelingly. If it is not, we should not be surprised that they refuse to read.

Children must know words with power. This power is most evident in literature, writing by lovers of language who work at putting the best words in the best order for the greatest effect. Powerful words have magical powers: they can cast a spell to hold readers and listeners in thrall, and as this happens, a measure of their power transfers to each reader and listener. Sometimes discouraged, we may think that nothing less than magic can fight illiteracy and aliteracy. Then we are prepared. In words with power there is powerful magic. Our challenge is to see to it that children encounter these words.

Resources for Teachers

American Library Association
www.ala.org
The ALA provides a number of publications useful in choosing and evaluating children's books, among them *The Booklist, Picture Books for Children, Children's Books of International Interest, Let's Read Together: Books for Family Enjoyment, A Multimedia Approach to Children's Literature,* and *Beyond Fact: Nonfiction for Children and Young People. Top of the News* is an ALA periodical that discusses national and international issues relating to children's literature.

The ALA sponsors the annual Caldecott and Newbery awards. Lists of the winners and runners-up (honor books) for both awards since their inception are posted on the organization's website.

Bookbird
www.ibby.org
The International Board on Books for Young People (IBBY) has headquarters at Nonnenweg 12 Postfach, CH-4003 Basel, Switzerland. Its quarterly periodical on international literature is available in most libraries. Refer to www.ibby.org for information.

R. R. Bowker
www.bowker.com
The public library is a good source for publications by Bowker, which include *Children's Books in Print, Subject Guide to Children's Books in Print, Paperbound Books for Young People: Kindergarten through Grade 12, Best Books for Children: Preschool through Middle Grades.* These lists are available online.

Bulletin of the Center for Children's Books
Graduate Library School, 501 E. Daniel Street, Champaign, IL 61820

This monthly bulletin contains reviews of new books, including comments on those not recommended.

CM: Canadian Materials for Schools and Libraries
Canadian Library Association
151 Sparks Street, Ottawa
Ontario, Canada KIP 583
Reviews books, films, games, and periodicals published in Canada.

Children and Books, 9th edition
Zena Sutherland
New York: Longman, 1997
A distinguished textbook of children's literature containing excellent bibliographies, discussion of various genres, and critical commentary on selected works.

The Children's Book Council
www.cbcbooks.org
The official sponsor and headquarters for National Children's Book Week, the Council is a nonprofit organization devoted to bringing children and good books together. A one-time charge puts a name permanently on the mailing list to receive a description of materials available for Book Week and the publication *CBC Features*, which includes articles by authors and illustrators, topical bibliographies, and lists of sources of free materials such as posters, press sheets, and book marks. The Council, open to the public during business hours, maintains an examination collection of new books.

The Children's Literature Association
ebbs.english.vt.edu/chla/
An organization committed to scholarly publications on children's literature, including *The Quarterly* and *Children's Literature*—the annuals of the Modern Language Association Division on Children's Literature and the Children's Literature Association.

Christopher-Gordon Publishers
www.christopher-gordon.com
Christopher-Gordon publications deal with practical issues related to choosing and using books in the classroom.

Great Books Foundation
www.greatbooks.org
Established in 1947, the Great Books Foundation is an independent, nonprofit educational corporation whose mission is to provide people of all ages with the opportunity to read, discuss, and learn from great works of litera-

ture. For a nominal fee, individuals may enroll in one of the two-day Basic Leader Training Courses offered regularly throughout the United States. Whether or not an individual wishes to lead official Great Books discussions, the training is helpful to anyone who helps children learn to read literature. Central to the program is a method of discussion called "shared inquiry," in which participants and discussion leaders work together to formulate and discuss interpretive questions that focus on important problems of meaning in a literary work.

The Horn Book Magazine
www.hbook.com

An entertaining and reliable way to learn what is happening in the world of children's books is through subscription to *The Horn Book Magazine*. Each issue contains articles by authors, illustrators, and critics; reviews of the best books published; and news about awards and conferences. The magazine publishes a selection of books and pamphlets on children's literature, including *The Horn Book Guide*, a biannual selection guide to children's and young adults' hardcover trade books.

International Reading Association
www.reading.org

The IRA publishes a wide array of references for educators, librarians, and parents, as well as periodicals such as *The Reading Teacher*, which—like all IRA periodicals—comes with membership in the Association. Besides articles and features on teaching and learning, *The Reading Teacher* contains reviews of new children's books.

Listening Library
www.listeninglibrary.com

Superb presentations of fine youth literature in unabridged recordings.

National Council of Teachers of English
www.ncte.org

Membership in the NCTE, which sponsors professional conferences and publishes books and periodicals on the teaching of English, is an excellent way to stay current on matters of importance in the field of English teaching. Subscription to *Language Arts*, a periodical published September through April and which includes book reviews, articles by teachers, and Council information, is available as part of membership. The NCTE publishes regularly updated versions of comprehensive booklists such as *Adventuring with Books* (pre-K through Grade 6), *Your Reading* (middle school/junior high), *Books for You* (senior high), and *High Interest/Easy Reading* (junior/senior high reluctant readers); and special interest publications such as *In the Middle* and *School Talk*.

New York Public Library, Children's Services
8 East 40th Street, New York, NY 10016, (212) 340–0906
A number of pamphlets and booklists are available from the children's services division of the New York Public Library, notably *The Black Experience in Children's Books* and *Libros en español*.

Recorded Books
www.recordedbooks.com
Superb presentations of fine youth literature in unabridged recordings.

Weston Woods
teacher.scholastic.com/products/westonwoods
Now owned by Scholastic, The Weston Woods catalogue, entitled *Children's Literature in the Audiovisual Media*, reflects a focus on videocassettes, motion pictures, sound filmstrips, and recordings of children's literature. Quality picture books are superbly rendered on film and filmstrip. Kits of recordings with accompanying booklets are designed for independent reading/listening.

The H. W. Wilson Company
www.hwwilson.com
The Wilson Company produces a wide variety of reference materials for libraries, many on CD-rom. Among them is the *Wilson Library Bulletin*, which features a monthly column of reviews of children's books, and *Children's Catalog*, a listing of recent children's books issued every 5 years. Also available through Wilson is an *Index to Poetry for Children and Young People*, in several volumes. Poems are indexed by title, first line, author, and subject.

Literary References

Andersen, Hans Christian. (1974). *The complete fairy tales and stories.* Translated by Erik Haugaard. Garden City, NY: Doubleday.

Armstrong, William. (1969). *Sounder.* New York: Harper & Row.

Atwater, Richard & Florence. (1938). *Mr. Popper's penguins.* Boston: Little, Brown.

Babbitt, Natalie. (1977). *The eyes of the Amaryllis.* New York: Farrar, Straus & Giroux.

Bauer, Marian. (1986). *On my honor.* New York: Clarion.

Baylor, Byrd. (1974). *Everybody needs a rock.* Illustrated by Peter Parnall. New York: Macmillan.

Brittain, Bill. (1984). *The wish giver.* New York: Harper & Row.

Brooke, Rupert. (1915). *The collected poems of Rupert Brooke.* London: John Lane.

Byars, Betsy. (1981). *The winged colt of Casa Mia.* New York: Avon.

Caroll, Lewis. (1865/1988). *Alice's adventures in wonderland.* Illustrated by Anthony Browne. New York: Knopf.

Chase, Richard. (1943). *Jack tales.* Boston: Houghton Mifflin.

Christopher, John. (1967). *The white mountains.* New York: Simon & Schuster.

Christopher, John. (1994). *A dusk of demons.* London: Macmillan.

Clifford, Eth. (1981). *Help! I'm a prisoner in the library.* New York: Dell.

Clinton, Cathryn. (2002). *A stone in my hand.* Cambridge, MA: Candlewick.

Conrad, Pam. (1986). *Holding me here.* New York: Harper & Row.

Conrad, Pam. (1995). *Call me Ahnighito.* Illustrated by Richard Egielski. New York: HarperCollins.

Cooper, Susan. (1973). *The dark is rising.* New York: Atheneum.

Cormier, Robert. (1983). *The bumblebee flies anyway.* New York: Knopf.

Cunningham, Julia. (1965). *Dorp dead.* New York: Pantheon.

Cushman, Karen. (1994). *Catherine called Birdy.* New York: Clarion.

Cushman, Karen. (1995). *The midwife's apprentice.* New York: Clarion.

De la Mare, Walter. (1959). *Tales told again.* New York: Knopf.

De la Mare, Walter. (1983). *Molly Whuppie*. New York: Farrar, Straus & Giroux.

Dickens, Charles. (1843/1952). *A Christmas carol*. Illustrated by Arthur Rackham. New York: Lippincott.

DuBois, William P. (1947). *The twenty-one balloons*. New York: Viking.

Ehrlich, Amy. (1988). *Where it stops nobody knows*. New York: Dial.

Ellis, Deborah. (2000). *The breadwinner*. Toronto, Ontario: Groundwood.

Ellis, Deborah. (2002). *Parvana's journey*. Toronto, Ontario: Groundwood.

Emberley, Barbara. (1967). *Drummer Hoff*. Illustrated by Ed Emberley. Englewood Cliffs, NJ: Prentice-Hall.

Farley, Walter. (1941). *The black stallion*. New York: Random House.

Fitzhugh, Louise. (1974). *Nobody's family's going to change*. New York: Farrar, Straus & Giroux.

Fleischman, Sid. (1987). *The whipping boy*. New York: Greenwillow.

Frost, Robert. (1978). *Stopping by woods on a snowy evening*. Illustrated by Susan Jeffers. New York: Dutton.

Gág, Wanda. (1928). *Millions of cats*. New York: Coward McCann.

Gardiner, John. (1980). *Stone fox*. New York: Crowell.

Garner, Alan. (1968). *The owl service*. New York: Walck.

Gramatky, Hardie. (1939). *Little toot*. New York: Putnam.

Greenfield, Eloise. (1978). *Honey, I love and other love poems*. New York: Harper & Row.

Grimm, Jakob & Wilhelm. (1886/1972). *Snow White and the seven dwarfs*. Translated by Randell Jarrell and illustrated by Nancy Berkert. New York: Farrar, Straus & Giroux.

Harley, Avis. (2000). *Fly with poetry: An ABC of poetry*. Honesdale, PA: Boyds Mills Press.

Heide, Florence. (1971). *The shrinking of Treehorn*. New York: Holiday House.

Henry, Marguerite. (1948). *King of the wind*. Chicago: Rand McNally.

Hesse, Karen. (1997). *Out of the dust*. New York: Scholastic.

Hoban, Russell. (1967/2001). *The mouse and his child*. Illustrated by David Small. New York: Scholastic.

Holm, Ann. (1965/1984). *North to freedom*. Translated by L. W. Kingsland. New York: Harcourt Brace Jovanovich.

Holman, Felice. (1974). *Slake's limbo*. New York: Charles Scribner's Sons.

Hughes, Monica. (1981). *The keeper of the Isis light*. New York: Atheneum.

Hunt, Margaret. (1983). *Grimm's household tales*. New York: Penguin.

Hutchins, Pat. (1968). *Rosie's walk*. New York: Macmillan.

Jones, Diana Wynne. (1995). *The crown of Dalemark*. New York: Greenwillow.

Keats, Ezra Jack. (1962). *The snowy day*. New York: Viking.

Keats, John. (1956). *Keats: Poetical works*. Edited by H. W. Garrod. London: Oxford University Press.

Kimmell, Eric. (1994). *Anansi and the talking melon*. New York: Holiday House.

Kipling, Rudyard. (1902/1987). *Just-so stories*. Illustrated by Safaya Salter. New York: Holt.

Langton, Jane. (1980). *The fledgling*. New York: Harper & Row.

Lasky, Kathryn. (1995). *She's wearing a dead bird on her head!* New York: Hyperion.

Lattimore, Richmond. (1951). (Trans.). *The Iliad of Homer*. Chicago: University of Chicago Press.

Le Guin, Ursula. (1968). *A wizard of Earthsea*. Illustrated by Ruth Robbins. New York: Parnassus.

Lively, Penelope. (1973). *The ghost of Thomas Kempe*. New York: Dutton.

Lowry, Lois. (1979). *Anastasia Krupnik*. Boston: Houghton Mifflin.

MacLachlan, Patricia. (1986). *Sarah, plain and tall*. New York: Harper & Row.

Martin, Bill, & Archambault, John. (1989). *Chicka chicka boom boom*. New York: Simon and Schuster.

Mazer, Norma Fox. (1982). *Mrs. Fish, Ape, and me, the dump queen*. New York: Avon.

McCord, David. (1962). *Take sky*. Boston: Little Brown.

McCord, David. (1970). *For me to say*. Boston: Little Brown.

McCord, David. (1974). *One at a time*. Boston: Little Brown.

McDermott, Gerald. (1977). *The voyage of Osiris: A myth of ancient Egypt*. New York: Viking.

McDermott, Gerald. (1978). *Arrow to the sun*. New York: Puffin.

McGovern, Ann. (1967/1992). *Too much noise*. New York: Scott Foresman.

McKinley, Robin. (1985). *The hero and the crown*. New York: Greenwillow.

Merriam, Eve. (1965). *Do you want to see something?* New York: Scholastic.

Merriam, Eve. (1974). *Out loud*. New York: Atheneum.

Merrill, Jean. (1964). *The pushcart war*. New York: Young Scott.

Mikaelsen, Ben. (2002). *Red midnight*. New York: HarperCollins.

Millay, Edna St. Vincent. (1924). *The harp-weaver and other poems*. New York: Harper and Brothers.

Milne, A. A. (1924). *When we were very young*. New York: Dutton.

Mosel, Arlene. (1968). *Tikki Tikki Tembo*. Illustrated by Blair Lent. New York: Holt.

Murphy, Jim. (1995). *The great fire*. New York: Scholastic.

Neil, Philip. (1986). *Drakestail visits the king*. New York: Philomel.

Norton, Mary. (1953). *The borrowers*. New York: Harcourt Brace Jovanovich.

Nostlinger, Christine. (1977). *Konrad*. Translated by Anthea Bell. New York: Watts.

Noyes, Alfred. (1902). *Collected poems of Alfred Noyes*. New York: Lippincott.

Osborne, Mary P. (1987). *Beauty and the beast.* Illustrated by Winslow
    Pels. New York: Scholastic.
Osborne, Mary P. (2001). *Christmas in Camelot.* New York: Random
    House.
Paterson, Katherine. (1978). *The great Gilly Hopkins.* New York: Crowell.
Paulsen, Gary. (1985). *Dogsong.* New York: Bradbury.
Paulsen, Gary. (1988). *Hatchet.* New York: Bradbury.
Paulsen, Gary. (1993). *Nightjohn.* New York: Delacorte.
Peck, Richard. (1977). *Are you in the house alone?* New York: Dell.
Peck, Richard. (1983). *The dreadful future of Blossom Culp.* New York:
    Delacorte.
Perrault, Charles. (1981). *Cinderella.* Illustrated by Marcia Brown. New
    York: Macmillan.
Perrault, Charles. (1990). *Puss in boots.* Illustrated by Fred Marcellino.
    New York: Farrar, Straus & Giroux.
Pfeffer, Susan. (1987). *The year without Michael.* New York: Bantam.
Picard, Barbara. (1966). *One is one.* New York: Holt, Rinehart and Win-
    ston.
Pinkwater, Manus. (1976). *Lizard music.* New York: Dodd, Mead.
Polacco, Patricia. (1994). *Pink and Say.* New York: Philomel.
Potter, Beatrix. (1902). *The tale of Peter Rabbit.* London: Warne.
Potter, Beatrix. (1912). *The tale of Mr. Tod.* London: Warne.
Pringle, Laurence. (1997). *An extraordinary life: The story of a monarch
    butterfly.* New York: Orchard.
Pullman, Philip. (1995). *The golden compass.* New York: Knopf.
Ritchie, Alice. (1949). *The treasure of Li Po.* New York: Harcourt Brace
    Jovanovich.
Sachs, Marilyn. (1971). *The bears' house.* New York: Doubleday.
Sawyer, Ruth. (1936). The flea. In *Picture tales from Spain.* New York:
    Lippincott.
Sebestyen, Ouida. (1979). *Words by heart.* Boston: Little, Brown.
Sebestyen, Ouida. (1988). *The girl in the box.* Boston: Little, Brown.
Sendak, Maurice. (1963). *Where the wild things are.* New York: Harper
    & Row.
Sendak, Maurice. (1967). *Higglety, pigglety, pop!* New York: Harper and
    Row.
Sendak, Maurice. (1993). *We are all in the dumps with Jack and Guy.* New
    York: HarperCollins.
Seuss, Dr. (1938). *The 500 hats of Bartholomew Cubbins.* New York:
    Random House.
Shepard, Aaron. (1995). *The gifts of Wali Dad: A tale of India and Paki-
    stan.* Illustrated by Daniel San Souci. New York: Atheneum.
Siebert, Diane. (1989). *Heartland.* New York: Crowell.
Sis, Peter. (1996). *Starry messenger.* New York: Farrar.
Sleator, William. (1999). *Rewind.* New York: Dutton.

Slobodkina, Esphyr. (1947). *Caps for sale.* New York: Scott.

Smith, Robert. (1972). *Chocolate fever.* New York: Dell.

Speare, Elizabeth. (1983). *The sign of the beaver.* Boston: Houghton Mifflin.

Sperry, Armstrong. (1940). *Call it courage.* New York: Macmillan.

Spinelli, Jerry. (1997). *Wringer.* New York: HarperCollins.

Staples, Susan. (1996). *Dangerous skies.* New York: Farrar.

Steig, William. (1969). *Sylvester and the magic pebble.* New York: Simon and Schuster.

Steig, William. (1972). *Dominic.* New York: Farrar, Straus & Giroux.

Steig, William. (1986). *Brave Irene.* New York: Farrar, Straus & Giroux.

Steinbeck, John. (1976). *The acts of King Arthur and his noble knights.* New York: Farrar, Straus & Giroux.

Steptoe, John. (1987). *Mufaro's beautiful daughters.* New York: Lothrop.

Sterling, Dorothy. (1954). *Freedom train: The story of Harriet Tubman.* New York: Doubleday.

Stone, A. Harris. (1967). *The last free bird.* Englewood Cliffs, NJ: Prentice-Hall.

Swift, Jonathan. (1726/1985). *Gulliver's travels.* New York: Avenel Books.

Tashjian, Virginia. (1969). *Juba this and Juba that.* Boston: Little Brown.

Tashjian, Virginia. (1974). *With a deep sea smile.* Boston: Little Brown.

Taylor, Mildred. (2001). *The land.* New York: Phyllis Fogelman/Penguin Putnam.

Taylor, Theodore. (1995). *The bomb.* New York: Harcourt.

Tsuchiya, Yukio. (1988). *Faithful elephants.* Illustrated by Ted Lewin. Translated by Tomoko Dykes. New York: Houghton.

Updike, John. (1975). *Picked-up pieces.* New York: Alfred Knopf.

Van Allsburg, Chris. (1981). *Jumanji.* Boston: Houghton Mifflin.

Voight, Cynthia. (1982). *Dicey's song.* New York: Atheneum.

Waugh, Sylvia. (2000). *Space race.* New York: Delacorte.

Whelan, Gloria. (2000). *Homeless bird.* New York: HarperCollins.

White, E. B. (1952). *Charlotte's web.* New York: Harper & Row.

White, E. B. (1970). *The trumpet of the swan.* New York: Harper & Row.

Wolfe, Humbert. (1962). The gray squirrel. In Louis Untermeyer (Ed.), *Modern British poetry* (7th rev. ed.). New York: Harcourt Brace Jovanovich.

Yashima, Taro. (1976). *Crow boy.* New York: Puffin.

Young, Ed. (1997). *Voices of the heart.* New York: Scholastic.

Zindel, Paul. (1968). *The Pigman.* New York: Harper & Row.

Zindel, Paul. (1980). *The Pigman's legacy.* New York: Harper & Row.

General References

Adams, H., & Searle, L. (1986). *Critical theory since 1965*. Tallahassee, FL: Florida State University Press.

Anderson, R. C., Hiebert, E. H., Scott, J. A., & Wilkinson, I. A. G. (1985). *Becoming a nation of readers: The report of the Commission on Reading*. Washington, DC: National Institute of Education.

Apol, Laura. (1998). "But what does it have to do with kids?" Literary theory and children's literature in the teacher education classroom. *Journal of Children's Literature*, 24(2), 32–46.

Applebee, Arthur. (1978). *The child's concept of story*. Chicago: University of Chicago Press.

Applebee, Arthur. (1992). The background for reform. In J. A. Langer (Ed.), *Literature instruction: A focus on student response* (pp. 1–18). Urbana, IL: National Council of Teachers of English.

Arnold, Matthew. (1896a). *Literature and dogma*. New York: Macmillan.

Arnold, Matthew. (1896b). *Essays in criticism* (Second series). London: Macmillan.

Ashton-Warner, Sylvia. (1964). *Teacher*. New York: Bantam Books.

Atwell, Nancie. (1987). *In the middle*. Portsmouth, NH: Heinemann.

Baghban, Marcia. (1984). *Our daughter learns to read and write*. Newark, DE: International Reading Association.

Barbe, Walter. (1961). *Personalized reading instruction*. Englewood Cliffs, NJ: Prentice-Hall.

Barthes, Roland. (1977). From work to text. In R. Barthes, *Image–Music–Text*. Translated by Stephen Heath. New York: Hill and Wang.

Barton, Bob. (1986). *Tell me another*. Portsmouth, NH: Heinemann.

Beach, Richard. (1993). *A teacher's introduction to reader-response theories*. Champaign, IL: National Council of Teachers of English.

Bennett, Jill. (1979). *Learning to read with picture books* (3rd ed.). Stroud, England: The Thimble Press.

Bettelheim, Bruno. (1976). *The uses of enchantment: Meaning and importance of fairy tales*. New York: Knopf.

Bleich, David. (1978). *Subjective criticism*. Baltimore: Johns Hopkins University Press.

Bloom, Benjamin. (1956). *Taxonomy of educational objectives handbook I: Cognitive domain*. New York: David McKay.

Bridges, Lois. (1995). *Assessment*. York, ME: Stenhouse.

Brooks, Cleanth. (1947/1968). *The well-wrought urn: Studies in the structure of poetry* (Rev. ed.). London: D. Dobson.

Bruner, Jerome. (1960). *The process of education*. Cambridge, MA: Harvard University Press.

Cai, Mingshui, & Traw, Rick. (1997). Literary literacy. *Journal of Children's Literature. 23*(2), Fall, 20–33.

Calkins, Lucy. (1986). *The art of teaching writing*. Portsmouth, NH: Heinemann.

Carr, J. (1982). *Beyond fact*. Chicago: American Library Association.

Carr, J. (1987). Filling vases, lighting fires. *The Horn Book Magazine, 63*, 710–713.

Childers, Joseph, & Hentzi, Gary. (Eds.). (1995). *The Columbia dictionary of modern literary and cultural criticism*. New York: Columbia University Press.

Chomsky, Carol. (1972). Stages in language development and reading exposure. *Harvard Educational Review, 42*, 1–33.

Chomsky, Carol. (1978). When you still can't read in third grade: After decoding, what? In S. Jay Samuels, *What research has to say about reading instruction* (pp. 13–30). Newark, DE: International Reading Association.

Chomsky, Noam. (1957). *Syntactic structures*. The Hague: Mouton.

Clay, Marie. (1980). *Reading: The patterning of complex behavior* (2nd ed.). Auckland, Australia: Heinemann.

Cohen, Dorothy. (1968). The effect of literature on vocabulary and reading achievement. *Elementary English, 45*, 209–213, 217.

Cohen, Elizabeth. (1986). *Designing group work*. New York: Teachers College Press.

Copeland, Jeffrey. (1993, 1994). *Speaking of poets*, Volumes 1 and 2. Champaign, IL: National Council of Teachers of English.

Cormier, Robert. (1997). *Books remembered*. New York: Children's Book Council.

Crook, Patricia, & Lehman, Barbara. (1991). Themes for two voices: Children's fiction and nonfiction as "whole literature." *Language Arts, 68*, 34–41.

Culler, Jonathan. (1978). *The pursuit of signs*. London: Routledge and Kegan Paul.

Culler, Jonathan. (1982). *On deconstruction: Theory and criticism after structuralism*. Ithaca, NY: Cornell University Press.

Culler, Jonathan. (1997). *Literary theory*. New York: Oxford University Press.

Cullinan, Bernice, Jagger, Angela, & Strickland, Dorothy. (1974). Language expansion for black children in the primary grades: A research report. *Young Children, 29*, 98–112.

Cullinan, Bernice, Scala, Marilyn, & Schroder, Virginia. (1995). *Three voices: An invitation to poetry across the curriculum.* York, ME: Stenhouse.

Curran, Karen. (1987). *A study of the effect on children's writing of selected folk tales read aloud.* Unpublished Master of Education paper, School of Education, Queens College of the City University of New York.

Dahl, Roald. (1997). *Books remembered.* New York: Children's Book Council.

Daley, P. A. (2002). Iser, Crutcher, and the reader: Creating the world of Sarah Byrnes. *Journal of Children's Literature, 28*(1), 32–38.

Daniels, Harvey. (1994). *Literature circles: Voice and choice in the student-centered classroom.* York, ME: Stenhouse

de Man, Paul. (1979). *Allegories of reading.* New Haven, CT: Yale University Press.

Dressel, Janice. (1988). Critical thinking and the perception of aesthetic form. *Language Arts, 65,* 567–572.

Eagleton, Terry. (1996). *Literary theory: An introduction.* Minneapolis, MN: The University of Minnesota Press.

Eckhoff, Barbara. (1983). How reading affects children's writing. *Language Arts, 60,* 607–616.

Eells, J. S. Jr. (1955). *The touchstones of Matthew Arnold.* New Haven, CT: College and University Press.

Eldredge, J. Lloyd, & Butterfield, Dennie. (1986). Alternatives to traditional reading instruction. *The Reading Teacher, 40,* 32–37.

Fish, Stanley. (1980). *Is there a text in this class? The authority of interpretive communities.* Cambridge, MA: Harvard University Press.

Fleming, Carolyn. (1981). *Small is heroic.* Unpublished master's thesis submitted for the degree of Master of Arts, School of Humanities, The Flinders University of South Australia.

Fox, C. (1983). Talking like a book: Young children's oral monologues. In M. Meek (Ed.), *Opening moves: Work in progress in the study of children's language development.* London: University of London Institute of Education.

Fox, C. (1985). The book that talks. *Language Arts, 62*(4), 374–384.

Freeman, Edward. (1887). Literature and language. *Contemporary Review, 52,* October, 566.

Freund, Elizabeth. (1987). *The return of the reader: Reader-response criticism.* New York: Methuen.

Frye, Northrop. (1956). Poetry. *University of Toronto Quarterly, 25,* 290–304.

Frye, Northrop. (1957). *Anatomy of criticism: Four essays.* Princeton, NJ: Princeton University Press.

Frye, Northrop. (1963a). *The educated imagination.* Toronto, Ontario: Canadian Broadcasting Corporation.

Frye, Northrop. (1963b). *The well-tempered critic*. Bloomington, IN: Indiana University Press.

Frye, Northrop. (1963c). The developing imagination. In *Learning in language and literature*. Cambridge, MA: Harvard University Press.

Frye, Northrop. (1970). *The stubborn structure: Essays on criticism and society*. Ithaca, NY: Cornell University Press.

Frye, Northrop. (1976a). *The secular scripture*. Cambridge, MA: Harvard University Press.

Frye, Northrop. (1976b). *Spiritus mundi*. Bloomington, IN: Indiana University Press.

Frye, Northrop. (1982). *The great code: The Bible and literature*. New York: Harcourt Brace Jovanovich

Frye, Northrop. (1988). *On education*. Markham, Ontario: Fitzhenry and Whiteside.

Frye, Northrop. (1993). *The eternal act of creation: Essays 1979–1990*. Bloomington, IN: Indiana University Press.

Gallo, Donald. (Ed.). (1977). Teaching writing: Advice from the professionals. *Connecticut English Journal, 8*(2).

Geller, Linda G. (1985). *Wordplay and language learning for children*. Urbana, IL: National Council of Teachers of English.

Goodman, Kenneth. (1968). The psycholinguistic nature of the reading process. In Kenneth Goodman, *The psycholinguistic nature of the reading process*. Detroit, MI: Wayne State University Press.

Goodman, Kenneth, Shannon, P., Freeman, Y., & Murphy, S. (1988). *Report card on basal readers*. Katonah, NY: Richard Owen.

Goodman, Yetta. (1989). Evaluation in whole language classrooms. *Teachers Networking, 9*(4), Katonah, NY: Richard Owen.

Goodman, Yetta, Watson, Dorothy, & Burke, Carolyn. (1987). *Reading miscue inventory: Alternative procedures*. Katonah, NY: Richard Owen.

Graves, Donald. (1983). *Writing: Teachers and children at work*. Portsmouth, NH: Heinemann.

Greene, Ellin. (1996). *Storytelling: Art and technique*. New York: Bowker.

Guthrie, J. (1981). Reading in New Zealand: Achievement, volume. *Reading Research Quarterly, 17*, 6–17.

Halliday, M. A. K. (1975). *Learning how to mean: Explorations in the development of language*. London: Edward Arnold.

Hardy, Barbara. (1977). Towards a poetics of fiction: An approach through narrative. In M. Meek, A. Warlow, & G. Barton (Eds.), *The cool web: The pattern of children's reading* (pp. 12–23). New York: Atheneum.

Harste, J., Woodward, V., & Burke, C. (1984). *Language stories and literacy lessons*. Portsmouth, NH: Heinemann.

Heard, Georgia. (1989). *For the good of the earth and the sun: Teaching poetry*. Portsmouth, NH: Heinemann.

Heard, Georgia. (1999). *Awakening the heart*. Portsmouth, NH: Heinemann.

Heath, Shirley B. (1985). Literacy or literate skills? Considerations for

ESL/EFL learners. In P. Larson, E. Judd, & D. Messerschmitt (Eds.), *On TESOL*. Washington, DC: TESOL.

Henke, Linda. (1988). Beyond basal reading: A district's commitment to change. *The New Advocate, 1*(1), 42–51.

Hickman, Janet. (1986). Children's response to literature. *Language Arts, 63*, 2.

Hill, B. C., Johnson, N., & Noe, K. (1995). *Literature circles and response*. Norwood, MA: Christopher-Gordon.

Hill, B. C., & Ruptic, C. (1994). *Practical aspects of authentic assessment: Putting the pieces together*. Norwood, MA: Christopher-Gordon.

Holdaway, Don. (1979). *The foundations of literacy*. Auckland, Australia: Scholastic.

Holdaway, Don. (1984). *Stability and change in literacy learning*. Portsmouth, NH: Heinemann.

Holland, Norman. (1975). *5 readers reading*. New Haven, CT: Yale University Press.

Huck, Charlotte. (1961). *Children's literature in the elementary school* (1st ed.). New York: Holt.

Ingarden, Roman. (1973). *The cognition of the literary work of art*. Translated by Ruth Ann Crowley and Kenneth R. Olson. Evanston, IL: Northwestern University Press.

Iser, Wolfgang. (1978). *The act of reading: A theory of aesthetic response*. Baltimore: Johns Hopkins University Press.

Jacobs, Leland. (1965). *Using literature with young children*. New York: Teachers College Press.

Jakobson, Roman. (1972). *The prison house of language: A critical account of structuralism and Russian formalism*. Princeton, NJ: Princeton University Press.

Jauss, H. (1982). *Aesthetic experience and literary hermeneutics*. Minneapolis, MN: University of Minneapolis Press.

Kernan, Alvin. (1993). Helpful things to say about literature. In Susan Gubar & Jonathan Kamholtz (Eds.), *English inside and out: The places of literary criticism* (pp. 9–28). New York: Routledge.

Koch, Kenneth. (1970). *Wishes, lies, and dreams*. New York: Chelsea House.

Koeller, Shirley. (1981). 25 years advocating children's literature in the reading program. *The Reading Teacher, 34*, 552–556.

Langer, Judith. (1995). *Envisioning literature: Literary understanding and literature instruction*. New York: Teachers College Press.

Larrick, Nancy. (1987). Illiteracy starts too soon. *Phi Delta Kappan, 69*, 184–189.

Lehr, Susan. (1991). *The child's developing sense of theme*. New York: Teachers College Press.

Livingston, M. C. (1991). *Poem-making: Ways to begin writing poetry*. New York: HarperCollins.

MacDonald, Margaret R. (1993). *The storytellers start-up book*. Little Rock, AR: August House.

Makaryk, Irena. (Ed.). (1993). *Encyclopedia of contemporary literary theory*. Toronto, Ontario: University of Toronto Press.

Meek, Margaret. (1982). *Learning to read*. Portsmouth, NH: Heinemann.

Miller, George A. (1962). Some psychological studies of grammar. *American Psychologist, 17*, 748–762.

Moss, Joy. (1984). *Focus units in literature*. Urbana, IL: National Council of Teachers in English.

Nodelman, Perry. (1996). *The pleasures of children's literature* (2nd ed.). White Plains, NY: Longman.

Oliver, Mary. (1994). *A poetry handbook: A prose guide to understanding and writing poetry*. New York: Harcourt Brace.

Opie, Iona & Peter. (1959). *The lore and language of school children*. New York: Oxford University Press.

Padgett, Ron. (2000). *Handbook of poetic forms*. New York: Teachers and Writers Collaborative.

Probst, Robert. (1990). Literature as exploration and the classroom. In E. J. Farrell & J. R. Squire (Eds.), *Transactions with literature* (pp. 27–37). Urbana, IL: National Council of Teachers of English.

Rabinowitz, Peter. (1987). *Narrative conventions and the politics of interpretation*. Ithaca, NY: Cornell University Press.

Rabinowitz, Peter, & Smith, Michael. (1998). *Authorizing readers*. New York: Teachers College Press.

Rigg, Pat, & Allen, Virginia. (Eds.). (1989). *When they don't all speak English: Integrating the ESL student into the regular classroom*. Urbana, IL: National Council of Teachers of English.

Robb, Laura. (1993). A cause for celebration: Reading and writing with at-risk children. *The New Advocate, 6*, Winter, 25–40.

Robb, Laura. (1994). *Whole language, whole learners: Creating a literature centered classroom*. New York: Morrow.

Roe, B. D., Alfred, S., & Smith, S. (1998). *Teaching through stories: Yours, mine and theirs*. Norwood, MA: Christopher-Gordon.

Rogovin, Phyllis. (1985). *Poetic devices in children's speech*. Unpublished Master of Education paper, School of Education, Queens College of the City University of New York.

Rosen, Harold. (1985). *Stories and meanings*. Sheffield, England: National Association for the Teaching of English.

Rosenblatt, Louise. (1938). *Literature as exploration*. New York: Appleton-Century.

Rosenblatt, Louise. (1978). *The reader, the text, the poem: The transactional theory of the literary work*. Carbondale, IL: Southern Illinois University Press.

Schertle, Alice. (1996). Up the bookcase to poetry. *The Horn Book Magazine, 4*, July/August, 430–435.

Scholes, Robert. (1985). *Textual power.* New Haven: Yale University Press.

Seashore, C. E. (Ed.). (1919). Fourth report of the Committee on Economy of Time in Education. In *18th Yearbook of the National Society for the Study of Education* (Part 2). Chicago: University of Chicago Press.

Short, K., & Pierce, K. (Eds.). (1990). *Talking about books: Creating literate communities.* Portsmouth, NH: Heinemann.

Shuy, Roger. (1981). A holistic view of language. *Research in the Teaching of English, 15*(2), 101–111.

Skinner, B. F. (1957). *Verbal behavior.* New York: Appleton-Century.

Sloan, Glenna. (1972). A delicate balance. *Elementary English,* April, 596–599

Sloan, Glenna. (1975). *The child as critic* (1st ed.). New York: Teachers College Press.

Sloan, Glenna. (1980). Developing literacy through literature. *The Reading Teacher, 34*(2), 132–136.

Sloan, Glenna. (1981). Eve Merriam: A profile. *Language Arts, 58*(8), 957–964.

Sloan, Glenna. (1984). *The child as critic* (2nd ed.). New York: Teachers College Press.

Sloan, Glenna. (1988). *Literature-based instruction in six elementary classrooms.* Unpublished research.

Sloan, Glenna. (1991). *The child as critic.* (3rd ed.). New York: Teachers College Press.

Sloan, Glenna. (1995). Questions of definition: Teachers' perceptions of literature-based teaching and learning. In M. Sorenson & B. Lehman (Eds.), *Teaching with children's books.* Urbana, IL: National Council of Teachers of English.

Sloan, Glenna. (1997). Toward literacy through literature. *Journal of Children's Literature, 23*(2), 47–51.

Sloan, Glenna. (1998). Poetry and linguistic power. *Teaching and Learning Literature, 8*(1), 69–79.

Sloan, Glenna. (2001a). But is it poetry? *Children's Literature in Education, 32*(1), 45–56.

Sloan, Glenna. (2001b). Poetry Applied. *The Dragon Lode, 20*(1), Fall, 10–13.

Sloan, Glenna. (2001c). *Teachers to teachers in bringing poetry and children together.* Urbana, IL: National Council of Teachers of English.

Sloan, Glenna (2003). *Give them poetry!* New York: Teachers College Press.

Smith, Frank. (1978). *Understanding reading* (2nd ed.). New York: Holt.

Smith, Frank. (1983). *Essays into literacy.* Portsmouth, NH: Heinemann.

Smith, Frank. (1986). *Insult to intelligence: The bureaucratic invasion of our classrooms.* New York: Arbor House.

Snow, Charles P. (1959). *The two cultures and the scientific revolution.* New York: Cambridge University Press.

Sorensen, M., & Lehman, B. (Eds.). (1995). *Teaching with children's books.* Urbana, IL: National Council of Teachers of English.

Soter, Anna. (1999). *Young adult literature and the new literary theories: Developing critical readers in middle school.* New York: Teachers College Press.

Soter, Anna, & Letcher, Mark. (1998). Literary theory and appreciation: Learning about the literary craft. *Journal of Children's Literature, 24*(2), 22–31.

Spack, Ruth. (1985). Literature, reading, writing, and ESL: Bridging the gaps. *TESOL Quarterly, 19,* 5–14.

Stein, N., & Trabasso, T. (1982). What's in a story: An approach to comprehension and instruction. In R. Glazer (Ed.). *Advances in instructional psychology* (Vol. 2, pp. 213–254). Hillsdale, NJ: Erlbaum.

Sutherland, Zena. (1997). *Children and books* (9th Ed.). New York: Longman.

Tompkins, Jane. (Ed.). (1980). *Reader-response criticism from formalism to post-structuralism.* Baltimore: Johns Hopkins University Press.

Traw, Rick. (1998). Literature-based programs can work: Large-scale assessment of two school districts. *The New Advocate, 11*(2), Spring, 135–151.

Tuleja, E. (1998). Understanding *Morning Girl* through Judith Langer's "envisionment" model. *Journal of Children's Literature, 24*(2), 56–65.

Tunnell, Michael. (1986). The natural act of reading: An affective approach. *The Advocate, 5,* 156–164.

Tyler, Ralph. (1977). Reading aloud: Is it time for a revival? *Bookviews, 1,* 16–20.

Veatch, Jeanette. (1959). *Individualizing your reading program.* New York: Putnam.

Veatch, Jeanette. (1968). *How to teach reading with children's books.* Katonah, NY: Richard Owen.

Walcutt, Charles, & McCracken, Glenn. (1981). *Jumping up.* Lippincott Basic Reading. New York: Lippincott.

Wellek, René, & Warren, Austin. (1949). *Theory of literature.* New York: Harcourt, Brace & World.

Wells, Gordon. (1982). Story reading and the development of symbolic skills. *Australian Journal of Reading, 5,* 3.

Wells, Gordon. (1986). *The meaning makers: Children learning language and using language to learn.* Portsmouth, NH: Heinemann.

Wilkinson, Andrew. (1971). *The foundations of language.* New York: Oxford University Press.

Willard, Thomas. (1994). Archetypes of the imagination. In Alvin Lee and Robert Denham (Eds.), *The legacy of Northrop Frye* (pp. 15–27). Toronto, Ontario: University of Toronto Press.

Williams, Paul, et al. (1995). *Reading: A first look.* Report of the National Assessment of Educational Progress. Washington, DC: Office of Educational Research and Improvement, U.S. Department of Education.

Willinsky, John. (1991). *The triumph of literature/The fate of literacy.* New York: Teachers College Press.

Wimsatt, William, Jr., & Beardsley, Monroe. (1954). *The verbal icon: Studies in the meaning of poetry.* Lexington, KY: University Press of Kentucky.

Yan, Peter. (2002). Frye and I: On the 11th anniversary of his death. *Northrop Frye Newsletter, 9*(1), 30–31.

Zarnowski, Myra. (1990). *Learning about biographies: A reading-and-writing approach for children.* Urbana, IL: National Council of Teachers of English.

Index

About the Author

Glenna Sloan earned a B.A. from the University of Toronto, M.A. and doctoral degrees from Teachers College, Columbia University, and an associate's diploma (ARCT) in Speech and Drama from the Royal Conservatory of Music of Toronto. A specialist in literacy development and children's literature, Dr. Sloan taught for 16 years in elementary and junior high schools. She now teaches graduate courses in children's literature in the School of Education at Queens College of the City University of New York.

In addition to *The Child as Critic*, Professor Sloan has published numerous articles in professional journals, a series on reading and study skills for junior high school students, a sixth-grade language arts text, and three novels for young people. She was an author and consultant for the Harcourt Brace Jovanovich series, *Literature: Uses of the Imagination*.

A member of the National Council of Teachers of English (NCTE), Dr. Sloan was elected to a 4-year term on the Elementary Section Steering Committee. She was a member of the Council's Committee on Literature-Based Language Arts Instruction and Chair of the committee to administer the NCTE Excellence in Poetry for Children Award. For the Children's Literature Assembly of NCTE, she chaired the 1998 Committee to Choose Notable Children's Books in the Language Arts. She was president of the International Reading Association's (IRA) Reading and Children's Literature Special Interest Group (SIG) and has chaired the SIG's committee to select Notable Books for a Global Society. She also has served twice on the board of the International Children's Literature Association and is editor of the children's book column for *Bookbird*, the publication of the International Board on Books for Young People (IBBY).

In 2001, Dr. Sloan was recipient of the International Reading Association's Arbuthnot Award for an Outstanding Teacher of Children's and Young Adult Literature. As a consultant for school systems, she evaluates programs and also designs and leads in-service seminars and workshops for teachers.